D1499683

Nothing Quite Like It

Nothing Quite Like It

IAN WALLACE

ELM TREE LONDON

First published in Great Britain 1982
by Elm Tree Books Ltd
Garden House, 57–59 Long Acre
London WC2E 9JZ

British Library Cataloguing in Publication Data
Wallace, Ian
    Nothing quite like it.
    1. Wallace, Ian, *1919–*   2. Singers—
    Correspondence, reminiscences, etc.
    I. Title
    782.1'0924   ML420.W/

    ISBN 0-241-10853-5

Photoset in Baskerville by
Rowland Phototypesetting Limited
Bury St Edmunds, Suffolk
Printed in Great Britain by
by Billing and Sons Limited
London and Worcester

Dedication

To Pat, whose reaction to another book was to buy me a huge length of high duty cable to bring heat, light and power for the typewriter to the garden summerhouse where there is no 'phone. She greeted my frequent departures to the solitude of North Norfolk by coming out to the car staggering under the weight of a survival carton of rations and alcoholic stimulants.

I know she'll not mind sharing this dedication with two people, one a close friend, one unknown to me; John Partridge for all sorts of help and encouragement during 40 years, near as dammit – and the unknown? It's the chap who invented 'lift off' tape for IBM typewriters. These magically easy corrections make even a two-finger operator like me capable of an unblemished paragraph.

Acknowledgements

The author and publishers would like to thank the following for permission to use copyright photographs:

The Chester Chronicle (photo number 7); Central Press Photos Ltd (8); Glyndebourne Opera (18); Guy Gravett (19); *The Scotsman* Publications Ltd (17); Lord Snowdon (20); Associated Newspapers Ltd (11 and 21); Bryan and Shear Ltd (22); BBC Copyright Photographs (25); PIC Photos Ltd (26); Thames Television Ltd (27, 28, 29, 34); Sophie Baker (31); MGM (14).

Other photographs are by:

John Vickers (5); Angus McBean (9); Photo Functions (10); Oscar Savio (15); Wilfred Newton (23); Sheila van Doren (24).

Every effort has been made to contact the holders of copyright in the photographs in this book. Should any omission have been made, we apologise and will be pleased to make the necessary acknowledgement in any future edition.

Chapter One

I looked myself in the shaving mirror dead in the eye.

'Why on earth have you agreed to write another volume of your autobiography?' I demanded.

I tried to avoid my gaze and let my eyes wander to a long hair just below my left nostril that the electric shaver had missed since last Tuesday.

'Come on, don't change the subject. It can't be the money.'

'Why not?'

'Well, your publisher has certainly combined generosity with optimism, but it's not exactly a couple of hundred thousand.'

'I don't happen to be an ex-cabinet minister who kept a diary or a film star with seven notches on his wedding ring.'

'There's no need to be defensive. Answer the question.'

I treated myself to the ghost of a smile. 'I enjoyed writing the first one.'*

'Is that all?'

'Not quite. My grandfather was a journalist and his father before him, so writing's in the blood.'

'Hmmm.'

'What's that supposed to mean?'

'I'd have thought you'd enough to do already singing and broadcasting, and aren't you always saying you want to do more acting? It isn't as if you're a trained writer.'

'I wasn't a trained actor or singer when I started.'

'You're spoiling for a fight this morning.'

'No I'm not, but in a roundabout way you're accusing me of self-indulgence and I don't like it.'

'The truth is always painful.'

'Now look here . . . Oh, all right, I admit it; but don't forget I told the readers of the first one that if I sold six copies I'd write volume two.'

* *Promise Me You'll Sing Mud (John Calder 1975)*

'Yes, I remember that rather sickening example of false modesty.'

'Thank you for reading so far. It was on the last page but one.'

'Oh yes I read it all right, but what about the people who didn't? Are you going to fill them in about your early days or plunge straight in around 1950?'

'Yes.'

'I see. Well, there's no time like the present.'

'Right.'

I reached for the after-shave, pulled on a pair of slacks and the blue jersey with the gold Arsenal Football Club motif that my daughter Rosie gave me for Christmas and made my way downstairs to my studio where the plastic cover on the type-writer looked more of a reproach than a protection.

*   *   *

The journey to Byron House School didn't take very long on my fairy cycle. There was only one quiet road to cross so I was allowed to go to school on my own, a pleasant mile of large red-brick houses standing back from the road in an attractive, leafy north London suburb.

There are still one or two very old people in Highgate who can recall meeting this plump little cyclist homeward bound at the age of seven or thereabouts. They remember him propping his bike against a fence and offering to sing them a song as, quite unabashed, he produced a small ukelele from its case in the handlebar basket. It must have been an offer as irresistible as it now feels embarrassing in retrospect.

The origins of this extrovert infant provide some sort of explanation for what might have been dismissed as precocious or even eccentric behaviour. It wasn't really either of those. You could call it a fresh chapter in a long story.

Let's go back to the beginning, which might just as well be 1882, when a boy called John Wallace started in the counting house of a linoleum works in Kirkcaldy, a grey Fife seaport on the Firth of Forth. He was fourteen years of age and his wages were ten pounds a year.

The firm was Michael Nairn & Company and it took John thirty-three years to become its London managing director. He did it by sheer determination plus a considerable talent for selling linoleum and getting on with his fellow man.

When he retired in 1947 at the age of seventy-nine he'd been with Nairns for an unbroken sixty-five years. He'd also represented a Fife constituency in Parliament in the Liberal interest for eight inter-war years and received a knighthood, which was even more of a tribute in view of the fact that he was not always one of those MPs who voted 'just as their leaders tell 'em to'. Yes, I'm very proud of my father.

He excelled at many things but two were beyond him. One was retirement. After eighteen months of it he just quietly slipped away. The other was music. He once told me that when he was a young man he volunteered to sing at a church social and his name was on the programme for two songs. He thought his offering in part one had gone down a treat. When the second half of the entertainment drew to a close without the master of ceremonies calling on him again, he indignantly enquired what had gone wrong. The MC must have been a man of tact.

'Well, you see, John, you're what I would describe as a satisfying singer.'

I only ever heard him sing while lathering his face in the morning. In all honesty it was not a sound that gave me any pleasure and, so far as I could ever discover, his two sisters hadn't a note of music in them. His parents were both dead long before I was born and my father never volunteered any information about their tastes or recreations beyond saying that his father was a lay preacher of hell-fire sermons and that he sometimes wondered how his dear mother had put up with him.

My mother's family was brimming with musical and histrionic talent which for two generations was never fully exploited. Her father was James Temple, a Glasgow journalist who could equally well have been a singer or actor. My mother was his eldest daughter May and though not at all musical she was the star pupil of the elocution class and took the leading part in the school plays, while her younger sister Margaret, my auntie Peggy, sang and played the piano exceptionally well for her age.

When the celebrated actor Beerbohm Tree adjudicated the school poetry reading competition he not only awarded May the first prize but offered her a scholarship at a London drama college. The family, as might be expected, threw up their hands in horror.

And in 1904 she had the longest hair in Great Britain. You don't believe me? A school-mate pulled one of them out by the roots. Then they wound it round a post card and entered it for a contest run by a shampoo firm determined to find the girl whose locks had currently outstripped the rest of the field.

The first prize was a trip to London where the winner, all expenses paid, would sit every day for a week in a window of Selfridges department store proudly displaying her tresses to the admiring Oxford Street crowds who would then have an opportunity to read the placards proclaiming the astonishing hair growing propensity of the shampoo.

May's hair won the contest in a canter. No wonder – she could sit on it.

When the letter bearing the exciting news arrived she was delighted – till she showed it to her mother.

Whoever eventually graced Selfridges window it was not the winner. Alas, girls who attended the Park School in the West End of Glasgow when King Edward VII was nearing the middle of his brief reign just didn't do those sort of things – even if they had amazingly long dark hair and talent pouring out of their ears.

Perhaps my maternal grandmother, whom I never knew – she died in 1910 – was also influenced by an earlier embarrassing incident that concerned a shop window.

When it was announced that Queen Victoria would drive through Glasgow as part of her Diamond Jubilee celebrations in 1897, the published route took her past the fish shop patronised by Mrs Temple. The owner of the shop suggested to his valued customer that with such large crowds it might be difficult for her two little girls aged seven and four to see the Queen at all.

'I'll tell ye what I'll do, Mrs Temple. I'll clear a' the fish off the marble slab, for there'll be nae customers that morn. The slab's nice and high, ye see, and after I've washed it doon I'll put three chairs for ye to sit on while ye're waitin'. Then ye can stand up when the auld lady comes by, and the wee lassies'll see fine.'

When the three arrived at the fish shop on the great day the expected crowds were nowhere to be seen. Perhaps there were better vantage points elsewhere, but whatever the reason there was hardly anyone about at all.

'Why can't we stand at the edge of the pavement, Mummy?' demanded May.

'Because dear Mr McKay has gone to a great deal of trouble and we can't let him down.'

To this day my mother, now ninety-two, remembers the embarrassment of sitting in the fish shop window for at least an hour to the amusement of passers by. When at last the Queen drove past she was sufficiently struck by the sight of three of her subjects waving union jacks from a spot normally reserved for cod fillets or Dover soles that she gave them a royal wave all to themselves.

The call of duty prevented my grandfather from joining his wife and daughters on the slab. He was covering the royal visit for his newspaper. He was a good reporter with an excellent turn of phrase, but instead of this talent inherited from his father he passed on to May and Peggy his musical and histrionic gifts which he scarcely used as an amateur and never professionally.

His sweet lyric baritone would have been an asset to any light opera company and his way of telling a story giving all the characters in it a different voice was made all the more effective by a natural dignity which invested the whole performance with unexpected hilarity.

While May inherited her father's histrionic ability – and never found any outlet for it beyond school theatricals, Peggy made a brave attempt to pursue a musical career after studying singing and piano at the Royal College of Music in London. Unfortunately she did her voice no good at all in a brief spell on the music halls with an act in which she did impressions of the likes of Alice Delysia, Harry Lauder and Count John McCormack.

Her Harry Lauder was a knock out, but in those pre-microphone days it was a murderous strain on her larynx, and even though her exhausted voice box, which lasted barely two weeks in the rigours of twice-nightly appearances, recovered with rest, she never pursued a professional career as a singer any further.

Grandad was over sixty when I first became aware of him; short and stout with close-cropped white hair and a clipped moustache under a big nose, he wasn't in the least formidable, something of an expert indeed at entertaining small boys.

One afternoon when I was about five or six he was left in sole charge, and between lunch and tea he taught me three basic chords on the piano and a song to go with them:-

'Old Mother Hubbard, she went to the cupboard
For something to quench her thirst.
When she got there the cupboard was bare
For her old man had been there first.'

Needless to say grandad was in the dog-house. But I'm getting ahead of myself; I haven't even got John Wallace and May Temple married yet.

They met in 1912 at a Scottish hotel, the Hydropathic at Kilmacolm, a pleasant Renfrewshire village near the Firth of Clyde only seventeen miles from Glasgow. John had become Nairn's Glasgow manager and had decided to stay in the Hydro for the summer and travel to the city each day. The attraction was the golf course for in those days he had a single figure handicap and he could play on the long summer evenings. May came to the Hydro with her father and Peggy for a holiday. While they were there John lost his mother. He adored her which may partly explain why he was still a bachelor at the age of forty-four. Perhaps an even more important reason was a line from Kipling's poem *The Winners* which he quoted to me more than once: 'He travels the fastest who travels alone.'

May was twenty-two and together with her father and sister was still recovering from the loss of her mother who had died young of pernicious anaemia a very short while before a cure was discovered. Perhaps it was mutual sympathy which first brought these two together. At any rate when the Temples returned to Glasgow after their holiday John became a regular visitor at their home near the West End Park and a year later he and May were married. They had only just set up house in Glasgow when he was promoted to London and May had to say goodbye to her father and Peggy.

I think the loss of his wife in her forties and his daughter May's marriage to a man twice her age who had taken her four hundred miles away must have knocked a bit of the heart out of Grandad for he retired soon after, and when Peggy's musical studies and her brief music hall career were at an end he and she went to live at the Kilmacolm Hydro as permanent residents. Although he was a good journalist he was really a singer and actor manqué. He wouldn't have retired from the theatre in his fifties as he did from journalism. The public would have seen to that.

In 1915 my father, too old for military service and cursed with poor sight since a bad go of measles in childhood, celebrated his promotion by buying a newly built house in Highgate and made a successful business debut in London. Grandad, always thinking of others, was convinced that everyone in wartime London was starving and used to send down perishable food parcels. In those pre-fridge days they were an embarrassment to my mother who told him he must let her know if something was coming, so that she could organise her shopping.

One day there was a ring at the bell and she opened the door to find a policeman on the step. In his hand was an opened telegram.

'Can you explain this, madam?' He sounded grave. It had been handed in in Glasow that morning and read, 'Sending sausages tonight love Father.'

My mother smiled and suggested that it was self-explanatory. 'Why have you brought it?' she asked.

The arm of the law told her that they suspected it was a code referring to a zeppelin raid on London. It may have been a somewhat primitive security precaution to intercept such a message, but if there had been an air raid that night grandad might have found himself in the nick. Incidentally the sergeant returned next day to see if the sausages had arrived, which they had, though my father pointed out that a spy who knew his job would have sent them anyway.

In 1918 my father was elected to Parliament as a Coalition Liberal and in July 1919 – six years after the wedding – I arrived on the scene. A suitable opportunity to ask either of my parents the reason for the delay has never arisen, but in October 1918 the war must have looked as good as won and some sort of celebration may have seemed in order. I was their

7

only child and inherited my father's caution and his eyebrows. As my mother's speaking voice has no quaver in her ninety-third year I can thank her for being able to sing at sixty-two much as I did when I was thirty.

Undoubtedly some of the best times in her life were the years when my father represented Dunfermline Burghs in the House of Commons from 1918–22 and from 1931–35. She was a doughty platform speaker, a winning canvasser and a regular visitor to the constituency between elections. They fought four in all. Grandad was pressed into service at one as a door to door canvasser. He noticed a row of doors behind a tenement and knocked on the first one. No reply. He tried again.

'Who's there?' cried a querulous voice.

'I'm canvassing for John Wallace.'

'Go to hell! This is no a hoose, it's a water closet.'

My mother was also good at taking constituents on a tour of the Palace of Westminster. Sometimes my father, whose knowledge of the history of the Mother of Parliaments was sketchy at best, accompanied her. In the Crypt, where I had the good fortune to be christened, someone admired the large brass candlesticks on the altar.

'Ah yes,' said my father, 'they're very heavy. In fact if any man can carry one of them at arm's length from the altar to that door over there he can keep it.'

'I'll have a go,' quietly observed a herculean miner from Lochgelly. Before anyone could stop him he'd performed the feat with ease and was not in the least amused when his embarrassed Member of Parliament explained he was only joking. That was at least one vote down the drain.

My childhood was as happy as my parents could make it, but it was a drawback to have a father approaching sixty while I was still at kindergarten school. Golf and bridge were his relaxations and he thought nothing of spending all Saturday and sometimes part of Sunday at the golf club, either on the course or at the card table with his male cronies.

He was also an enthusiastic member of the famous Reform Club, becoming its chairman for the whole of the second war period, and he certainly subscribed to the sentiment that the House of Commons is the best club in London. Add to these preoccupations his frequent business and political visits to

Scotland and it's easy to understand why I was never bowled at in the garden or taken on exciting childhood expeditions by my father.

I was aware of great affection and concern from this reserved, secretive man – capable of occasional moments of relaxation and laughter, but mortally terrified of showing emotion. He'd probably married a bit too late to be able to change the bachelor style of life he'd enjoyed for more than twenty years, and at times my mother must have wished for more of his company.

She was a good, generous hostess who enjoyed entertaining and quickly built up her own circle of women friends, all of whom played either golf or bridge. The latter game at which she excelled was invariably played at any evening party in our house. Astonishingly my father would often invite three men into bridge after dinner, which banished my mother from the drawing room. I have no card sense whatsoever and never even mastered the intricacies of the scoring of contract bridge, so that their passion for the game was frustrating.

My mother shared the job of keeping me amused and occupied with various cooks and house parlourmaids – never a nanny, except odd girls who were temporarily engaged to keep an eye on me when we went on holiday, enabling my mother and father – usually at St Andrews – to play golf and bridge with one another for a change. At other times she took me to theatres and cinemas from a very early age, for holidays à deux when my father was too busy to join us and of course she was a splendid reader of adventure stories from *Tiger Tim's Annual* or, a little later, *The Boy's Own Paper* when I was battling with more than my fair share of chest colds and bronchitis in my childhood.

Like many only children I was starved of company my own age out of school hours. The youngest of the six Walker brothers next door was two and a half years older – a vast gap when you're five and not much better when you're ten. Though I experienced some loneliness I did have the benefit of the most up to date home entertainments of the 1920s.

They consisted of a table-sized wind-up gramophone in a mahogany case and a crystal set wireless called a Gecophone which also lived in a small mahogany box. In the drawing room was an upright piano from T. G. Payne, London (Gold Medal

9

Glasgow Industrial Exhibition 1904) which was only played by auntie Peggy when she stayed with us and sang beautifully to her own accompaniment, and by me – execrably – as I reluctantly practised for the succession of piano teachers who failed to get me beyond the most elementary stages of keyboard technique and musical theory.

Most of the records for the gramophone were of Harry Lauder and it was only by bitter experience that I discovered that the frying noise which preceded favourites like *Roamin' in the Gloamin'* lasted further and further into the song the more often it was played.

As well as Harry Lauder there was Sir Charles Santley singing *Simon the Cellarer*. He must have been very old at the time because the record has survived and this singer who was undoubtedly magnificent in his prime sounds like a quavering gnome.

We also had a record of the National Anthem and I got into serious trouble when I accidentally sat on it. Brought up as I was on a diet of steak & kidney pie, sausage & mash, roast beef & Yorkshire pudding, trifle, steam puddings and apple tart & custard *God Save the King* hadn't a hope in hell. Records in those days were about as tough as Dresden china and at seven I was politely described as well built.

I can't think why we had that record and why there was such a row when I broke it. We were a patriotic family but not to the extent of standing to attention round the gramophone.

The Gecophone provided a tremendous interest in my life every afternoon at 5.15 when, if I carefully manipulated the cat's whisker on the crystal, I could just hear – through ear-phones – *Children's Hour* from 2LO at Savoy Hill.

This was only possible because we had a good aerial. It was a length of cable that stretched from the back of the house high over the lawn to an oak tree at the top of the garden.

The lawn was the size of a tennis court – just; but undeterred by its limitations, my mother had persuaded my father to buy all the equipment, including nets all the way round the court, despite the fact that at one end the baseline was within three feet of a bank made into a rock garden, and at the other a similar distance separated it from a steep grassy slope down to the french windows of the drawing room.

If Jean Borotra or Suzanne Lenglen had been invited to one of my mother's tennis parties they would have discovered in two minutes that any attempt by their opponents to return a deep lob would result in their being netted like butterflies and probably sustaining a broken ankle into the bargain.

But of course it was not Madame Lenglen who was invited to play on our cramped court but Mrs Scott, Mrs Turnbull and Mrs Thornton, local ladies who, one sunny afternoon in the 1920s made up a tennis party doubles match with my mother. All wore the white, sleeveless knee-length frocks of the period. Mrs Scott had an eyeshade to match.

I watched them from the dining room window, having dispatched the last Japanese biscuit and slice of Battenberg cake left over from their tea to while away the time till the magical hour of 5.15.

My mother was about to serve, her dark brown hair gathered in a tight bun at the back of her head. She impatiently pushed her ivory bangle up her arm before delivering one of her underarm specials.

Mrs Thornton – a little overweight but energetic – made a wild effort to return my mother's low, looping serve. She struck it with the middle of her racket high into the air and by a thousand to one chance hit the wireless aerial a stinging blow.

It vibrated from end to end and then dramatically parted company with the oak tree. The cable, blackened by a year or two of soot, grime and pea-soup fogs, descended on the tennis players snaking wickedly like a snapped ship's hawser. It coiled round Mrs Scott and Mrs Turnbull and as my mother rushed to their aid it embraced her as well.

No one was hurt, but their tennis dresses looked as if the wearers had been flogged with a tarry whip.

For that afternoon it was game, set and match and though I hopefully twiddled the cat's whisker the voices of Uncle Mac and Auntie Sophie could no longer be heard.

Maybe it was the abrupt loss of my receiver that pushed me into being a transmitter. Even in those early days, inspired by my visits to the theatre and the annual trip to the Lyceum pantomime, I was attracted to any school theatricals like iron filings to a magnet. I had a good treble voice and, as already indicated, was only too ready to show it off. Though I wasn't aware of it the three talented Temples who had settled for school plays or charity concerts must have all been waiting with bated breath to see what would happen to me.

Chapter 2

What sort of education did I get at the end of that fairy cycle ride? The teachers were all women and the classes co-educational. It's surprisingly easy to conjure up pictures of some of these colourful ladies more than half a century later.

The tall, angular Miss Mason who took 'the little ones' had brown hair plaited into earphones, and her serene face was often lit with a smile of angelic bliss. With her it was all little pots of water, paint brushes, plasticine and sticking red stars with gummed backs in patterns on large sheets of stiff white paper.

She would draw a cat on the blackboard and write the word beside it. Then came the day when she decided we were ready to be stretched and boldly chalked up THE. I can still recall her wheeling round and saying triumphantly,

'Now then, what about *that* for a word!'

The 'big boys' went to Miss Griffin – an alarming lady with a deeply lined brownish face and lips slightly flecked with foam who stood no nonsense and ran the wolf cubs like a sergeant major. Inexplicably her propensity for losing her rag one minute and roaring with laugher the next made us all very fond of her.

By the time I had exchanged my dark blue Byron House cap for the Lincoln green of Heath Mount Preparatory School in Hampstead I could boast that my theatrical career had begun. I had the roles of King Alfred and Bottom the Weaver under my belt.

I went to my new school on the other side of Hampstead Heath sometimes in my father's newly acquired, chauffeur driven Austin 20 limousine, but more often in the single decker bus. It was a man's world where there were playground war games and a kick up the bottom was always on the cards.

Fortunately the headmaster, the Rev. A. R. K. Wells, a retired naval chaplain and an old Etonian whom we all feared, especially when he was being dangerously and quietly polite, set great store by a play at Christmas time. So my theatrical career continued. As a new boy I had to drop back to being a mere soldier in Henry V, but soon returned to feature billing as Friar Tuck.

Heath Mount, like all such schools, had hanging over it the necessity to get you up to the mark for some prestigious public school. The importance of doing well in the Common Entrance exam was reiterated to the point of paranoia. I had no particular anxieties on that score but I did wonder how I'd get on at boarding school when the time came. All the talk was of how tough it was at Sedbergh or how brainy they were at Winchester. No one seemed to know much about Charterhouse, where I was due to go in the summer of 1933.

My mother was convinced that without her care my chest colds in a draughty dormitory would swiftly relapse into pneumonia. In the event the opposite was the case. A rather more rigorous existence on the top of a Surrey hill at Godalming chased them away and I never had a bad one in five years.

Undoubtedly life at a boarding school like Charterhouse in the 1930s was mental torture to a small minority, tolerable to some and positively enjoyable to a sizeable number. After a short and occasionally painful period of adjustment I joined the last group. The constant companionship of boys my own age (not just in school hours as before) was, to an only child like myself, a much needed contrast to the adult world I knew at home.

I was ragged a good deal at first; not because I was a new boy, they were sympathetically treated on the whole. It stemmed from my background. My father was now sixty-five and his friends who visited our home tended to be in the same age group. I had inherited auntie's dangerous facility for mimicry, often exercising it unconsciously and expressing myself in an adult way that caused some amusement and ridicule. Once after I'd been to see the housemaster that shrewd, kindly man was heard to remark, 'Wallace never had a childhood, he was born an old man.'

The phase soon passed or people decided to accept my pompous delivery as a permitted eccentricity. I don't know which. Charterhouse was and is a friendly place.

In the fullness of time I became a sort of licensed jester, singing with my new banjolele at scout campfires as well as taking part in plays and play reading.

My mediocre performances in the compulsory games never diminished my enjoyment of them and I was an enthusiastic spectator whether the heroes of the first eleven did battle with Eton or Harrow on the beautiful cricket ground in summer or the footballers took on the flower of Lancing or Repton before we returned to our boarding houses in the fading winter twilight to warm our hands round huge mugs of tea and jockey for position at the fire with a doorstep of new bread on a long wire toasting fork.

It was a monastic, sheltered existence where privileges connected with the wearing of certain garments or walking on hallowed stretches of turf increased with seniority, but they carried increased responsibilities. Many activities that were compulsory in those days are now the choice of the individual and probably the emphasis of responsibility has changed too. For example I never knew that near Godalming railway station was a large and famous home for epileptic women and I'm certain none of my contemporaries did either. The present generation of boys almost certainly do, as a part of their increased awareness and concern for the community in which they spend five impressionable years.

Our masters all seemed personalities in their own right and far more relaxed in our company than the uneasy disciplinarians at Heath Mount. I can recall with affection and respect at least half a dozen who by word or deed influenced me profoundly.

Of them all the one who did most to steer me towards my ultimate destination was the musical director, Dr Thomas Fielden, a brusque, tactless man going very deaf. I didn't learn an instrument with him but he picked me for the choir and decided to assume responsibility for my musical wellbeing. After my voice broke he taught me songs of a much more serious nature than those I sang with my banjolele. Instead of *Never have a bath till you need one* or *Waggon Wheels* I was struggling with *Lord God of Abraham* from Mendelssohn's *Elijah* and the *Erlkönig* of Schubert. It was a violent change of emphasis. He knew nothing about voice production but in his spare time taught me the notes and something about interpretation. There wasn't a penny added to the school bill.

It never crossed my father's mind that I might one day sing or act professionally. I didn't dare let it cross mine because I knew I was destined to be a barrister. It was a matter of quiet pride to my father that by the sweat of his brow he could afford to give me such a good education. Had he been able to go to university as a young man, law would have been his choice.

At any rate when I went to Trinity Hall in the autumn of 1938 Tommy Fielden insisted on putting me in touch with a friend of his, Billy Drew, who was a respected singing teacher.

'Even if you're only going to sing for pleasure,' he said, 'You might as well learn how to do it properly.'

I was enthusiastic and my father was prepared to pay for the lessons. So far as he was concerned it was assisting me with a hobby. As for my mother? As one of those talented Temples she was probably already, though silently, bowing to the inevitable.

After the cosy existence of a house at Charterhouse and the final year with all its perks and privileges, the isolation of a set of rooms at Trinity Hall, Cambridge with the services of a 'gyp' or college servant to bring in breakfast and 'do' the fire inspired in me a mixture of emancipation and loneliness – added to the unaccustomed exercise of organising one's own work programme. I gravitated to the Amateur Dramatic Club and Billy Drew's studio, found I was a stiff, ungainly oarsman, was welcomed by the college football eleven – they only had ten till I arrived – and did enough work as a freshman to get a second. But in the first year of the war with all its distractions I could do no better than a third. I knew long before I entered the examination room that I'd never be much of a lawyer.

After five months at a Royal Artillery Officer Cadet Training Unit at Catterick I emerged with a pip on my shoulder and posted to the 98th Field Regiment Royal Artillery, a splendid outfit that had been the Sussex and Surrey Yeomanry and who fought their way through most of the major campaigns in Italy and France. I wasn't with them. After a few months – and before they left England – I contracted genito-urinary TB (probably due to infected milk) and had a couple of alarming and intimate operations. Then I was down-graded and put to work with the Army Entertainment Branch at South Eastern Headquarters in Reigate. I was very happy there till I succumbed to a TB spine. The tubercle bacillus really had it in for me.

I lay on a bed of plaster of paris, immobile for nearly two years. The whole contraption was mounted on a trolley so that I could be pushed round the hospital grounds. Many people died of this complaint at that time. There are now effective drugs to treat it, but then the best odds I could get for recovery was even money, which wasn't all that bad in the middle of a world war when you're twenty-two.

Dr Johnson once said that if a man knows he is to die in a fortnight it concentrates his mind wonderfully. I had much longer to contemplate the same possibility and the good doctor was quite right. I decided very early on that if I were lucky enough to get to the tote window to collect my winnings on that even money bet, they would take the form of abandoning my reluctant pursuit of a barrister's wig. Instead I would chance my arm with my first love – the theatre.

Apart from lying on my back the only other thing they could do was to encourage me to eat – and drink pints and pints of fluid each day. Every three months the two diseased vertebrae in my lumbar region were X-rayed, the only way of finding out if my chances of survival had improved. Eventually they decided I'd licked it and what they got on to his feet was a seventeen stone monster with legs that felt like sacks of potatoes. None of my clothes fitted and there was rationing! What matter! I was alive and when I cautiously bent over, the searing compelling pain I had known for so long had completely gone.

I convalesced at a guest house in Kilmacolm (the Hydro had become a naval hospital) in the winter of 1944 and, despite wearing a spinal jacket next my skin made of leather with steel reinforcements, I secured the all important first break – a leading part in a play for a small company in Glasgow which attracted critical acclaim and led to work for the BBC in

Scotland and the Glasgow Citizens' Theatre. I had never been inside a drama school or a music college and I couldn't believe my luck.

In Glasgow I got wind that the Scots actor and film star Alastair Sim was about to produce *The Forrigan Reel*, a James Bridie play with music, in London. On my return home I got hold of his address and rang his door bell to ask for an audition. To my joy he invited me in and eventually offered me a part. The run was brief but led to a part in a Christmas show at the St James's Theatre which in turn brought forth an invitation to audition for the Royal Opera House, Covent Garden, then starting up after the war.

Though the manager David Webster and his musical director Karl Rankl made encouraging noises and spoke of my singing the part of Papageno in *The Magic Flute* I felt out of my depth. It was one thing to be an actor with a couple of songs in your part. Grand opera was infinitely more formidable, yet I couldn't help being intrigued as I walked away through the fruit barrows in Floral Street that my voice might be up to it.

I decided to audition for another company which was about to start life just up the road at Seven Dials. This was the New London Opera Company at the Cambridge Theatre – a much more sensible size for a beginner. I sang the same audition song – an aria from Handel's opera *Berenice* – it was the only operatic aria I knew. Again it did the trick and certainly my luck was in. Their vocal adviser, the celebrated Italian tenor Dino Borgioli told me that a singer with a similar voice whom they'd engaged for their first production had had to withdraw earlier that day.

The impresario, a Russian business man, Jay Pomeroy, short and stocky with dark eyes that blinked rapidly when he was thinking of a suitable reply to an awkward question was mounting the opera season for his girl friend Daria Bayan, a musical comedy actress. It was financed by profits he'd made on whisky deals during the war which had been made heavily taxable by retrospective legislation and the Inland Revenue were suing him for about £400,000! Unfortunately for them we'd used most of it up by the time they'd won their case in the House of Lords. Unfortunate, too, for poor 'Pom' as we called him, because in the end he died a bankrupt. But the litigation

17

was hardly begun when on 12th June 1946 he presented Puccini's opera *La Bohème* and I made my opera debut as Schaunard.

The tenor was an American army captain Lester Ferguson and apart from Daria Bayan the rest of us were British and we sang in English. All the subsequent operas were in Italian and there was the frightening occasion when we sang *La Bohème* in English one night and in Italian two nights later. This was to enable the management to engage singers from abroad – especially Italians who would give the company an international flavour.

I've never had any cause to regret deciding to start in a smaller theatre. In the two years of the company's life (1946–48) I was given some marvellous parts and sang them alongside Italians, Germans, Jugoslavs as well as the British contingent who were mostly, like me, making operatic debuts. The Italians taught us how to pronounce their beautiful language correctly as well as imparting that indefinable element of an operatic performance, style. It was a wonderful opportunity to learn in the best of schools, the public arena, and I seized it with both hands.

You may be wondering how anyone could just walk into an opera company after a few singing lessons at Cambridge and a long major illness. I find it hard to explain myself. It would probably have been impossible if we had had any other conductor than Alberto Erede, who turned out to be not only a fine musician but a patient teacher as well.

He and the Italian chorus master George Coop taught me my roles along with a meticulous Polish coach Professor Maliniak. My inherited mimicry helped with the Italian, but I hardly had a singing lesson in the two years which was as remarkable as it was foolhardy, but Dino Borgioli was completely taken up with producing the first few operas and maintaining his practice of private pupils. He helped me with the interpretation of my biggest role, Dr Bartolo in *Il Barbiere di Siviglia*, but that was all. Dr Bartolo has featured in my career many times and in many places. Both Dino and Maestro Erede emphasised that the crusty old lawyer in love with his pretty young ward and outwitted by her and the handsome Count Almaviva must be played straight to gain the best comic effect. In this way both the character and the amusing situations can be sustained throughout the performance. It is fatal to go for easy laughs. What good advice to a young inexperienced artist, not averse to the sound of laughter.

I wasn't the only Scot in the Cambridge Theatre *Barber*. The Figaro and Almaviva were William and Murray Dickie from the west of Scotland, both with strikingly good voices in quite different ways. Bill, who died just after this book was finished, had the classic Italian high baritone timbre, while his brother's tenor has a unique lyric quality that made him the automatic choice as David in *Die Meistersinger* all over the world for many years and a permanent member of the Vienna State Opera for the rest of his career. We three have been lifelong friends. Bill retired into management many years ago, where he was, quite literally, loved and respected by the many artists who passed through his hands. He was a man of total integrity who never dissembled; in some people that can make for uncomfortable relationships, but Bill possessed an enormous sense of fun which invested even his most robust comments with an accompanying salve of humour. Not all the great names in entertainment are to be found at the top of bills. Our Cambridge Theatre reunions, which we've organised over the years on the flimsiest of excuses, will never be the same.

Despite all the help I received I still can't really explain how I managed to sing a role like Dr Bartolo after studying it from a standing start for only about a couple of months, but somehow singing on a stage in Italian with a full orchestra seemed to plug me in to a source of energy and concentration which was accompanied by the odd sensation of watching myself do it from a disembodied spot somewhere above my right ear!

Happily my father lived long enough to see me launched on this exotic path. He was proud and perhaps bewildered. Certainly one visit to the opera, the first of his life, was enough. The talented Temples? Generously delighted.

A reversal of my fortunes had begun with a vengeance and now, in retrospect, the best possible thing happened. Carl Ebert, the celebrated Glyndebourne artistic director was engaged to produce *Rigoletto* at the Cambridge Theatre. I took his eye in a small part and when he directed *Don Giovanni* for us I had the part of Masetto, the young peasant who makes a show of defiance to the Don and is beaten up for his pains. When the Cambridge Theatre season finally ended early in 1948 I got a letter inviting me to sing Masetto for Glyndebourne Opera at the Edinburgh Festival in August – under the direction of Carl Ebert. It was the start of a long association with that opera house in a fold of the Sussex Downs which, one way and another, continues to this day.

When Glyndebourne were kind enough to offer me a part in Verdi's *Un Ballo in Maschera* the following summer and Dr Bartolo in *Le Nozze di Figaro* the one after that, my life began to take on a pattern of opera in the summer and almost anything else from films to pantomime for the rest of the year. But it also took on a much more permanent pattern. On the 26th June 1948 (just before my first Glyndebourne season at Edinburgh) in the Bow Kirk in the heart of Fife I married Patricia Gordon Black – the second daughter of a friend and business colleague of my father. Though we lived four hundred and fifty miles apart we had met a number of times since we were children.

As Pat, fair haired with a complexion that knows not make-up is still looking after me, she'll forgive it if, just for the time being, I leave her in the little flat we rented in Highgate, cooking splendid meals, longing for a garden to tend, but keeping the place spick and span in spite of having to empty my ashtrays fairly often – yes, I smoked – without inhaling – until ten years ago, which she must have hated. I know she'll forgive me because for so long it was often her lot to be left behind. Wives in this profession have to be very special to stay for thirty-three years – I'm one of the lucky ones. Incidentally I had to tell her before we got engaged that as a result of my illness the chances of our having a family, though not ruled out, were slim.

Chapter 3

Alberto Erede became a close friend and in February 1950 he offered me a part in two performances of *Don Giovanni* at the Teatro Reggio, Parma, Italy! The role was, as you've guessed, Masetto.

Nothing more exciting or unexpected could have come my way; it was also frightening because Parma opera-goers give singers the bird with great regularity. The rehearsals in that city noted for cheese and violets were perilously short for such a difficult masterpiece – three days instead of five weeks. Apart from Casinelli who sang the title role, none of the others had sung the opera before. They stared at me in disbelief when Alberto told them I'd done it over fifty times.

The opera house was full for the first of the two performances. *Don Giovanni* hadn't been heard in Parma for seventy-four years!

Alas, one of the sopranos did get the bird that night. Admittedly she was not in her first youth but her only crime was to falter momentarily at the top of one or two very demanding phrases. It was heartless and cruel from her point of view and nerve-wracking from mine as I had yet to make my first entrance. I was safe enough in a comparatively minor role with no big display aria to reveal any fatal shortcomings.

To my delighted surprise the paper next day gave me an excellent write up and I realised then the advantage of being originally produced in the part by Carl Ebert. All the moves in Parma were different, but the character and the feeling for it that he'd given me worked just as well.

I went into the second and final performance with much more confidence, though the poor soprano had to have half her part cut to save her from further humiliation. She was very brave to appear at all and keep the curtain up for the rest of us.

*   *   *

It was a pleasant surprise to find a bank in Milan open in the early evening. The clerk accepted the modest wad of lire notes I wished to deposit, peeled one off the top and held it up to the light. His expression never changed as he produced a pair of scissors and cut it diagonally in half.

'Non e buono', he explained with a sympathetic smile. I watched anxiously as the whole of my travelling and hotel expenses while singing at Parma were given the same scrutiny. To my relief the rest were all buono.

I was completely exhausted. The last performance of *Don Giovanni* had ended at about a quarter to one that morning. Then there had been dinner at a local restaurant where, around half past two, I had been called upon to make a speech in my halting Italian. After a few hours sleep Maestro Erede and I had caught an early train to Milan. Bless his heart, the Maestro wanted to launch me into an international opera career, but it had to be done in the hour and a half at his disposal before he was obliged to dash off somewhere else to pursue his own.

We went straight from the station to a magnificent apartment where lived, he told me, an Italian Count married to an American lady of great wealth who was a patron of opera. Every morning, apparently, her salon was where singers and impresarios congregated, hopefully, to their mutual advantage.

A butler divested us of our coats and gravely conducted us up the elegant marble staircase. The salon was large – the sort of room you walk through, suitably awed, at Fontainebleau. The central feature was a concert grand piano – the lid shut to accommodate on top of it a positive library of opera vocal scores. Nearby, flexing his finger joints, was a typical olive complexioned, blue jowled, curly black haired repetiteur or opera coach. These are the pianists who work in opera houses like George Coop at the Cambridge Theatre to teach singers their parts, and who can play anything from the operatic repertoire straight off the bat, making the piano sound like the orchestra into the bargain. Many opera conductors started life as repetiteurs, including Alberto Erede.

The only other occupant of the salon recognised the Maestro and the two shook hands. He was Laszlo Halasz, director of the City Centre Opera, New York. Surely this was the sort of opportunity that only presents itself in one's dreams.

Our hostess arrived a moment later. I can't remember her name, but she was kind, informal and obviously very, very rich; otherwise she would never have appeared in public with a vital button missing from her blouse and one of her stockings spectacularly laddered. She called for coffee which was served in gold cups.

Maestro Erede had hoped that the salon would be full of people useful to me and was upset that we'd picked such a slack morning, though I thought a New York impresario wasn't bad for a start. When Erede suggested I might sing, Mr Halasz at once made it clear that he was only there to hear someone who would be arriving later. Undaunted, I ploughed through Masetto's short aria from *Don Giovanni* – just about the last thing anyone in his senses would choose to impress an opera house manager. I think Erede and I must have been so tired that its inadequacy as audition material didn't strike us until it was too late. Mr Halasz was brutally non-committal. On our way out we passed on the stair a handsome young man with a jewel in his tie-pin and the look of someone ready to sing himself aboard an airliner to New York.

Erede and I parted in the street, his sad, lugubrious face betraying the same feeling as I had about our expedition. It was the epitome of life in this profession – a personal success one day and the necessity to start all over again the next. I walked along the Galeria near the Scala Opera House where singers gather to discuss past triumphs and future prospects. I didn't recognise a soul, but Erede had arranged for me to see over the famous theatre and I passed through the stage door that had admitted Caruso, Chaliapin and Toscanini to some of the great nights of their lives. Standing on the empty stage and looking into the dimly lit auditorium was like a dream. I always have a shyness about being in a theatre where I'm not working, so it cost me a good deal to take a breath and sing a scale. The acoustic was perfect. Mine is not a big voice as operatic voices go but, with the orchestra sunk in that deep pit, it must be a joy to sing there. Even a whisper would be audible in that resonant arena. Since that day when any compere or toastmaster announces, as they sometimes do, that I've sung at the Scala Milan, I don't need to embarrass them by denying it.

I had decided to bank the proceeds of the Parma engagement in Italy against a possible future holiday, as I was returning to London by train and boat the next day. When I got back to my hotel I realised that I'd left myself with very little money for the next twenty-four hours. After an appalling dinner at the cheapest restaurant I could find I was nearly asleep on my feet and decided on an early night. My train didn't leave until next afternoon, but just to make sure that I wouldn't oversleep I set my alarm for ten o'clock and went out like a light.

It seemed like no time at all before the alarm jangled me awake. Good grief, I thought, it must be the end of the world. Ten o'clock and it's still pitch dark. It wasn't the end of the world – I'd gone to bed at nine and with unbelievable stupidity set my clock to go off one hour later. I lay in bed shaking with laughter – it seemed the perfect end to my Italian debut.

But I came back from Italy to face a problem. How could I pursue an operatic career without belonging to an opera company? Glyndebourne was a summer festival and when Covent Garden had re-auditioned me after the Cambridge season ended in 1948 they'd turned me down on the grounds that my voice was too small. This was an inexplicable decision in view of their interest in me two years earlier when I was a far less experienced singer, though I did get some sort of explanation over lunch about a quarter of a century later with Sir David Webster, the General Administrator.

'You know,' he said, 'at that time I was in the position of saying no to this one and yes to that one. I believe that if I'd done it the other way round we'd have been just as well served by the people we'd have engaged.' Those who say this is a precarious profession will nod sagely at this point.

I hadn't started out with the slightest intention of being an opera singer, I wanted to act, but I'd been carried along by the momentum and excitement of two years continuous opera at the Cambridge Theatre and the three Glyndebourne engagements at Edinburgh; yet I had to face the fact that a voice like mine was best suited to the comic roles in Italian opera which are not all that thick on the ground in the repertoire of most companies – and there weren't all that many opera companies in Britain anyway.

To make it even more of a problem I'd not had the years at a music college to equip me for the concert or recital platform – the mainstay of most singers' careers. Still I did have the possibility of doing theatre and film work between operas, though that raised another imponderable. Both opera and concert engagements have to be accepted as much as a year or even eighteen months ahead – whether for a short season or a single night, whereas notice of work in the theatre or in films is seldom more than a few weeks at the most. Therefore the chance of appearing in a long running play, a film or a musical might have to be turned down because of a couple of weeks of opera or even one or two concerts contracted many months before.

Yes, it was painfully obvious that an operatic and musical career could not be combined with one in the theatre and films. In five years I had established a couple of toes in each camp. Surely the time had come to leave one and put all my effort into the other. But which? Common sense indicated a total commitment to opera and maybe some sort of crash course in musical studies and repertoire to open up concert possibilities.

The more I thought about it the more I realised that there was something of my tone deaf father about me to counterbalance my musical grandfather on the other side of the family. The thought of abandoning all idea of working in the theatre was unbearable. That was probably the bit of my mother in me.

Give up opera and wait for someone to recognise me as an actor? Crazy. The demand for my services in that department was hardly overwhelming, though enough work had come my way to give me modest hopes. So I decided – not to make a decision, and to accept work in any field. One day, I assured myself, the decision would make itself. It never has.

There was another reason why I couldn't have abandoned an opera career in the 1950s, and his name was Rodolfo Mele (pronounced Maylay). He was a Neapolitan who had become naturalised before the war and was one of the most consistently successful backers of horses I've ever met. Not that I've met many, but Rodolfo had that rare distinction of having to change his bookmaker quite regularly. A large number closed their account with him because he won too often. He was also a magnificent singing teacher.

An old friend of Alberto Erede's, he'd been a frequent visitor to the operas at the Cambridge Theatre, but because it was part of my contract that all vocal matters were the responsibility of Dino Borgioli, Alberto had felt in honour bound not to introduce us until the contract had ended, even though I was, as I've said, getting no vocal tuition at all.

As soon as the company's final fling at the Stoll Theatre and a cinema in Croydon in 1949 was over Erede introduced me to Rodolfo and Meg, his charming Scots wife, and strongly advised me to have some singing lessons with him. I needed no second bidding. Rodolfo had come to London many years before the war and despite his failure to have the sort of singing career his voice would have justified, he never considered returning to Italy. He used to explain why he had never sung at Covent Garden very simply.

'I killed Blois. Colonel Blois was the artistic director and I wenta to see 'im and to singa for 'im. Mele, 'e said, I will give you a contract next season. Within a week he was dead. I don'ta dare see the next one in case the same thing 'appen to 'im as well!' Dear Rodolfo, that wasn't the only blow he had.

'I get a letter from an agent who invite me to England and I think that I am to sing in many opera 'ouses. When I get 'ere it turns out that I am to sing in Lyons Corner 'ouses at Leicester Square and the Strand – fourteen arias every day, and the money is notta very good.'

Anyway he stayed. He was rather below medium height, broad and deep chested. He had a cherubic face with high cheek bones and when he smiled or laughed, which was often, his eyes almost disappeared. He also possessed a fiery temper and an outspokenness which made him a few enemies, but endeared him to his friends.

It would be impossible to describe his teaching methods in a few sentences, not easy in a chapter, but he made singing easy and he did it very quickly. He often bemoaned the fact that he was incapable of spinning it out and making a lot of money from pupils.

'I makea them sing very quick and they say thank you very much, goodbye!' I didn't. I went to him pretty regularly till he died, and that was nearly thirty years later. I always took a new operatic role to him and anything else with which I was having problems, and often I'd just go for a check up. Every singer needs someone they can trust to hear them regularly and draw their attention to the faults and mannerisms that creep unconsciously into the performances of even the most experienced. Every now and then he'd ring me up.

'Ian, listen, I don'ta want your money for a lesson, but lasta night I 'eard you on the radio – you're singin' witha the larynx too 'igh and that makes the voice get smaller. Don'ta worry, you were OK, but I'm just warnin' you. Goodbye.' What a man and what a service!

He often said that a teacher worth his salt has to be able to 'make' outstanding pupils. He 'made' many including Ina Souez who can be heard on the pre-war Glyndebourne recording of *Don Giovanni* and Marion Studholme, whose splendid singing both in opera and on the concert platform will be well known to many readers. Oddly enough he can give me a lesson even now. If I have a vocal problem, I only have to sit down and think back on the many hours I spent in his studio and suddenly I recall an exercise or a piece of advice that enables me to produce the correct sound. When this happens I can hear again his cry of 'Ecco!' that expressed the exquisite satisfaction that overwhelmed him when a pupil had comprehended and could translate that comprehension into a vocal sound.

At night after his last pupil had gone he got out his form books and a list of the runners for the following day. He kept careful records of each horse's performance and awarded them points for what had happened last time out based on time, weight carried, the going, the wind and the differences between the various courses. He knew what to allow in his calculations for straight, flat courses as opposed to undulating tracks with a bend. Before the war a national newspaper offered him a job as their tipster with a good salary. He wasn't interested. Another time a bookie approached him with a fascinating proposition.

''E saya to me, Ian, whena they are all tryin' in a race you tell us whicha will win and whena they're not all tryin', we'll tella *you*.' He wasn't interested in that one either. He was a singing teacher who loved his job and backed horses as a relaxation. Despite his skill and scientific approach, I have to report that he did not die a rich man. As the famous theatrical impresario Sir Charles Cochrane once said about putting on shows, 'People remember your successes and forget that your failures swallow up an awful lot of your profits.'

Rodolfo put it another way. 'The number of times I lose by a short 'ead's amazin'.'

In the spring of 1950 I was really reaping the benefit of his teaching. I was invited to sing in a performance of Bach's *St Matthew Passion* at Glyndebourne, one of the events in the Lewes Music Festival, and a totally unexpected honour as far as I was concerned. The other soloists were Margaret Ritchie, Kathleen Ferrier, Eric Greene and Richard Standen, all highly experienced oratorio singers. The orchestra was to be conducted by Dr Reginald Jacques, a Bach expert, and included such illustrious names as Leon Goossens and Gareth Morris, to say nothing of Dr Thornton Lofthouse on the harpsichord. I had never sung a note of the solo part in my life – only the choir items in a school performance – and to say that I was apprehensive was no exaggeration. As the day of the performance approached I began to regret accepting the invitation to join such distinguished company in such a demanding work.

A visit to Dr Jacques' flat to go through my aria *Make thee clean, my heart, from sin* did nothing to allay my fears. Though he was extremely polite he couldn't conceal some irritation at my lack of experience in interpreting Bach and it was obvious that whoever had engaged me for this concert, it wasn't him.

'Go away and work at it. Bach isn't easy, you know,' were his parting words. I was only too well aware of it.

I noticed in the concert column of *The Daily Telegraph* that there was a performance of the work at Southwark Cathedral a couple of days before ours in which William Parsons, a highly regarded oratorio singer, was appearing in the part I was to sing at Glyndebourne. I decided to go and hear him. If I thought it would boost my confidence I had made a big mistake. Bill Parsons' interpretation was effortless and serene – something that could only come from a great experience, not only of the work, but of a style of singing about which I knew next to nothing. It was not at all operatic – just a beautiful voice singing Bach's music with all the intensity and musicianship of an instrumentalist. His words were clear but not dramatised. I had heard of the 'coolness' of oratorio singing; now I was watching and listening to someone demonstrating it to perfection. For me to acquire anything approaching it in two days was out of the question.

I did my best – not a good best, I fear, for I wasn't so much nervous as petrified and it must have shown. It bore out the truth of a statement attributed to the Polish pianist Paderewski, 'Nerves are guilty conscience.' Everyone was very nice to me afterwards which is not always a good sign. One of the nicest was Kathleen Ferrier, perhaps the sweetest and most modest artist I've ever met. It was my first and last *St Matthew Passion*.

I dare say I could have learned how to do justice to such a great work, but I couldn't imagine myself spending long hours in cathedrals, churches and concert halls all over the country – a suitably grave expression on my face – awaiting my solos in the *St Matthew Passion* or other similar works like Mendelssohn's *Elijah* or Handel's *Messiah*. My musical talent, such as it is, seems better suited to cheering people up than uplifting them spiritually.

It was therefore with some relief that I found myself within a month doing a comedy programme on television with Bobby Howes – one of the pre-war musical comedy stars I had enjoyed during school holidays in shows like *Jill Darling* and *Mr Cinders*. I don't recall much of my own contribution except that I sang an absurd Victorian oddity by Gounod entitled *Vulcan's Song*. The lyric is about Realms of Endless Night – Glowing Furnaces and Heavy Hammers. While I was singing it they did a camera trick which turned everything white black and vice versa. Nobody listened to the song. They were too busy trying to adjust their sets.

The show was televised live (as they all were then) from the BBC studios at Alexandra Palace in north London. The designer was Stephen Bundy. At the end Bobby, a small man with a winsome smile and an uncertain temper, was to blow up Ally Pally, as it is affectionately called, and this effect was to be achieved by using a table model of the buildings containing a small explosive charge which was to be set off at the turn of a switch. Of course the explosion couldn't be rehearsed – there was only one model, but we were told it couldn't fail to work. When the moment arrived the viewers first saw Bobby pushing down the plunger of an old fashioned detonator, then the camera cut to the model, which looked convincingly like the real thing – but there was no explosion. The producer held the shot of an unscathed Ally Pally as long as he dared, and finally his patience was rewarded. A tiny wisp of smoke appeared from one corner of the model. No one even thought of shouting 'bang!', but Bobby's despairing voice could be heard accusing the hapless and blameless designer.

'Oh bungling Bundy!' he cried. Thirty years later in 1980 poor old Ally Pally did go up in flames – accidentally.

Live television was much more of a strain than any other form of entertainment, especially when there was only one channel seen by the whole nation. You knew that any disaster would be the main topic of conversation in every commuter train the following morning and for a few years after the war no one had devised a way of prompting an actor who'd 'dried' (forgotten the words) during a play. The studio manager had a script in his hand, but all his preoccupations were, as they are today, with technical matters – ensuring the cameras don't collide, that the microphone or its shadow doesn't encroach on the screen, that the performers are correctly positioned and so on. Actors' lines were low on his priority list until the worst happened – by then it was too late.

Singers could have the words written on a board at the side of the camera, but your eyes looking to one side could take on a fixed stare and, as only so many words will go on a board in large enough letters to be readable, more than one was often required. This could lead to various hazards. The board not being changed quickly enough or, even worse, the wrong one appearing. Anything going wrong with a crib is worse than no crib at all. 'Idiot boards' as they are called are still in use but my sight is not good enough to see them without glasses, which gives the game away!

Eventually in those days when plays and musicals were still presented live on television an ingenious device was invented to help artists in trouble. A prompter was introduced into the studio: he held the script in one hand and a bulb connected to the control panel in the other. If anyone dried he pressed it cutting off the sound on your set. He called out the actor's line and then released the bulb. Simplicity itself, and it may have originated from the presence of mind shown by the late Harold

Warrender who forgot his lines during a TV play, but instead of standing there frozen with horror could be seen silently mouthing words.

The producer in the control box concluded that the sound system had broken down and ordered the display of the card 'Normal Service Will Be Resumed As Soon As Possible' which viewers frequently saw in the late 1940s and early 50s. In the ensuing confusion Harold grabbed the script, found his line and the play continued. I believe he didn't appear on TV for a year as a punishment, poor chap, but maybe he sowed a useful seed in some technician's mind.

Nowadays autocue has taken much of the terror out of the live television that still happens every day, as well as smoothing out the problems in certain types of recorded programmes. The words come up on a roller caption which, by a system of mirrors, is visible as you look straight into the camera. The speed of it is controlled by the operator who hears the broadcaster talking through earphones. Of course it can break down. That's why news readers always have the script there as well.

*   *   *

One advantage singers have over actors is the large number of private individuals and organisations who need our services at functions of all kinds from public dinners and Masonic Lodge meetings to concerts at music clubs and choral societies all over the country. We're not wholly dependent on the media or theatrical managements. Much of the work is straightforward, but every now and then you find yourself asked to do something out of the ordinary. In 1950 I was just beginning to get a few concert offers, mostly from folk who wanted something operatic. Out of the blue I received a letter from the Spiritualist Association of Great Britain inviting me to sing at public seance in Hornsey Town Hall. I live in the borough of Hornsey. I rang up the writer of the letter and asked him how on earth they'd got hold of my name.

'No mystery about that,' he laughed, 'When we hold such seances we always ask the town hall we've booked for the name of a good local singer and they suggested you.'

'What do you want me to sing?'

'Oh, that's up to you – what about *The Toreador's Song* from *Carmen?*' He sounded very jolly. I decided against Bizet though what I did choose seemed, when I got there, even more incongruous. My accompanist was Bryan Balkwill – a friend from the Cambridge Theatre days who was steadily making a reputation as a conductor. His wife Susan came along too and joined Pat and my mother in the audience.

The Town Hall was packed. The majority of those present were female and the average age was on the high side. On the posters my name was prominently featured with the legend, 'Direct from Parma Opera House, Italy.' Bryan and I were to join the platform party and, as we entered the hall, we could hear the strains of *Nimrod* from Elgar's *Enigma Variations* being played on the piano, which was not on the platform, but down on audience level. The pianist was a middle aged lady wearing a large hat that boasted a quantity of artificial fruit.

Bryan and I took our places, determined not to catch one another's eye. The first part of the proceedings was interesting. A speaker frankly accepted that at such a meeting there must be many present who were sceptical about the possibility of establishing contact with those who had passed over. He would attempt to convince us how possible it was.

The story he told concerned the crash at Beauvais in 1929 of the British airship the R 101 with the loss of forty-eight lives out of fifty-six on board. Within a few weeks a medium at a seance suddenly started to speak with the voice of the captain of the R 101 and using the words 'Tell Eckener, tell Eckener!' Then followed a great deal of technical information which related to the crash – information that the medium had no conceivable means of knowing. Dr Hugo Eckener was the great German expert on airships and when he received a transcript of the medium's words he declared that they entirely explained the causes of the disaster.

We were all fascinated and impressed. It was a rivetting account excellently delivered and I sustained an awful jolt when in the next breath he added, 'And now Ian Wallace will sing for us.'

I got to my feet, Bryan clattered down the steps to the piano, and we gave them one of the Brahms *Four Serious Songs*: 'Though

I speak with the tongues of men and of the angels.' It left everyone rather bewildered.

Then it was time for the medium to appear. She was small, middle aged with short, untidy grey hair and a wrinkled face. She wore a shapeless, crumpled purple dress, but it was her eyes, bright and clear, darting here and there that held our attention. She seemed pretty jolly too and practically danced around the platform as she addressed us.

'Don't be alarmed, I shall not go into a trance or anything like that – what's that, dear?' She looked upwards, holding up a hand for silence as if she couldn't quite hear whoever it was who was speaking to her. Indeed her balletic entrance had inspired an excited twitter from the audience.

She held this listening attitude for a few moments, smiling and nodding as she listened to her silent interlocutor.

'Right, dear. Now, does the name Bob mean anything to anyone?'

'Yes!' called a voice from the hall. 'That'll be my husband. He died last week.'

'That's right, dear. Tell me, does the name Elsie mean anything to you?'

'Oh yes,' cried the same voice, 'That's my sister who lived with us. She died before Christmas.'

'Now, dear, would it be true to say that in this world Bob and Elsie didn't hit it off too well?'

'That's right. Fought like cat and dog they did.'

'Well, Bob says they're getting on like a house on fire where they are now, dear.' The audience rocked with laughter and the departed Bob and Elsie were not the only links established with the next world that night to produce laughter from the audience. Perhaps many people there were laughing for the first time since their bereavement. It was a mixture of relief and mild hysteria and I began to wish I'd brought one of my comic songs with me. That medium gave a long virtuoso performance which undoubtedly brought solace and reassurance to some of those present, and though she didn't remove my built-in scepticism, she did reinforce my belief in that remark addressed to Horatio about there being more things in heaven and earth.

Just before she finished she once more cocked her head

upwards into the listening position and looked expectantly towards the ceiling.

'Who's that?' Pause. 'I see. Is there anyone here who has lost someone who is allergic to fat people?' I sat very still and I saw my mother's head go down. That description fitted my father who had died the previous April. A kindly, reasonable man in every way, he did, for some reason, have a distaste for fat people and was most upset that my illness had left me very overweight. But I couldn't believe that it would be his style to announce himself at a public seance, and if he did, it wouldn't be to mention this one curious prejudice. A cockney lady in the audience saved us further embarrassment and suspense.

'That'll be 'Arry!' she yelled. 'Always goin' on abaht it 'e was.' What a relief!

I had to sing one more song to round off the proceedings. I only had the one with me and so couldn't change it, but it did raise a few smiles on and off the platform: *Oh Mistress Mine, Where are you Roaming?*

Although Glyndebourne was my operatic sheet-anchor, there was one other important source of work for British freelance opera singers in 1950 – the BBC Opera Department. Under its manager David Harris and its musical director Stanford Robinson it pursued an adventurous policy presenting a wide variety of operas, mostly in English, at its Camden Studio – a beautiful old theatre near Mornington Crescent Tube Station, alas, no longer rented by the BBC. These were concert performances not staged in any way, but the cast wore evening dress for the transmission, and an invited audience provided an added sense of occasion.

Within a few days of my Bobby Howes television show I was rehearsing for one of those BBC studio operas, Borodin's *Prince Igor*. I had quite a small part. Only a week before the performance the bass who was to sing the leading part of the Khan Konchak had to withdraw due to illness and I was asked to take it on. This was not such a daunting task as it sounds. Though the Khan is a dominant figure in the opera, his principal scene consists of a recitative with Igor followed by an aria with a beautiful, familiar melody.

I was told of my good fortune at the lunch break in rehearsals by the BBC repetiteur of those days, Leo Wurmser, a man whose perpetually anxious appearance reflected his disposition which was pessimistic.

'We haven't much time, do you think you can do it?'

I said that I'd have a bloody good try. Suddenly he snapped his finger and thumb.

'Ah! I have an idea. Go now to Colin Shreeve's shop in Newport Place and see if you can get a record of the scene by Chaliapin – it will be in Russian, but it will give you an idea of how it should be done.'

Colin Shreeve's Collector's Shop boasted a magnificent stock of rare opera records going back to the beginning of the gramophone era. He was more like a genial, knowledgeable mine-host than the owner of a shop, and his views on singers and singing were pungently entertaining. One of his customers ventured to criticise Melba. Colin's fruity tones of outrage could have been heard in Charing Cross Road.

'Sir! In this establishment we worship at the shrine of Melba. Kindly leave.'

He loved it when singers came in and sometimes produced a glass of sherry if business was slack. On this occasion it was a quick visit. He had what I wanted, I paid my pound and returned to the BBC in triumph with the precious second hand twelve inch 78 record.

Khan Konchak had been one of the legendary Feodor Chaliapin's great roles still remembered by those few who had seen him perform it at Drury Lane in 1914. In his big scene the Khan visits Prince Igor in his tent. He has defeated him in battle and taken him prisoner, but the Khan is chivalrous in victory and treats his captive well. He chides him for looking so downcast, praises him for his courage in battle and suggests that if they could only join forces they would conquer the world.

'Right,' said Leo, 'Let's listen to the great man and we'll follow him in the vocal score.'

The recitative was on one side of the disc, the aria on the other. As the engineer turned it over after side one I glanced at Leo. He shrugged his shoulders, his eyes regarded the ceiling and his eyebrows were as high as they would go. When we'd heard side two Leo shut his score and said, 'Will you promise me something? Will you promise me faithfully not to play that again until after our performances of *Prince Igor* are over?'

I'm sure that the great Russian bass would have been the first to admit that he took a few liberties with the music on that record, and it was probably exactly the way he sang it on the stage. In every respect but one it was no help to me at all. He was sometimes surprisingly out of tune, elsewhere he went at twice the speed indicated by Borodin, while he held on to some notes for so long that the conductor must have been tempted to look at his watch in an attempt to urge him on. If I had emulated that performance for Stanford Robinson he would have been looking for a second replacement, but it must be remembered that Chaliapin belonged to a generation of opera singers who had things very much their own way. The ascendancy of the conductor as the arbiter of musical taste in the opera house is a more recent development. Nevertheless what did come across clearly on that old record was the character of Konchak. That was a great help to me, and if old Feodor could get away with standing the music on its head to create that character, good luck to him!

When I told Rodolfo of my lucky chance I could see the light of battle in his eye. We worked on the part whenever I could get away from rehearsals. He showed me how to darken the colour of my voice, but one thing he couldn't do was convince me that when the moment came I would sing a splendid bottom F – the lowest note in the aria and an important one at that.

'You can do it, Ian!' he would say in exasperation. I could – in the morning with the voice still heavy with sleep, I could do it in the afternoon when nothing was at stake, but at night, under nervous tension, every voice goes up a little, and that was why I knew that I would never be able to call myself a true bass. There were too many bottom Fs in the bass repertoire, to say nothing of Es, E flats and, in the case of Osmin in Mozart's *Die Entführung* and Baron Ochs in Richard Strauss's *Der Rosenkavalier*, Ds!

A measure of the work that Rodolfo and Leo put in on my behalf that week was to be found in *The Listener* whose music critic was kind enough to write: 'Of the individual singers Gre Brouwenstyn with her even voice up to top C and her intelligent phrasing and Ian Wallace, who has the right kind of trolling bass for the Khan, gave the most distinguished performances.'

36

He must have been away putting the kettle on when I produced no more than a sort of strangulated death rattle on that lowest note.

Beecham stories have become a branch of musical folk-lore. There is one connected with *Prince Igor*, though not with that performance, and the Welsh baritone Bruce Dargavel.

One day Beecham invited him to his house to give an audition. Whatever it was Bruce sang delighted the bearded baronet who, as an afterthought, asked him if he'd ever sung the Galitsky aria from *Prince Igor*. Bruce knew it well, but thought he might impress Sir Thomas even more by a little subterfuge.

'No, I'm afraid not, Sir Thomas, but if you've got a spare copy by any chance I'll have a go at sight reading it.'

The copy (which Bruce had noticed lying on a table) was produced and off he went, holding it up but hardly looking at it. When he had finished Sir Thomas exclaimed,

'What a remarkable fellow you are, Dargavel! Not only do you read at sight but you translate from the Russian at the same time!'

Bruce had failed to notice that his copy was in Russian only. Beecham, of course, adored that sort of effrontery which was so in tune with his own character.

Bruce was also remarkable for the astonishing range of his voice. He could – and did – sing miscellaneous concerts starting with the Sarastro bass arias from *The Magic Flute* and, after working his way up through baritone arias like *Eri tu* from *Un Ballo in Maschera*, he would finish with *The English Rose* from *Merrie England* in the original tenor key including the top C! This astonishing facility may well have been his undoing because using the extremities of the voice too much takes its toll in the end. He had a distinguished career, but had he concentrated on the baritone register he would have been world class.

That summer Beecham was involved with Glyndebourne for the only time in his career. It was an ambitious project commissioned by the Edinburgh Festival – Richard Strauss's opera *Ariadne auf Naxos* combined with Molière's play *Le Bourgeois Gentilhomme* for which Strauss had composed incidental music and a ballet. Apart from the ballet, which was in the capable hands of Madame Rambert, Carl Ebert produced both the play and the opera as well as *Le Nozze di Figaro* for good measure.

The play had been translated into English by the actor Miles Malleson who also headed the cast.

I very much doubt if any director today would be prepared to produce two such major works at a top international festival opening on successive nights – or anywhere else for that matter! Not only that – in those days directors did their own lighting, sitting up most of the night before the dress rehearsal deciding every lighting change, giving detailed instructions to the electrician and stage manager. Now lighting has become a production skill in its own right and names like Richard Pilbrow or Andrew Bridge on the programme is part of the hallmark of a good production. Such experts take a considerable weight off the director's shoulders.

Ebert was sixty-two in 1950 and was to continue to perform this sort of feat regularly for Glyndebourne for many years with a much smaller staff of production assistants than is commonplace in the 1980s. He worked with great thoroughness and attention to detail, remaining with the company throughout the season and, where necessary, giving the cast notes after each performance. Jani Strasser, the head of music studies would follow him round the dressing rooms taking us cheerfully to task for any musical errors that night. Thus were the standards maintained.

Beecham was only partially in his element. He must have enjoyed conducting such a lavish and successful production, but he was born to be a number one, not equal first. Beecham with Glyndebourne at Edinburgh was a brilliantly successful experiment that might not have worked quite so well a second time.

Those of us concerned with *Le Nozze di Figaro* were not confronted by the most colourful and outspoken English conductor of this century. Instead Ferenc Fricsay, a young Hungarian maestro (also making his Glyndebourne debut) was in charge of a cast headed by the American baritone George London – who was to become one of the great Wotans, the Count was Marko Rothmuller who had been our Rigoletto at the Cambridge Theatre and the adorable Sena Jurinac from Bulgaria, whose Cherubino made every male member of the cast, married or single, her slave.

One afternoon the Figaro cast were engaged by the BBC to

record a short excerpt from the opera from the stage of the King's Theatre, where we were appearing in Edinburgh. This was to be done in our ordinary clothes and with no audience present. The BBC were sending the programme down a post office line to London where the recording equipment was operating. They didn't have many tape recorders in 1950. We stood in a tight group on two levels, some on the stage itself, the rest on an eighteen inch rostrum for better sound definition. Just as we were about to start a fault developed on the line and there was a delay. Murray Dickie, the Scots tenor who was singing Basilio said to me, 'We look just like a school photograph.'

I walked out in front of the group, took off my jacket, threw it over my head and, like an old-fashioned photographer, said, 'Look at the birdie!'

The cast laughed, the orchestra stood up to see what was happening and then they began laughing too. Mr Fricsay was not amused. He had very little English and didn't use any of it. He shouted and yelled in Hungarian, but at least twice I heard my surname. He was very, very angry. When he finally subsided I whispered to Marko Rothmuller, 'Do you understand Hungarian?'

'Yes.'

'What did he say?'

'I'd rather not repeat it.'

'Was he shouting at me?'

'Yes.'

'Was it pretty bad?'

'Yes.'

At that moment we got the all clear to record. When it was over the stage manager said, 'Mr Fricsay wants to see you in his room.'

My heart sank. That evening was the last performance and rows on performance days are particularly upsetting.

He was sitting with his wife looking at a road map.

'Hallo,' he said. 'You are Scottish, no?'

'Yes, maestro.'

'Good. You show me quick way to London out of Edinburgh. I go tonight after the opera.' My photographic act was never mentioned.

Such a frivolous anecdote may seem inadequate coverage of an engagement at the Edinburgh Festival in the days when it was regarded by travel agents all over the world as 'event number one'. But, just as a soldier after a battle can only speak of what befell his platoon, so I can only record my own impressions – and while I was doing my job without anything untoward happening there's nothing worth mentioning. This fact of showbusiness life was brought home to me much more recently when, shortly before he died, I sat next to the celebrated Shakespearean actor Sir Donald Wolfit at lunch in the Garrick Club. He had just returned from an Australian tour and felt aggrieved that the success of it had failed to inspire even a paragraph in the British press.

'We played to capacity everywhere – but not a word! – *not a word*!' He looked in vain to Sir Bronson Albery, the aged theatre owner sitting at the head of the table, for a sympathetic comment. I dared to break the embarrassed silence.

'Of course there wasn't, Donald,' I ventured. He slowly turned to me with the expression of baffled rage that he used in *King Lear* when Goneril and Regan were being particularly obstreperous.

'Explain yourself, my boy.' Donald was a kind, courteous man, but he was labouring under considerable emotion and I could have easily had his avocado and prawns as a head dress.

'Don't you see? There's no news value when you fill a theatre. Everyone expects you to do that – and you did it. If the theatres had been empty the papers would have been full of it.' The dear man looked ridiculously pleased. Then he frowned.

'But what must I do to get publicity for a tour like that?'

'Difficult. It's probably a choice between stopping a runaway horse and indecent exposure.'

Chapter 4

When the Festival was over Pat and I, blessing the fact that petrol rationing had ended that summer, pointed my dark blue Austin 12 towards Fife and a few days holiday at her mother's home near Cupar. Today the Forth Road Bridge makes light of this journey but it's possible to be nostalgic for the car ferry boats still operating in 1950 with their tough looking skippers and the crew men shoe-horning a surprising number of cars, lorries and buses on board for each trip.

The crossing took about ten minutes and then, winding our way up from North Queensferry, we headed east to Kirkcaldy, where my father was born in 1868 and from there another sixteen miles brought us to Edenwood, the sandstone house with a large conservatory standing in spacious pleasantly wooded grounds, a large paddock stretching away from the front, a marvellous walled garden one acre in size and a view of the distant Lomond Hills.

Pat's father Michael Black had died in his forties four years previously. He was a quiet, steadfast intelligent Scot with a natural dignity and charm of manner that many actors would have envied, who had married an Englishwoman, Gladys Temple Thomson. Slim, dark and vivacious, she was elegance personified in the hunting field and a skilled and generous hostess who had adapted well to Fife with its cold winters, shooting parties and hunt balls. She was also an indefatigable committee member for numerous good causes.

Michael had been a director of Nairns, the linoleum company where my father had started his business life as a boy. It was this connection that had brought about the friendship between our two families. He also cultivated the five hundred acres of Edenwood Farm, breeding pedigree Aberdeen Angus cattle and Pat, after she left school in the middle of the war, worked there as a land girl.

When Michael died Gladys had bravely decided to keep on

the herd – an expensive type of farming but one that was to bring a year of glory in the show ring (the Supreme Championship at both the Royal and Royal Highland Shows) before she was forced to break up the herd and farm commercially.

For Pat one of the joys of a visit to Edenwood was, of course, going round the farm casting a critical eye over those black aristocrats, the sheen and texture of their coats paying tribute to their first class condition. She would converse knowledgeably and enthusiastically with the cattleman, an irrepressible Aberdonian with a blue tweed cap at a perky angle above his shiny red face, and at such times I was very much aware of her love for country life and her gifts which in London could never be fulfilled.

We had been married for two years and it was becoming obvious that the surgeon's pessimistic predictions about my inability to provide Pat with children were correct. No one in Fife had been tactless enough to ask those arch questions about a family that can distress a childless couple, but we were meeting large families every day and the unspoken question was in the air. Despite my busy life we had made no attempt to postpone a family; at the same time we didn't feel like submitting ourselves to tests that might do nothing but remove our hopes for good.

We often spoke of adoption, but if the subject came up in conversation with Gladys or my mother, both were extremely discouraging. Both could quote instances where it had not been a success, neither was impressed by our argument that there were some pretty unsatisfactory people about who had been born in Holy Wedlock.

We didn't worry too much about it in 1950 because we knew that any adoption society, told that the adoptive father had only been pronounced fully recovered from genito-urinary and spinal TB two years earlier, would say no and quite rightly insist on a longer period of time in case I relapsed. This wait must inevitably have been more disappointing for Pat than for me with all the excitements of a career unfolding, but she never showed it.

The few days in Fife were soon over and we had to go home. This extraordinary year of Parma, *The St Matthew Passion*, TV comedy, *Prince Igor* and *Le Nozze di Figaro* still had one or two surprises up its sleeve.

We came back to London in one long day, sharing the driving in fifty mile spells, but our destination was not the place where we'd started our married life.

Then we'd been lucky enough to find the small flat (where I left her on an earlier page!) on the top floor of an old house in Highgate that had just been converted and, with the help of a thousand pounds which my father had given me within five minutes of hearing we were engaged, we had furnished it as nicely as we could. New furniture was rationed in those days and engaged couples had to apply for dockets to buy 'utility' bedroom and living room suites. There wasn't much choice but we were delighted with our eyrie high above north London with a view from the living room window of endless rows of terraced houses, shops and playing fields stretching away towards the docks and Essex. I'd even managed to get a ridiculously cheap reconditioned mini-piano in Harrods' sale.

Then, less than a year later, my father died leaving my mother alone in the large house they'd bought in 1915 when his promotion in Nairns brought him south to manage their London office. It was newly built and they were the first owners. Until I married Pat I had known no other home and I was fond of it. My mother's feelings went much deeper. It was her pride and joy.

This faced me with a problem. Though my father was eighty when he died, my mother was only fifty-eight; she might live for many years and the way things looked financially I couldn't see her being able to afford the running of the house on her own. For her to have to sell it after thirty-five years and find something smaller would be a great wrench.

So when Pat and I came back to London from Scotland our brief tenancy of our little flat was over and we were returning to half my family home where we had taken up residence a few months earlier. We had planning permission to divide it into two parts. Looking back it was not a wise decision on my part. Though the architect's plans were ingenious and looked well when complete, it wouldn't have been possible to make the two parts really self contained without the sort of radical changes to the existing house that in my mother's opinion (and it was hard to disagree with her) would have defeated the object of the exercise.

Thus we had embarked on the traditionally perilous home-sharing relationship with its inevitable tensions and difficulties. We all managed to make it work for nearly a decade, but it wasn't fair to either of the two ladies involved and, as I realised later when we'd got the financial side sorted out, unnecessary any way.

We had happy times there and some marvellous parties, but we shared the same front door – and I believe that as much for my mother – a woman of supremely independent spirit – as for Pat and myself, also well fancied runners in the independence stakes – that was a strain. I was entirely responsible, brushing aside my mother's misgivings when she said,

'Will you really be satisfied with it?'

'Of course,' I replied and meant it, though at the back of my mind I knew that trying to do the best for everyone is a risky business.

There was another odd consequence of this decision. Even though things were going quite well for me the leap from a two roomed flat to half a mansion in eighteen months would have been rash in the extreme if I'd had to face mortgage payments – always assuming that I could have got a building society to look at me!

Half that big house with its large garden, spacious rooms and good address was far more than I could have afforded at that early stage in my career. Comic basses, even those who earn a bit on the side doing other things on radio and television, don't earn star salaries and though I could afford to run our part of the house and pay for the alterations, that was as much as I could manage.

Most folk reading this would probably consider us extraordinarily fortunate to have had a comfortable home, never mind how it came about. But then not everyone has that puritanical streak in their make-up that besets many of those with connections north of the border. As an elderly Scots lady once told me,

'It doesn't prevent you straying from the path of righteousness – it just means that if you do you won't enjoy it.'

Even now some grain of my Scots ancestry makes me wish that we'd stayed in our little flat until we could have afforded to look for a house of our own. We have one now, still in Highgate and by a sort of irony it's also half of a much larger house. We love it very much, but I wish we'd come to it by a different route.

My father, as I've said, started work at fourteen and bought his London house thirty-two years later. It was a great achievement. I was starting off living in the style that had taken him half a lifetime to reach and I don't think I've profited from that as I should.

He left me a little capital – nothing like enough to live on, but enough to tide over a year or two if I'd been determined to follow one type of career at the expense of everything else. It could certainly have covered some sort of training.

Instead I accepted the steady stream of varying offers which has continued until the time of writing and which have gradually turned me into a freelance troglodyte – very thankful to be in demand, but pursuing a career rather like a music hall artist of the past called Sirdani, whose act was to keep about twenty plates or tumblers revolving on sticks as he dashed up and down giving each of them a stir as they threatened to wobble and fall.

I think I inherited my father's capacity for hard work but not his singleness of purpose. He fought his way to a higher standard of living. I've been a little too fearful of losing it.

* * *

Small opera companies doing one or two productions a year have always been a godsend to young singers and one of those in the early 1950s was the London Opera Club run by an Austrian singing teacher, Ernest Urbach. Apart from being a vehicle for his advanced pupils the object was to give an airing to lesser performed works. Nobody expects to make any money out of this sort of company but every now and then someone establishes a reputation.

In the autumn of 1950 they were presenting a double bill of *Le Pauvre Matelot* by Darius Milhaud and *The Night Bell* by Donizetti and invited me to sing in both at the Chester Festival. As my only other operatic engagement for that three months was two radio performances of *Der Freischutz* I was delighted. I enjoyed portraying the villainous forester Caspar in my dinner

45

jacket at the Camden Studio of the BBC, but it was no subsitute for opera on the stage.

The Night Bell was written by the famous Italian composer to rescue an opera company who had lost their leading tenor and takes place at the home of an elderly chemist who has just married a young girl.

An unexpected arrival at the wedding reception is Enrico (baritone), the girl's former lover whom she had given up for dead when he went to the wars. Enrico is furious with her for marrying such an old ninny and is determined that the chemist will never have a chance to climb into the marriage bed.

He engineers this by pushing through the chemist's letterbox a spoof government edict decreeing that all chemists must dispense medicines at night in person and not leave the job to their assistants.

Yes, you've guessed it. The night bell keeps ringing as a succession of patients arrive with prescriptions made up of scores of complicated ingredients. All of them are, of course, Enrico in a series of hilarious disguises which he sustains until dawn is breaking and a coach arrives to take the frustrated old apothecary to a chemists' congress miles away. Among those waving him goodbye are his wife and Enrico.

We were lucky to have the American baritone Bruce Boyce as Enrico with his roguish eye and subtle sense of comedy. Bruce is six feet five and broad, which made the disguises, all unsuspectingly accepted by the chemist, even more absurd and we had the advantage of a witty English translation by Christopher Hassall – Ivor Novello's lyricist – and a young producer making his name – Basil Coleman.

When I played the old chemist I was thirty-one and I played him absolutely straight – except for a little comic business with pill boxes, bottles and prescriptions several feet long – because the laughter is inspired by a real person in an unreal situation. I'd play him the same today but with a difference. Now I'm the age of that chemist and more conscious of the tears that are a hairsbreadth from the laughter.

There'd be another difference if it were produced today. In the 1950 programme Enrico was described as a gay young man.

The other opera is harrowingly sad and though my part was

more of a spectator to the high drama between my daughter, her husband and another man, I was for a short while on the first night of the Chester Festival embarrassingly the centre of everyone's attention.

I was an old sailor and the scene was the kitchen of my little house in a French seaport. According to the stage directions I had to enter long before I had anything to sing. Already in the kitchen were my daughter and another sailor (it is her husband missing for fifteen years and she has failed to recognise him), the time is early evening.

The producer was Joan Cross who had taken to direction most successfully after a distinguished operatic career, and she gave me some excellent business to fill in the time between my entrance and the moment I was due to open my mouth.

'You're old,' she said, 'So you can walk slowly.' I was beginning to realise that my operatic future lay in playing parts between the ages of fifty and the geriatric ward.

'Go over to the table and light the oil lamp, then take the chair from beside the table to the back wall, fetch the lamp, climb on to the chair (so this was to be one of my younger roles) and hang the lamp on a hook on the wall. Then take the chair back to the table and if you time it all right, that'll be about your first singing cue. The whole thing will give us a chance to change the lighting from early evening to night.'

At the dress rehearsal it worked perfectly, and my only worry on the first night was that I'd be clumsy with the matches. One is always shaking with tension on these occasions like a dog that has spotted a cat in the garden through the window. However, I managed to light the lamp without trouble and, as I came back for it after putting the chair against the wall Edward Renton the conductor gave me a nod as if to say,

'You're on time.'

It wasn't until I was standing on the chair and lifting the lamp above my head that I realised the hook wasn't there. I stood for a moment frozen with the lamp above my head as if I'd just won the FA Cup, except that I had my back to the audience. Then I simply had to get down off the chair and carry it back to the table. It must have looked like some strange fisherfolk ritual – totally without meaning.

My daughter and the sailor, Jennifer Vyvyan and Arthur

Servent, were fighting a fairly even battle between serious singing and hysteria. My own mixture of emotions was more varied – fury at the stage manager who'd rightly removed the hook after the rehearsal so that it wouldn't tear the canvas when the scenery was folded away, but had forgotten to replace it for the first night; embarrassment at looking like an idiot, fear of forgetting the words in the confusion or joining the other two in an explosive, uncontrollable fit of the giggles.

The stage manager is now an opera director of international renown. He's an old friend, so I'll leave you to guess his identity.

But as I stood on the chair with nothing on that damned wall capable of supporting a feather let alone an oil-lamp I could feel the audience at the back of my neck thinking to themselves,

'What's he *doing*?'

As it was a fairly highbrow festival and we were performing a connoisseur's opera I hoped that some of them might nudge their next door neighbour and knowingly whisper the word symbolism.

At Christmas time it was back to pantomime at the Princes Theatre (now the Shaftesbury) for Bert Montague – *Mother Goose* with Ethel Revnell in the title role and supported in the laughter making by veteran comedian Billy Russell; Hy Hazel with an acting talent to match her superlative long legs was the principal boy and Joe Arthur, at seventy-three part of a great tradition of pantomime animals and birds who not only play the parts but also make what they call 'the skin' was the goose.

Joe's goose was absolutely lifelike except that it was about five times the normal size. Snow white feathers, yellow webbed feet, soulful eyes and a beak that opened and shut to comic and poignant effect.

Joe, a martyr to lumbago, was doubled up inside and peered out through a square of white gauze low down on the neck. The goose never spoke, just looked from side to side, winked an eye and opened its beak. The kids loved it and the grown ups marvelled at the craftsmanship that must have gone into its making.

He played goose opposite many dames – Ethel was the only female so far as I know, but the one he never forgot was Bunny Doyle.

There's a scene where Mother Goose is dressed ready for a ball and pleads with the goose for reassurance that someone will fall in love with her. So far as I recall the bird is sympathetic but non-committal.

For this scene Bunny Doyle wore a dress with a long train. One night Joe, without realising it, had planted his webbed feet on the end of the train. At that moment Bunny took two rapid paces down stage crying,

'Belinda, tell me I'm young and beautiful!'

Belinda was taken somewhat by surprise. The train securely fastened to Bunny's shoulders had jerked forward and the unprepared goose was abruptly up-ended.

Bunny was playing the scene for all it was worth. Undeterred by the audience laughter at what should have been a moment of pathos, he continued his tragic pleas and redoubled his efforts to quieten them down.

'Belinda!' he yelled still facing the public, 'Give me a sign! Tell me what I want to know!'

He wheeled round to see Belinda lying on her side. She gave him a sign all right – straight from the bottom of her neck and the whole audience heard it.

'Put me on me bloody feet!'

Chapter 5

The Festival of Britain – roundly condemned in advance by many as a reckless extravagance at a time of austerity – was just what we all needed to convince ourselves that there was more to life than the spartan existence to which we'd been accustomed for so long, and we could bless Prince Albert for having encouraged equally cautious Victorians to hold the Great Exhibition in 1851.

The British can usually be tempted to indulge in a knees-up to celebrate a historical event, and we're real suckers for a centenary.

The specially built Royal Festival Concert Hall and the Exhibition on the South Bank of the River Thames with its intriguing Skylon and the elaborate Battersea Park Fun Fair grabbed the headlines, but it was what was happening all over the country that interested everyone connected with the arts.

Local authorities and the Arts Council of Great Britain were subsidising local festival events and we all hoped that if these were successful they might become hardy annuals like Edinburgh had done. Fortunately many did, inspiring other communities to follow suit.

At the beginning of May the Glasgow Grand Opera Society, an amateur group with a long history of successful productions, presented their Festival of Britain season for which they had obtained sufficient financial aid to book the Scottish National Orchestra, their celebrated conductor at that time Walter Susskind and two or three professional singers.

They had chosen two contrasting works, *Jeanie Deans* by the Scots composer Hamish MacCunn and *Mefistofele* by Arrigo Boito for which I was engaged to play the title role and Richard Lewis the part of Faust.

Boito, best known as Verdi's librettist, was a modest man and is said to have kept his finished manuscript in a drawer for many years afraid to publish it in case the great Giuseppe thought it presumptuous of his collaborator to compete with him.

When he finally plucked up courage and confessed to being a composer the great man roared with laughter and helped him to get it published.

Mefistofele is a powerful version of the Faust story with impressive scenes for the chorus. I was particularly pleased to be offered the title role because it was a serious bass part not a comic one; nor was it another of my doddering old men. The devil is as old as creation, but he always strikes me as being about forty-two.

After some of the parts I'd played the prospect of ageing ten years was flea-bite, but what about that mean, mocking evil countenance?

I went off to the Leichner make-up studio and showed them my chubby features.

'We'll do our best,' said the girl and set to work. I told her I'd be wearing a black wig with a prominent widow's peak and a pointed black beard.

'That should help a bit,' she murmured doubtfully, 'but you do look a bit jolly, don't you?'

I noticed that she was only making up one side of my face and asked why.

'Watch what I'm doing and then you can have a go at the other side. Afterwards we'll give you a little chart to remind you what to do.'

She gave my eyebrows a devilish curve and painted a touch of purple sensuality about the mouth, but I still looked depressingly jolly.

When I'd seen the music of the opera I'd been surprised to find that as bass parts go it wasn't all that low. I never accept any part until I've been through it to make sure that none of it will strain my voice. The odd very high or low note may not matter too much but what the Italians call the tessitura or general level is the deciding factor. That's the part of the voice you'll be using all night so it's got to be in the middle of your range or you're in trouble.

The tessitura of the part of Mefistofele was no problem, but after a few lessons on it with Rodolfo he said,

'Ian, thees ees too easy for you and eet don'ta sound right.'

I agreed with him. I had bought an old set of 78 records of the opera with a famous Italian bass called De Angelis in the title role. He had a dark voice of huge size and when he took his powerful instrument up to the top notes which I found so easy he obviously had to make a tremendous effort. The effect was formidable and I couldn't get anywhere near it.

'Thata part nearly keeled 'eem,' commented Rodolfo. 'Many basses won'ta do eet becausea for them eet's a voice breaker. You can do, but eeta sounda too light.'

So I sounded too light and looked too jolly. What a prospect!

'We musta darken the voice,' declared Rodolfo. We did and it certainly sounded much better, but it was an imitation of a deep bass not the real thing.

Were my fears about voice and appearance justified? Well two of the critics whose opinion I trusted were at the first night at Glasgow's Theatre Royal. Frank Howes in *The Times* wrote,

'Mr Ian Wallace conveyed the cynicism of Mephistopheles without making him a cardboard villain; he sang with power but was inclined to throttle his words in artificially darkening his tone.'

Christopher Grier in *Opera* also tried to be as nice as possible: 'Ian Wallace rightly shunned melodrama, but went too far in playing down his Infernal Powers. His urbane geniality did not give that edge of arrogance . . .'

I learned my lesson. Ever since I've confined my satanic ambitions to singing *The Song of the Flea*.

* * *

Robert Morley once said that the best training for an actor is to spend a few months selling vacuum cleaners round the doors. He did it himself and confessed that although he didn't get many orders he was often invited to stay for lunch.

Another good training – especially in audience control – is to play the same piece in a mixture of village halls, schools, town halls and convents; in other words a selection of completely different types of audience. Do it in an English county in early summer in a year when the weather is kind and you have all the elements of a most happy experience – provided, that is, that the play is enjoyable and your fellow performers are congenial.

I first saw the script of *The Four Men* in the elegant drawing room of Lord Duncannon's house near Hyde Park. He had dramatised Hilaire Belloc's book of that name which describes a westward journey through the author's beloved Sussex taken by four characters: 'Myself', 'The Poet', 'The Sailor' and 'Grizzlebeard'. All these are different facets of Belloc's persona and Eric Duncannon had skilfully made a play with them conversing about the history of Sussex, the beauty and character of its countryside, the merits of its inns and the brews of ale to be found in them interspersed with songs from 'The Sailor' – hence my invitation to take part.

The play was to be presented all over Sussex for six weeks in late May and the whole of June, opening at the Assembly Room in Chichester as part of Sussex's contribution to the Festival of Britain. There was no Chichester Theatre in those days, but the responsibility for coordinating festival events in Sussex was with a tall, shy young man who would have been politely incredulous if anyone had prophesied that his future would include being Director of the Edinburgh Festival or Head of Music of the BBC. His name was Robert Ponsonby.

The intellectual forces in that drawing room were formidable; though Eric Duncannon was every inch an aristocrat, tall, slim and possessing the sort of good looks that a recording angel would have envied, his modesty and politeness couldn't conceal the fact that he was a learned and serious writer.

With him was Robert Speaight, the original Becket in T. S. Elliot's *Murder in the Cathedral* whose career had been much associated with Shakespeare and other serious dramatists like Shaw and Ibsen. He was to direct *The Four Men* and play the part of 'Myself'.

Also there that morning – unless my memory has played me a trick – was Harold Hobson, drama critic for *The Sunday Times*, who had apparently encouraged the future Earl of Bessborough to adapt Belloc's book for the stage and was there to give the project his blessing.

After listening with awe to those three in conversation I was asked to read some of the Sailor's part with Robert Speaight playing the other three. I found it rather stiff and wordy.

After the reading, which was an ordeal in such august company, they kindly told me how it would be done.

There was to be very little movement on a small set easily transportable from place to place – just a few steps up to a rostrum and down again to an area where the only props would be a couple of wooden chairs, a table, a candlestick and some pewter tankards. At one side there would be a wooden pole on which different inn signs would be displayed to mark the stages of our Sussex pilgrimage. The choruses of the songs I'd sing were to be printed in the programme and – theoretically – the audience would join in with such ditties as *They brew good beer in Haslemere*, a troupe of little girls from a dancing school would appear on the rostrum behind us a couple of times to enact what we'd been talking about like the battle between The Men of Sussex and The Men of Kent. Eric Duncannon's cousin David

Ponsonby who had arranged the music would go round with us to play the piano.

As I listened to all this without much enthusiasm I noticed a pile of LPs (which were quite a novelty in 1951) on the window-sill. Where I would have expected to see Bach, Teleman and Brahms with, perhaps, a Mozart opera for light relief there were original cast recordings of *Oklahoma* and *South Pacific* plus a Frank Sinatra album for good measure. There must, I decided, be another side to my serious host.

I didn't have to wait long for an explanation. When we broke off for coffee I met Eric's wife Mary, a dark haired girl with a lively personality and an American accent.

Actors are notoriously bad judges of what will make a successful evening's entertainment and this was a case in point. I left that meeting with those charming folk convinced we were on to a loser. How wrong I was.

Belloc's prose has a splendid ring and in the event the simplicity of the set helped the audience to concentrate on the beauty of the words. Robert, as well as speaking his lines with the understanding of an actor and poet combined, directed us with the minimum of instructions and taught me that lack of movement, even in a play about a journey, is unimportant if the actors can release the imagination of the audience.

The part of The Poet was played by the sensitive and retiring John Leather who usually spent his summers with one or two kindred spirits taking the plays of Strindberg to remote Cornish villages, while Grizzlebeard (Belloc as an old man) was W. E. Holloway – father of David Holloway, literary critic of *The Daily Telegraph* and Anthea Holloway, the actress. With his tweed knickerbockers, receding hair and wildish beard (supplied by the management) he looked very like Bernard Shaw in late middle age.

Mr Holloway had been warned by his doctor to avoid anything strenuous and during rehearsals I wasn't altogether surprised to get a phone call from Anthea, who had married one of my school friends.

'Please say no if you can't manage it, but if you're going to drive to the dates could you possibly take my father? He's too proud to ask – but I don't think he'll be able to stand up to doing it all in the train.'

I said that of course I would, privately thinking that six weeks of picking up an elderly actor almost every day and driving him an average round trip of ninety miles might prove tedious. How often, I wondered, would I hear the same reminiscences.

W. E.'s companionship turned out to be an unexpected bonus of a blissfully happy engagement. He did reminisce – most entertainingly, and he never repeated himself. I eagerly awaited next day's instalment and if I had had a tape recorder running on those journeys I would have captured the material for a book that would have been unique.

He had toured with many actor managers not only in this country but in India and Australia. He spoke of their idiosyncrasies and foibles with a rare sense of observation and compassion. I got the impression that for the likes of Matheson Lang, Martin Harvey and Benson, my gentle and stimulating companion must have been a good man to have around. Apart from being an excellent actor he also understood the logistics of touring. I got the impression that when he was with these larger than life thespians far from home he would never venture an opinion unless asked. When that moment came – usually after some foreseeable disaster had struck, he was prepared to express himself so much to the point and so quietly as to make the lugubrious wearer of the coat with the astrakhan collar flinch.

Towards the end of rehearsals we were all invited to have lunch with Hilaire Belloc at his Sussex house.

He was a very old man living with middle aged relations who seemed to be rather scared of him. Before lunch he sat in the drawing room wearing an ancient black suit, his beard decidedly grizzled and regarding us all suspiciously from dark narrowed eyes. We all felt that this visit was about ten years too late.

I ventured to tell him that my father had known him before the war at the Reform Club.

'What was his name?'

'Sir John Wallace.' He shook his head and obviously didn't remember. There was no reason why he should. Once more silence fell, so I tried again.

'He was a Member of Parliament between the wars and used

to say that the old cliché was true about the House of Commons being the best club in London. I doubt if it is now.'

He considered my conversational gambit for a while and then said, 'No, the coinage of politics has been debased even more since then.'

Lunch was announced and he embarrassed his relations while delighting us by drinking his wine from a silver tankard and insisting on being served first – up to the brim.

He showed absolutely no interest whatsoever in our theatrical enterprise.

After lunch his grand-niece, an attractive girl of eighteen or so, volunteered to show us over the windmill next to the house. Wearing a light summer frock she started up the ladder.

I followed and was the only one to discover that she was wearing very little else. I hope she'll forgive me thirty years later for remembering.

When I came down from admiring the sweeps and the view I was, to my surprise, called to the phone.

Pat – almost as if she knew that I was pursuing a girl who wasn't even wearing a bonnet to throw over the mill – had told my agent where I was.

'Would you like to play the part of The Blind Harper in *The King of Scots* at Dunfermline Abbey during the Edinburgh Festival? Not much money but a lot of prestige.'

'It can't be less than I'm getting for *The Four Men* and I'm enjoying every minute. Yes.'

I seemed destined to get to that Festival one way or another. Glyndebourne had offered me the part of the Alcade in *La Forza del Destino* at Edinburgh that year. As it was the least important operatic role I'd been offered since I started in 1946 I'd turned it down, making it clear that I was grateful for their attempt to employ me for the fourth year running. I just felt it was a step in the wrong direction.

When they'd got over the shock of being turned down – especially by someone as unruthless as me – they were inclined to agree. Now, admittedly on the other side of the Forth, I would be in a Festival event after all.

The Four Men was scheduled to play at Chichester for three nights before the tour started and to save us returning each night to London during that period hospitality was arranged.

I arrived quite late at night after the dress rehearsal at the home of the poet and author Robert Gittings and his wife Jo, the sort of hosts who give the impression that they've lived in hopes that one day you'd turn up.

After preliminary greetings I was hushed to silence. It was a still, balmy night and the french window to the garden was open.

'With any luck,' said Jo quietly, 'we'll hear the nightingale in a minute.'

We did – the first time in my life. It was a good omen.

Next morning I had to go to the theatre for a final rehearsal and when I came back to the Gittings for lunch Robert appeared looking white and strained. I felt I already knew him well enough to ask if he was all right.

'Oh yes. But you see I've written a poem this morning and it takes it out of you.'

Actors and singers know how much a performance can drain them. This was proof that the act of poetical creation was also spiritually and physically exhausting.

After lunch the phone rang. It was Robert Speaight. Eric Duncannon's younger brother serving with the army in Germany had been killed in a road accident. Eric wouldn't be playing the part of the narrator for the first performance, but had insisted that we should go ahead.

He returned in a day or two saying that he could manage if none of us mentioned the tragedy. Possibly the long successful tour helped him to bear such a terrible bereavement. I can still see him sitting to the side of us on a Sussex wheelback chair, wearing a velvet jacket, his open book resting on his knees as he listened to the four of us between his spells of narrative.

Where did we go on that tour? Sussex folk over forty-five may remember. Storrington, Forest Row, Wadhurst, Eastbourne College, Arundel (where we were entertained afterwards in the Castle), Roedean (where the headmistress told us of the naval occupation during the war and the sailors' delight at notices in the dormitories saying 'If you need a mistress during the night, ring the bell'), the Girl Guides Hall, Crowborough where we had a standing ovation – from an adult audience, Mayfield Convent where the nuns joined resoundingly in the songs and slapped their stomachs on the line 'And a bellyful of good ale!', and many other places.

The press from *The Times* to *The Tablet* were full of praise and to make life easy for me dear David Ponsonby's first class arrangements were as good as his accompaniments.

We only had one disappointment. The last performance was in a barn owned by Lady Birley, wife of Sir Oswald Birley the portrait painter. This was for her guests, many of whom were Glyndebourne buffs, theatre people and artists. Just the sort of audience, we thought, to end with.

They sat in almost total silence and then gave it polite, muted applause. If it hadn't been for Michael Denison and Dulcie Gray who rushed round afterwards to tell us how marvellous it was and what a stuffy lot they'd been sitting with, I think we'd all have jumped into the Thames on the way home.

The BBC agreed with Michael and Dulcie. They hauled us in to record it – not only for immediate consumption but for the archives, though I think we all felt it needed the help of a village hall audience to recapture the magic of that English summer.

I do hope it will be revived one day. I'd love to do it again even if they had to rename The Sailor The Ancient Mariner.

*   *   *

The King of Scots was an entirely different sort of challenge. Since the beginning of May I had been an operatic devil, a singing sailor and a fleshly monk (a short notice emergency job for the English Opera Group at the Cheltenham Festival!). Now, in late August I was to be a blind Scots harper linking with songs the story of Robert the Bruce's flight from England, the Battle of Bannockburn, the death of Edward I and Bruce's coronation.

The blank verse play by Robert Kemp required a large scale production and a historic setting. The nave of Dunfermline Abbey was an inspired choice.

Playing a blind man of several centuries ago meant that I couldn't wear dark glasses. Also I had a small harp to carry which precluded a stick. If I'd decided to shut my eyes I'd have needed a constant guide and could have well become disorientated – so I opted for open eyes staring through and past everyone in the crowded scenes.

I can't play even a mini harp, so the music had to be recorded. This meant that I had to synchronise my mime of playing it with the start of a record (tapes were not in use in theatre performances then,) and woe betide me if I forgot the words. The harp chords would go blithely on whether I was singing and plucking away or not. Very funny to get it wrong in a comedy show, but not in this serious portrayal of a heroic chapter in Scotland's history. I had a few nightmares before we opened, but no disasters in performance.

Robert the Bruce was the Australian film star John Mc-Callum, who has Scots ancestry. One day at rehearsal he was called to the telephone. He had been offered a season with the Royal Shakespeare Company at Stratford.

'It's the sort of break most actors are praying for,' he told me over lunch, 'and I'd just love to get out of the studios and do a season there. The trouble is I don't think I dare.'

I thought that because the techniques of film and stage acting are so different he was worried about his long absence from the theatre.

'You're doing Bruce as if you'd never been away,' I assured him.

He laughed.

'That's very kind and not quite true. Projecting my voice in that abbey is quite a strain after working with microphones two or three feet away, but I think I can lick that problem. No, it's the tax man I'm worried about. Living up to the public's idea of star status leaves nothing over after the very high rates of tax I pay and I'll soon be getting a bill from the Inland Revenue for my last film. Unless I do another one next year I'll have to live a different sort of life altogether. I'm a sort of prisoner to the system. I'm loving this production – but it's only going to take a few weeks. Stratford would be months.'

Apart from John McCallum who, by the way, was a quiet, modest colleague never wanting 'star treatment' – and never likely to get it in a fairly rugged Scots company – there were some notable performances. I'm still haunted by Iris Russell as the Countess of Buchan whose reward for insisting on placing the crown on Bruce's head herself was to be exhibited by the English in an iron cage; and John Rae delivering the one prose passage in the play – Bishop Lamberton's actual sermon in

59

which he speculated on what might have happened to Scotland 'if the King's horse had not stumbled over the cliff at King-horn.' His noble address pointing out how vulnerable we are to the mere accidents that change the course of history is one of those cerebral videotapes I can play at will.

But most compelling of all was Edmund Willard as Edward I. Edmund grew a beard for this production and used it to spectacular effect. In the early scenes this ruthless monarch's beard was auburn, but when on his final expedition to harry the Scots he was carried into view by his soldiers a dying old man at Burgh on Sands it was pure white. The audience gasped at the transformation.

'Perfectly simple, old boy. My beard has grown in dead white for years – lack of pigment or something. The brown dye I use washes out in a couple of minutes.'

Both he and W. E. Holloway were dead within a year or two and belonged to that large group of actors who don't play star parts but crop up again and again in the theatre and on television playing a range of supporting roles so varied that it's all too easy not to notice them or appreciate that they are the backbone of the profession.

Poor Matthew Forsyth our director was killed by a car while out for a walk near his home not long afterwards. I had never met him before this production and was a bit scared of him at first. All through the first morning of rehearsal this sombre faced man with grey curly hair did not smile and sounded grim.

At the lunch break he asked me to stay behind. I immediately assumed that I was about to be sacked or told to pull my socks up at the very least. Everyone in this profession, whatever confident exterior they present, is plagued with insecurity.

'Come and have lunch,' he said when we were alone. 'I'm rather low today and I'm sure you'll cheer me up.'

At one rehearsal the recorded music missed a cue and despite our being on hallowed ground he exploded.

'Right!' he yelled at the end of a row of colourful expletives. 'We'll take it again.'

This time the music came in half way through the record, stopped abruptly and then instead of the harp we heard at full amplification that terrible *whoop*! of the needle travelling rapidly across the record.

The coronation of Robert the Bruce disintegrated as the King, the Countess of Buchan and the bishops shook with silent laughter.

Matthew made an enormous effort of self-control and pointed at me – my eyes had lost that faraway look –

'You're the musical one,' he barked, 'go and find out what the hell's happening.'

I made my way to the little cubicle where the record player was discreetly hidden from the public. I found the operator, a local man, shaking from head to foot.

'Oh, Mr Wallace,' he whispered, 'I don't know what to do. You see when Mr Forsyth shouts like that my hands shake and I canny put the needle on the right bit o' the record.' (The sophisticated equipment used by disc jockeys now which deals with that problem was still in the future.)

I decided not to give Matthew the real reason until later, so I told the operator to go home (it was late afternoon any way) and I'd say the equipment had broken down, which was true enough!

Over a drink that evening I told Matthew and his wife what had happened as if it were a bit of a joke.

He put his head in his hands.

'Oh God, why do I go off like that? Poor man – he's done a marvellous job and now I've frightened him out of his wits. I don't mean anything by it. I just get nervous so near the first night.' He got to his feet. 'I know where he lives. I'll go right round and apologise.'

He looked so full of remorse it was comical and very endearing. His peace mission was much appreciated and the needle never faltered again.

Matthew must have been happy with the final result for *The King of Scots* not only had good notices, it had a very wide coverage and we played to large audiences. Like *The Four Men* this play may have stood up to the ravages of time and be worth considering for some future Scottish festival.

Chapter 6

At this stage in my career I seem to have cut a curiously highbrow figure quite out of character with my everyday tastes and interests. With my inability to sight read or play the piano, I must have spent many hours that autumn with repetiteurs knocking the notes of operas and songs into my head, for my schedule for the last three months of the year, taking into account my musical illiteracy, was on the tight side.

On October 7th there was a live broadcast of *The Four Men*. On the 9th I was in Glasgow singing in a broadcast of Sir Walter Scott's *Marmion*. On the 12th back in London I sang in a broadcast performance of a very intricate one act opera by Martinu *Comedy on a Bridge*, and a week later I was concerned in a broadcast of *Hippolyte et Aricie*, an opera by Rameau in French conducted by Roger Desormière.

Immediately after that it was time to start rehearsing (and therefore to have words and music perfect) a large part in a rarely performed opera by Haydn called *Life on the Moon* for my old friends the London Opera Club who were starting a week's season on November 8th. Three operas in a month was quite good going and I was already having to work on Britten's *Let's Make an Opera* which I was to do at the Lyric Theatre Hammersmith for a Christmas season. But at least that would not, like *Life on the Moon* mean my playing yet another of those elderly eighteenth century idiots who have provided a great deal of work for nineteenth and twentieth century comic basses.

Though I was getting a little weary of playing these bumbling buffo characters there was one ageing operatic buffoon about to come my way who would transform my life so far as opera was concerned.

I had just got back from Glasgow in mid-November where, immediately after *Life on the Moon*, I'd been singing some excerpts from *Die Meistersinger* and *Parsifal* – the first and last

Wagner I've ever sung – when the telephone rang one morning early enough to wake me up.

'Harold Neden here, BBC. I think I've got something right up your street. Baron Stonybroke in an operatic pantomime.'

I thought I must be still asleep. 'Oh yes?' I grunted interrogatively.

'It's *Cinderella* by Rossini and Geoffrey Dunn has translated it brilliantly. In the first act the baron sings a comic aria about a nightmare. It's a bit like Figaro's aria in *The Barber of Seville* except it's for a buffo. It'll be part of a Rossini opera concert. Would you like to do it?'

He mentioned a date only about ten days ahead. I was free and you don't turn down the BBC unless you have to, but my first reaction was almost despair at having yet something else to learn at such a busy time.

What I didn't know was that Glyndebourne were going to do *Cinderella* – or *La Cenerentola* – in the original Italian version next season and were more than a little interested in how I would sing that aria on the radio. Up to now all the parts for which they'd engaged me had been middling in size. The baron, or Don Magnifico as he's called in the opera, is a major role and the first act aria a pretty testing piece.

Perhaps it was as well I didn't know what was at stake when I stepped up to the microphone in the Camden Studio to do that live broadcast, though I doubt if it would have made much difference. You can really only be nervous about one thing at a time and a live broadcast of something new and difficult is enough to be going on with. But it was one of those cases where luck was on my side. Harold Neden knew nothing of Glyndebourne's plans and there were other buffos he might have invited to do the broadcast.

Any way the result was that Moran Caplat, Glyndebourne's general manager asked me if I'd be prepared to relearn the aria in Italian and sing it for Maestro Gui. If he was satisfied the part was mine.

Vittorio Gui had conducted *Un Ballo in Maschera* at the 1949 Edinburgh Festival in which I'd sung one of those middling sized parts and on the first night he had paid my friend, the late Hervey Alan and me a frightening compliment. We had a big ensemble with the chorus which the maestro had insisted

63

should be at a certain tempo to be really effective. We had rehearsed it a great deal. When the moment for it arrived on the great night he beat out the first few bars and then smiling broadly laid down his baton and folded his arms. He didn't pick it up again until the end of the number three or four minutes later.

He'd come to Glyndebourne in 1948 to conduct Mozart's opera *Così fan Tutte* at Edinburgh and with this, his first collaboration with Carl Ebert, he had made an excellent impression. He was not at all most people's idea of an Italian maestro. Approaching sixty he had something patrician about him. His Roman nose, small piercing eyes and large forehead gave him, particularly in profile, a slight look of an elephant. It wasn't something to laugh about – it just fitted in with his round, clean shaven face and husky speaking voice.

Though much of the time he was placid and fatherly towards singers and musicians he could show flashes of Latin temperament. I recall him twice leaving the podium in a fury, once in Edinburgh for ten minutes, once in Austria for the rest of the day; but he was as much a scholar as a performer and though not given to criticising other Italian conductors in words, his silence and slight elevation of eyebrow when they were mentioned dared one to dwell on the subject.

Much of his scholarship had been devoted to the works of Rossini and for some time he had been trying to persuade Glyndebourne to extend their Italian repertoire beyond Verdi and Donizetti. Now with *La Cenerentola* he'd got his way.

I willingly agreed to sing for him on his next visit to London in a week or two's time. Not only did I have a great respect for him, I found it very pleasant, as did many of my colleagues, that he treated us, who were half his age, with equal respect – always provided we didn't try his patience too far!

When I told Rodolfo he was as excited as if it was his career that might be taking a step forward rather than mine. Certainly to have one of his pupils singing such a role could do him no harm – unless I messed it up.

'Now listen, Ian, don'ta be offended but I'm goin' to be very tougha with you. You pronounce Italian very well buta not perfect. For Gui it musta be perfetto, understand?'

I certainly did. He bullied and cajoled me for hours insisting

64

that I learn the second act aria which hadn't been mentioned and he wasn't satisfied until that was perfetto as well.

When I sang for the maestro I was seized with audition nerves and felt that I'd not sung the first act aria anything like as well as I had on the radio. When I asked if he'd like to hear the one from the second act he shook his head.

'Oh hell!' I thought, 'I've muffed it.'

'No point in it,' he called across the hall. 'We will not be doing that aria in the production. We do instead a scene for Don Magnifico in a wine cellar. Go and learn the rest of the part very well and we meet at Glyndebourne in the summer, no?'

He noticed my obvious relief and laughed. Then he pointed to Moran Caplat and Jani Strasser, Glyndebourne's head of music studies.

'It was they who wanted to hear you not me. I knew you could do it.'

That was typical of him. It wasn't true, of course, but it was a boost to my confidence which was what he intended. What was equally good for my morale was that Carl Ebert, who was producing *La Cenerentola*, had approved my casting without being at the audition.

So there I was with a plum opera role at Glyndebourne to work at and a year of great activity behind me, yet at the end of January 1952 I was at Merton Film Studios doing a part (I can't remember what) in a film called *Wide Boy* – and the press release announcing this mentioned that the film was by Rex Rienits writer of *Assassin for Hire* in which I had also appeared as a cockney cafe proprietor. Both films starred Sidney Tafler.

Assassin for Hire was a 'B' picture that enjoyed feature film success and eventually was shown on pretty well every TV network in the world – at no personal gain to the cast.

The last time I saw it I wanted to run out of the house, as a sixteen stone Ian Wallace wearing an apron advanced ponderously into close-up and asked his customers who'd ordered coffee,

'Mocha or Kenya?'

'Wot's the difference?'

'There ain't none.'

Why did the opera singer continue to be a bit player in films when he was so busy in other ways? We've been over all that

65

already, but at that moment it was probably because in all that busy year the rewards had been in prestige and enjoyment and looked as if they always would be. Though the film work was also unexciting financially I think I had dreams of ending up as a sort of Scots Spencer Tracy.

Behind my artistic exterior was the business sense inherited from my father. I hadn't the acumen only the belief that the labourer is worthy of his hire.

But I was spending many hours with Rodolfo and Rossini and looking forward to Sussex in May with great anticipation. For *La Cenerentola* was to be my Glyndebourne debut – at Glyndebourne. In four years with the company I'd never sung a performance south of Edinburgh.

Thirty years ago performances of *La Cenerentola* were comparatively rare. Rossini wrote the title role for a coloratura mezzo, a rare voice at that time and even now there are never many outstanding ones about.

Glyndebourne had found one with just the right quality of wistful sadness in Marina de Gabarain – a Spanish singer living in London.

The high baritone role of Dandini is altogether different from Figaro in *Il Barbiere di Siviglia*. Although the famous *Largo al Factotum* calls for agility, breath control, diction, panache and sheer staying power, the rest of the part for an experienced professional is no more than a good strenuous sing. Dandini, without having anything as showy as the *Largo*, has to cope with long passages of coloratura singing all through the evening. It's a role for a specialist.

Our specialist was Sesto Bruscantini, a young Italian who, like me, had studied law and abandoned it for the stage. His acting is as good as his singing and he's a very good singer.

Coloratura passages are familiar territory for lyric tenors but are normally confined to their arias where the cascades of notes and cadenzas are rather like the display of a courting bird. Ramiro, the Prince Charming of the story, has, like Cinderella and his valet Dandini, a great deal of agile singing in the ensembles as well as having to produce some quiet sustained ingratiating tones in between.

Another Spaniard was engaged for this role, Juan Oncina – a gentle, handsome brown eyed young man with the touch of an aristocrat in his manner to make him a convincing prince.

The Ugly Sisters were from Italy. Alda Noni, whose delicious charm and enormous expressive eyes had captivated audiences at the Cambridge Theatre in 1946 when Pomeroy presented *Don Pasquale* and Fernanda Cadoni, a mezzo with an equally beguiling personality. They were to portray the uglies as pretty girls ugly of heart.

Their father Don Magnifico also faced vocal tests that stretched me well beyond the part of Dr Bartolo which I'd done at the Cambridge Theatre and was the only other major role I'd sung so far. Again it was a matter of agility and a slightly higher tessitura. But the principal challenge was on the acting side. Dr Bartolo is a serious, jealous old man. Don Magnifico if you're not careful can appear as shallow as a pantomime buffoon.

The principals are completed by a shadowy benevolent magical character, Alidoro. He's the one who turns up in the kitchen and provides the coach and the dress so that Cinders can go to the ball. He's also on hand late in the opera to ensure that the prince's coach overturns in a storm (Rossini loved writing storm music) outside Magnifico's house bringing Ramiro and Cinderella (Angelina for the purists) face to face.

This bass part was in the safe hands of Hervey Alan with whom I'd sung that unconducted ensemble in 1949.

Rehearsing an opera is inevitably a case of two steps forward and one back. At Glyndebourne it's obligatory to arrive for the first rehearsal word and music perfect. This is different from rehearsing a play where actors like to have the script in their hands and write in the moves and business; but you can't carry vocal scores the size and weight of phone directories round the stage and what is more the music determines the exact moment a line is delivered, leaving the singer to time the stage business around the music. The actor has to work out both the timing of the lines and business.

Singers are often faced with the same words repeated over and over again, which is seldom an actor's problem.

The first steps forward are the musical rehearsals which start by a repetiteur taking you through your part and checking that you have everything secure down to the last semi-quaver rest. At Glyndebourne if the opera is in Italian there will be an Italian repetiteur in residence as well as the British members of the music staff. He will also check pronunciation – not only for the British artists but for all non-Italians in the cast.

The next stage is ensemble musical rehearsals for the principals, probably under the supervision of the conductor. Some of the ensembles in *La Cenerentola* were so strenuous and required such breath control that Bruscantini suggested we sing them running up and down the rehearsal room so that they'd seem easier when we stood still in performance. It worked quite well – but didn't do much for our interpretation!

The step back takes place when, after all that musical rehearsal, production rehearsals begin. As we worked with the dynamic Carl Ebert on the stage our concentration on moves, business and expressing the correct emotions inevitably caused our musical precision and interpretation to slip. Then we would be hauled back round the piano for a couple of three hour sessions to repair the damage. If we weren't aware of how far we had deteriorated the incisive nasal tones of Jani Strasser would soon plug that gap in our knowledge.

Occasionally in the five weeks of preparation we would have a day or two off while the music and production staff concentrated on one of the other operas in the season. I always went back to London on such days – to sit in the garden and let what I had been doing sink in, but I would also book an hour with Rodolfo in case my step back had been vocal as well as musical. Often he would urge me to sing something else.

'Listen, Ian, I thinka you should singa me *O tu Palermo* to broaden the voice. Eet will helpa you with Magnifico, you know.'

Other challenges to our powers of concentration came with the arrival about a week before the dress rehearsal of the basic scenery, props and at least part of our costumes. It was marvellous to have these added preoccupations so early when we could take them in our stride and get accustomed to them. For some of these late rehearsals we had the orchestra as well.

Many opera and theatre companies only produced all these things at the dress rehearsal on the day before the performance which made tremendous, sometimes insurmountable problems for singers and actors. 'It'll be all right on the night' was a phrase invented to cover up an old, inefficient and stupid way of mounting a theatrical venture, which also had a good deal to do with trying to pinch every penny before money actually came in at the box-office.

So far as orchestral rehearsal was concerned we worked with the splendid Royal Philharmonic Orchestra for something like twenty-one hours starting with a sitz probe where the singers sit and sing their parts, their scores on their knees, pencils at the ready to mark in any notes from the conductor, and progressing right through the later stage rehearsals to the dress rehearsal itself. Many other companies would only be able to afford six hours of orchestra time in all.

Stage rehearsals with Carl Ebert I've described elsewhere.* I owed him so much, as did all the generations of singers who worked with him. He refused to accept that because God had endowed someone with a beautiful voice this made it impossible for them to be able to act as well. Like all great teachers and producers (he was both), he knew that a stage performance was a matter of self confidence. He could impart that as well as a full exposition of the character to be portrayed, he gave maximum encouragement making it clear that he did not expect singers to act in a way that would interfere with their excellent voice production. This simple psychology worked wonders. He died in 1980 at the age of ninety-three.

Glyndebourne was – and is – a marvellous place to work, and given so much careful preparation we all felt that if we did not succeed we had only ourselves to blame.

There's a charming first night custom there. On every principal singer's make-up table is placed a half bottle of champagne – a gift from Mrs Christie, the wife of John Christie who originally built the opera house. (Incidentally her son George has continued the tradition though his mother died many years ago.) Most singers drink it after the performance or keep it as a souvenir.

The first night of *La Cenerentola* was very hot and after my first aria I had to make a rapid return to my room for a costume change. I was panting with exertion and feeling temporarily exhausted. I badly needed a drink of water but there was no tumbler in my room and no time to look for one. So I just slipped the wire off the bottle and drank it as if it was lemonade.

* *Promise Me You'll Sing Mud*

69

Within minutes I was back on the stage taking part in a recitative. After a moment or two it became painfully obvious that someone had forgotten a line and the silence was embarrassing.

I felt quite angry that someone had let us down when the performance was going so well. At that moment Bruscantini crossed the stage to where I was standing, placed a patronising hand on my shoulder in exactly the right manner for a servant masquerading as a prince and whispered something in my ear – my line for which everyone was waiting.

Whilst I had been wondering which of the 'bloody foreigners' was to blame they all knew it was the 'bloody Scotsman'!

I'm sure it wasn't because I'd used beautiful champagne as a thirst quencher – or almost sure – I had no more blank spots that night, but it underlined the sense of my rule never to drink before or during a performance.

When my mother and Pat resumed their seats after the long dinner interval of approximately an hour and twenty minutes they overheard a conversation between two members of the audience sitting immediately in front of them.

'That really is an amazing effort Ian Wallace puts in when you realise he's sixty-three.'

This was too much for my mother who was sixty-two at the time. She tapped the wretched fellow on the shoulder.

'Indeed and he's not. I'm his mother!'

There's no answer to that one.

Standing behind the curtain waiting to begin the second half of the opera I realised the value of the dinner interval. Whether the audience had sampled the excellent food and wine provided in the restaurant by Vernon Herbert or set out a picnic in the grounds, lowering bottles of hock into the lake in string bags moored precariously to the bank before the performance, their animated chatter was music to my ears.

The first scene of Act Two is a wine tasting at which Don Magnifico rapidly becomes magnificently sloshed and is eventually carried out singing at the top of his voice, and I could be forgiven for feeling a tremor of excitement mingling with first-night nerves which, contrary to belief, do *not* disappear the moment the show begins; I'd been told that if the applause justified it I was to take a solo call at the end of the short scene.

In fact it was hoped that I might get more than one to give more time for a complicated scene change that would be taking place behind the curtain. I managed two, though the second one was 'milking it' a bit as we say.

There remained one small anxiety. Late in the opera Don Magnifico gets his come-uppance when Dandini reveals to him that he is not the prince, only his servant, and that neither Clorinda or Thisbe (the uglies) have a chance with the real one.

The duet works up to a furious pace and Bruscantini and I had worked out with Ebert the trick of banging my stick on the stage in a temper and letting go of it so that it bounced in the air; Sesto then caught it and handed it back all in time to the music. In rehearsal it worked about three times out of five. Before we went out to play the scene that night Sesto insisted on spitting (hygienically) on each of my shoulders and on the ferrule of the stick. It worked a charm and the roar of laughter it produced was much more than we'd hoped for. He repeated the spitting for every performance but three out of five remained the stick's success ratio.

At the end of the duet the applause was gale force, but there was no curtain call, it would have held up the action at that moment, but I think that both of us would put down singing *Un segreto d'importanza* to a Saturday night Glyndebourne audience high on our list of enjoyable experiences – even when the stick refused to co-operate.

Sesto Bruscantini, Juan Oncina and I became, as a result of that performance, a team that remained together for three Glyndebourne productions of Rossini's operas adding *Il Barbiere di Siviglia* and *Le Comte Ory* to *La Cenerentola*. We also became firm friends and on the stage developed the sort of rapport that is a rare and exciting element in a performance.

The whole thing was a personal triumph for Maestro Gui whose faith in Glyndebourne audiences warming to Rossini was completely justified. It was a major triumph for Bruscantini and the ladies were all splendid; it was also a triumph for Oliver Messel whose designs had transported us to an elegant fairyland and Ebert saw to it that we behaved accordingly.

According to *Punch* it was 'a minor triumph' for me, but

Frank Howes in *The Times* made sure that I didn't get above myself by writing:

'Mr Ian Wallace, the pure buffo of Don Magnifico, which needed one final degree more crispness to make his delivery synchronise with the orchestra.'

Had I really sung out of time all night?

'No,' replied Jani Strasser, 'but you were a little out for a couple of bars in your first aria.'

That gives some idea of the high standard critics rightly expect from opera singers at that level.

Hamburg Opera had been engaged for the Edinburgh Festival in 1952. So once again I had nearly a year before I would sing another opera. The undoubted success of *La Cenerentola* brought no offers from any other opera company.

But once more I was destined to be at Edinburgh Festival, this time in *The Highland Fair*, a ballad opera to be presented at the Assembly Hall in the round. Written by Joseph Mitchell three years before *The Beggar's Opera* it was to be directed by Tyrone Guthrie who had had a phenomenal success on the same stage with *The Thrie Estates*. The challenge of acting and singing to an audience on three sides of the rectangular stage which could only be approached by the same aisles as the public used to reach their seats was stimulating to say the least.

Although it was set in Scotland I was an English soldier Sergeant Swilly with some good sturdy songs by Cedric Thorpe Davie and a colourful drunk scene in Act Two.

Guthrie, a very tall Irishman with a moustache and short back and sides that gave him a slightly military flavour invariably changed into carpet slippers for rehearsals. He revelled in bringing off the difficult and could have made a success of *Hamlet* in a Maori clearing with a native cast.

At the first rehearsal after I had sung through my first song he clapped his large hands together making a sound like a pistol shot.

'Right! That's the first encore number of the show and you'd better get it because I won't take the chorus off the stage until after it.' The thought of mild applause, no encore and the chorus trudging up those aisles in silence spurred me on to the sort of effort he wanted.

We had an amateur chorus whom he dealt with quite

differently from the hired help. He chose one delightful girl, a little older than the rest to be the butt, and gave them their instructions by gently ribbing her.

'Now come along, Grace, you're not buttering bridge rolls in Tantallan Road now, dear, you're a rough peasant at a fair hundreds of years ago.' Grace made a valiant effort to shed her look of refinement. When they were all to sit simultaneously on a music cue and missed it Grace got the blame.

'Grace, didn't you hear me? I said, one, two, three, *behinds* on the floor. You *must* set an example!' Grace smiled radiantly and flung herself to the ground – early.

After two or three nights of the three week run I went to him for advice.

'You know that long speech on my second entrance, Tony?'

He nodded.

'There are two laughs in it but if I get one I can't get the other. Which should I go for?'

'Edith Evans would get them both,' he said and gave me the characteristic single nod which meant that the ball was in my court.

It took me a week of experiment but one night I found out how to do it. He happened to be in the audience. When I met him afterwards in the dressing room passage he said nothing but repeated that single nod which unmistakeably said, 'Told you so.'

In the end it wasn't a serious rival to *The Thrie Estates* but the audiences loved it. James Cairncross and the late Roddy McMillan gave superb performances and among some young singers who made a good impression were Marion Studholme, Niven Miller and a quiet spoken, ambitious young tenor called Kenneth McKellar.

After the glamour of Glyndebourne and Edinburgh where within three months I'd worked with two of the best directors in the world the autumn looked like being a complete anticlimax.

Chapter 7

Registered letters marked 'Private and Confidential' can be the bearers of unwelcome tidings. I opened it with some misgivings.

'Dear Mr Wallace, We are now compiling a programme for the Command Performance at the Palladium on Monday evening, November 3rd, and I am writing to ask you if you would like to appear on this occasion and sing at least the chorus of a patriotic song leading into the big finale of the show.'

It was signed by Harry Marlowe, organising secretary of the Variety Artistes Benevolent Fund and dated October 3rd 1952. Even then the penny didn't drop.

'That can't be *the* Royal Command Performance,' I said to Pat.

I'd often listened to it on the radio as a kid – one marvellous act after another: Elsie and Doris Waters, The Western Brothers, Arthur Askey, Robb Wilton, George Formby, Nellie Wallace (no relation), as well as famous jugglers and acrobats whose routines had to be described for radio listeners by a commentator. For those whose lives were spent touring the theatres that made up the Moss Empire circuit it was like being picked to play in a glittering show business Test Match.

But the letter in my hand did refer to *the* Command Performance – so how had I, an opera singer of only six or seven years standing been honoured in this way? I didn't stop to think. Once I realised that this was what the Americans call 'The Big One', I was delivering a delighted acceptance to Mr Marlowe's office by hand. The thought of entrusting it to the pillar box at the end of the road never occurred to me.

The patriotic song arrived a few days later. It was *Soldiers of the Queen*, and I was to sing one verse and one chorus solo. Then I'd be joined by the entire company including the Band of the Coldstream Guards for a repeat chorus. There would be four hundred people on the stage and I would be bang in the middle.

The thought of it pressed the starter on a succession of emotions familiar to all performers when a totally unexpected exciting offer comes out of the blue. Incredulity gives way to elation, impulsive phone calls to friends and cries of 'Where's that champagne we won on the tombola?'

The euphoric phase is short lived. Soon, summoned from dark recesses in the subconscious, nagging doubts and fears arrive to torment every waking hour until the job is over. They penetrate the chinks in your professional armour and remind you of them again and again. Horrifying fantasies of a last minute loss of voice or a frog in the throat are interspersed with fears of going out of tune, cracking on a vital top note or making a disastrous musical mistake. Admittedly with a simple rousing melody like *Soldiers of the Queen* only two things could go wrong – forgetting the words or failing to hear the orchestral introduction through the applause for the previous act and starting the song too early – or too late!

Anything like that on such an occasion would take some living down.

The next excitement was when the full list of names of those taking part was in all the papers. Among those with whom I'd be appearing were Gracie Fields, Beniamino Gigli, Vic Oliver, Arthur Askey, Tony Hancock, Max Bygraves, Jimmy Edwards, Jerry Desmonde, Ted Ray, Vera Lynn, Reg Dixon. After my name they had put in brackets (Baritone, Glyndebourne Opera) which brought it home to me that I was something of an invited interloper who needed to be explained away. Also in the list were those veteran comedians Bud Flanagan, Naughton and Gold, Nervo and Knox – known collectively and affectionately as The Crazy Gang.

Reading those five names stirred old memories. The antics of Nervo and Knox and Naughton and Gold were among my earliest theatrical experiences. I had seen them at the London Coliseum with my mother when I was no more than six years old and could still recall with pleasure Nervo and Knox's slow motion routine – a brilliant impression of the silent films, helped by revolving discs over the spotlights to give a flickering effect. Naughton and Gold also made a small boy laugh though quite how has faded from the memory save a lingering image of two balding little Scotsmen being extremely energetic.

Flanagan and Allen sparkled in my schooldays. Struck from the classic double act mould of comedian and straight man, they possessed two great assets: extreme likeability and a unique singing style. Chesney Allen's delivery was *quasi parlante*, yet it provided something of a double bass backing for Bud's winning cockney croon. *Underneath the Arches* won them a small niche of immortality in recording history. When Chesney quit the boards for theatre management, Bud and the other two double acts amalgamated as the Crazy Gang. They were joined from time to time by the splendidly eccentric Monsewer Eddie Gray. As a schoolboy in the middle 1930s I saw them at the Palladium and was convulsed by their slapstick routines which one critic described as 'lambent lunacy'.

'Can you direct me to His Majesty's annoyed?'
'His Majesty's annoyed? There's no such place.'
'Yes, there is – King's Cross! Oi!'

Bud's amiable leer from beneath the broken brim of his ancient straw boater which crowned an even more dilapidated fur coat invested such simple gags with irresistible hilarity. The thought that one day I might join him on the stage of that show business mecca did not and could not have entered my head.

But those five names sparked off another memory which set a few alarm bells ringing. I was back in Reigate ten years earlier in 1942 working as assistant Command Entertainment Officer, South Eastern Command under Major Jack Hobbs – not the famous cricketer but a musical comedy star of the twenties and thirties.

Jack had a fund of theatre stories. One evening in the Castle Hotel near Reigate Station where we were billeted someone asked him what was his most embarrassing moment during a performance.

'No doubt about that,' he said. 'It was in a Royal Command Performance – and if ever I'm asked to appear again with the Crazy Gang I'll ask for danger money. I was appearing in a musical with Evelyn Laye that year and one of the big production numbers from it was chosen for the royal show. I was dressed as an officer in the Hussars of some imaginary country – a glamorous sky-blue outfit with tight breeches, the tunic frogged with gold braid, a high collar, plumed fur hat – the lot. The climax of the scene was Miss Laye and I whirling round in an elaborate waltz routine with the chorus and dancers.

'The Crazy Gang were appearing later with a spectacular water act, but they kept coming on stage throughout so I didn't think anything of it when I noticed some of them standing near me at the back of the set as I waited for my entrance cue to come up. I still don't know if they planned it in advance or did it on the spur of the moment – but just as my cue arrived a powerful jet of water from one of their hoses hit me slap in the buttocks so that I literally shot into view at the top of the staircase which led down into that glittering ballroom!

'From then on it was a nightmare. God knows I was nervous enough already, but now all I could think of was whether the audience could see water dripping off me and what they would make of it on such an important occasion! I swaggered down those stairs all smiles and devil-may-care trying desperately to think of a way to do the waltz routine without turning my back to the audience, for it was a racing certainty that by now there would be a dark stain on the seat of my elegant breeches. No one seemed to notice anything wrong until we started the dance. Every time we had to make a turn I steered Miss Laye behind one of the chorus couples. She thought I'd gone off my head as we wrestled our way through the dance. "Boo" Laye was the star, the centre of attention, yet I kept pulling her out of sight. Worse was to befall. Suddenly my legs wouldn't work properly and my dance steps became mincing and clumsy. You see my saturated breeches had started shrinking and all I could hope for now was to get to the end of the scene before they split wide open at the rear.

'"What's the matter with you?" hissed Boo through a loving smile. My reply mystified her completely. Leaning forward as if to whisper a sweet nothing in her shell-like ear I put her in the picture.

'"My arse is wet."'

We'd laughed a great deal in that hotel lounge but I wasn't laughing now. This was a great chance in a new field for me. Like Jack I would be appearing in uniform in a big scene. So I added to my growing list of anxieties the necessity to see that five incorrigible, irreverent, elderly schoolboys were not behind me in the nervous moments before marching down the stage to sing *Soldiers of the Queen.*

There was a rehearsal the day before the performance and what is called in the theatre a dress parade. Everyone puts on their costume and comes on stage to let the producer see it. In a new production the designer would be there with the wardrobe mistress and there would be considerable discussion among the production team to make sure that everything is right down to the smallest detail. It's very different for a rush job like a Command Performance. I was bitterly disappointed with the costume that had been hired for me as a result of my sending in my measurements to the theatre a week or so previously. It barely fitted and though it was quite correct for a recruiting sergeant in the Brigade of Guards at the turn of the century, it looked as if it had done duty then and lain fading in a cupboard ever since. I protested to Charles Henry, the producer, a kindly and efficient man with, that day, a huge load of responsibility. He shrugged.

'This is a charity show, Ian, we can't spend a lot on the production.'

'Can I try and find something better?'

'Up to you.'

I went to Nathan's – one of the best theatrical costumiers in London.

'I want the impossible and I need it tomorrow for the Command Performance.' That's the sort of challenge to which costumiers are quite accustomed. I had used the word impossible because in those days I weighed close on sixteen stone, though my height is only an average five foot ten and a half.

'You may be in luck,' said John Nathan. 'We did a uniform like that for a film and it's just come back. I think Martin Boddy wore it so it may need a bit of shortening.' I tried it on. It was superb. The bright red short jacket, dark blue trousers with a red stripe and a saucy pill-box hat. John threw in a pair of sideboards and a military moustache, saying that they'd work on the alterations – all night if necessary. The only part of the old uniform I would need to use was the recruiting sash.

I cheerfully returned to the Palladium for a run-through and to collect the four tickets I'd ordered for the following evening. When the manager handed them to me I thanked him thinking that they were the usual allocation of artists' first night complimentary seats.

'Will you make the cheque out to the Variety Artistes Benevolent Fund, please,' he said as I started to leave his office.

'Cheque?'

'For the tickets.'

'Oh, I thought . . .' He looked at me with contempt.

'No "comps" for the Command, son – surely you know that?' I didn't, though on such a great fund-raising night when everyone appears for nothing it should have been obvious.

'How much are they?'

'Fifteen pounds each – sixty pounds the four.' Thirty years ago that was a lot of money. I wrote the cheque in a daze wondering why I'd been so free with my invitations.

At the dress rehearsal on the following afternoon Charles Henry took one look at my resplendent uniform and nodded.

'That's more like it,' he murmued. By this time the Band of the Coldstream Guards were getting into position backstage as well as other regular troops who were to march up the aisles of the theatre in the finale. The warrant officer in charge of them approached me.

'Where are you from then?'

'I'm a singer.'

'Thought you must be something like that. Where did you get those boots?'

'They're mine. I had them in the war.'

'They're a bloody disgrace.'

'They're not bad. I polished them this morning.'

'You could have fooled me, and I tell you this. You're not marching on with our lot with 'em looking like that. Take 'em off and I'll get one of the lads to do a *proper* job on 'em.'

'Thank you.'

'Thank you, *sir*.'

'Yes, sir. Sorry, sir.' I was right back in the army and I hadn't the heart to tell him that I'd finished up with a commission. Anyway he hadn't finished.

'Your boots'll be all right, but I think we'd better soak your sash. It's hanging off your shoulder something chronic – looks terrible. They all have to be soaked, you know. It's the only way to get it to cling to you proper.' The performance was only hours away and after Jack Hobbs' story this reference to plunging part of my costume in water was unnerving.

'Let's see what the wardrobe mistress can do,' I suggested. Though harassed by almost everyone appearing she gave me and the warrant officer a few minutes of her great skill and pinned the sash in half a dozen places until he was reluctantly forced to admit that it would do. Meantime 'one of the lads' had done a great job on my boots, though he didn't think so.

'Takes hours to do a *real* job,' said the young soldier gloomily. The warrant officer looked me up and down with narrowed eyes.

'All right. You'll just about pass in a crowd, but for God's sake stand up straight when you're out there. Right, dismiss.'

There was no doubt that John Nathan and the warrant officer between them had ensured that I would *look* right. So I had nothing to worry about except nerves, words, voice and maybe the Crazy Gang.

Because I was only on for the last few minutes I wasn't required to be in the theatre all that much during the two days rehearsal and you only get in the way if you hang about. I hardly knew anyone taking part except Jimmy Edwards from Cambridge days before the war. I came from a different world, though I was on nodding terms with one or two others I'd met doing the odd singing spot in variety broadcasts – but this didn't include the big names like Gracie Fields, Gigli, Maurice Chevalier – the last minute surprise addition to the list – or the redoubtable Crazy Gang. So I was alone with my fears and suppressed excitement most of the time.

After the final run-through I went home to rest. Pat, my mother, my agent Richard Stone and his actress wife Sara Gregory – my supporters club for the evening – set off in good time for the 7.30 start. I decided to arrive quite a bit later. The thought of waiting in a dressing room for at least three hours was not inviting. I soon found that the empty house was equally scaring and I began to work out a scenario of punctures or mechanical failure that would be sure to occur if I left my departure too late. I had planned to leave home about a quarter to nine and get to the Palladium half an hour later. It was no good. I left soon after the others, parked near Broadcasting House and walked to Argyll Street coming through the stage door about 7.50. The voice of Tony Hancock could be heard through the tannoy. He was in the middle of a naval sketch that had a few digs at a member of the Senior Service sitting just behind the Queen. Tony was getting huge laughs, though even without seeing him it was obvious that he was fighting an attack of nervous giggles.

The tension in that theatre was more evident than anything I've experienced before or since. An invariable sufferer from nerves, I've known bigger personal ordeals than that night, but it was seeing so many famous people visibly under stress that was unusual. I went up to my dressing room which I was sharing with a seaside comic, George Cameron, who had been as amazed as I was to be included in the show and now – ten minutes before his act (which went well) – would have given anything to be back in the cosy atmosphere of some south coast pier pavilion. I opened the door and stepped inside but immediately retraced my steps, coughing and spluttering. The small, unventilated room was a blue fog of cigarette smoke. Poor George must have been in there for hours chain-smoking and feeling miserable.

Things were just as tense in the wings. The great Italian tenor Beniamino Gigli in white tie and tails was standing near the small grand piano that would be wheeled on to the stage for his spot. I had several of his records at home and to me it was awe-inspiring to be so near one of the greatest opera singers of this century. I wondered if dared shake his hand. He moved to the keyboard and quietly played a chord then, almost in a whisper so as not to disturb the act on the stage, he sang the words 'Vesti la giubba, – 'On with the Motley' – from Leoncavallo's opera *I Pagliacci*. He shook his head, groaned and said to no one in particular,

'Che nervoso son io.' ('I'm so nervous.')

As I'd picked up some Italian during my brief operatic career I addressed him in an approximation of his native tongue. I told him that I had sung once in Italy at Parma. He smiled.

'A dangerous place – they liked you?'

'Thank God yes!' We at least had in common the reputation of the Parma audiences.

'They will like you here tonight, maestro,' I said. 'In bocca lupo.' ('Into the wolf's mouth' – or 'good luck'.) We shook hands and so ended my one conversation with the great man, who not only sang *Vesti la giubba* but in duet with Gracie Fields gave an account of *Come back to Sorrento*, in which each of them egged on the other to tackle the highest notes in their respective ranges.

I had an even briefer conversation with Maurice Chevalier, another of my heroes. It is usually forbidden to stand in the wings unless you are concerned in the scene, but I wasn't going to miss this. He walked on to the stage looking exactly as I remembered him from the films I'd seen before the war. He sang a verse of *Louise* and half a chorus, then he broke off and walked twice across the stage waving his straw hat in the air to thunderous applause while the orchestra played a chorus and a half on their own. As he came off I had to move to one side to let him pass, so engrossed had I been that I was practically on the stage with him. He gave me that infectious gallic smile and said,

'Would you beeleev eet! I meesed ma words!' That sent me racing back up the stairs to the dressing room to check mine.

The tension I've described is easily explained. All performers are apprehensive about charity shows because the kind and generous people who support them are not necessarily the audience who would pay to see us in the ordinary way. Therefore they may not like our style of humour or singing and it may be hard to get a good reaction out of them. Add to this the necessity to find some new and unfamiliar material, the brief rehearsal time, the presence of the media and you can realise that the sympathetic group in the Royal Box are really the least of our worries.

Eventually – at approximately ten minutes past eleven – my great moment arrived. I stood behind a gauze curtain, my heart thudding well over seventy-two to the minute. The gauze flew away, a battery of lights picked me up, I heard the music, saw Woolf Phillips, the conductor give me a smile as I marched downstage and then I was singing my heart out. I had again that curious sensation of being outside myself watching the performance and occasionally giving a word of warning like, 'Don't hit it too hard, you'll be all in before the end' or 'Don't think ahead, just sing the words as they come.' This time it was 'Don't look at the Royal Box until you've finished and then for goodness sake bow to Her Majesty before the rest.'

How did it go? Cecil Wilson of *The Daily Mail* was kind enough to write:

'But the most exciting moment in an uncommonly smooth and well balanced bill came at the end when four hundred people – forty of them stars – lined up on the stage to sing their tribute to the Royal Box.

'It was a stranger to music hall – Ian Wallace, the Glyndebourne baritone, dressed in the scarlet tunic and pill box hat of a Victorian Guardsman who led them in *Soldiers of the Queen*. Behind him massed the stars and the Ilford Girls Choir, and, playing away in the background the Band of H.M. Coldstream Guards.

'Then as Gracie Fields stepped forward, the song merged into the National Anthem and sixty sturdy soldiers of various regiments marched down the aisles of the stalls in uniforms ranging through the ages to the khaki of today. The glory of that one scene would have justified all the effort that had gone into the evening.'

I was a bit disappointed not to be one of those presented to Her Majesty, but they had to draw the line somewhere and we all attended a nice party in the theatre at which the principal emotion was one of enormous relief that it was successfully over. There, for the first time I met some of the other singers in the show, Josef Locke, the Deep River Boys and Gerry Brereton who had been blinded serving with the Commandos and, of course, Vera Lynn. Yes, there was a great deal of singing in the show and many of the other big names like Jimmy Edwards, Reg Dixon, Norman Wisdom and Max Bygraves provided a medley of songs from the golden days of music hall. Like me they were in the show for one verse and one chorus.

When it was all over Gigli went back to Italy, Gracie to Capri, Chevalier to finish his career in a blaze of glory and most of the others to top bills, make films or invade the expanding world of television.

What did I do? Well I couldn't go back to Glyndebourne. I wasn't due there till May and this was November, so I went off to play a cockney character part in a play called *Worm's Eye View*

which was being revived at the Grand Theatre, Croydon. A bit
of a comedown? Not in my book. It had enjoyed a very long run
at the Whitehall Theatre with Ronald Shiner in the part I was
to play, and also in that London run in the role of a father-figure
RAF officer was my old friend Jack Hobbs.

That reminds me. The Crazy Gang were as good as gold and
sabotaged no one. In fact one or two critics felt that in this, their
ninth Royal appearance, they might have had more to do.

Chapter 8

A surprising number of actors and musicians declare that they
never read press notices about their performances. I've always
been unable to resist the temptation and used to subscribe to an
agency that covered every publication in the country and sent
me clippings from any which mentioned my name. For twenty
years or more they gave me faithful and efficient service then
suddenly they began to send me reports of pop concerts where a
drummer called Ian Wallace had done well and occasional
snippets about a noted ornithologist of the same name, while
friends from Scotland would refer in letters to a nice article
about me by Gordon Hislop in the Scottish *Sunday Express*,
complete with photograph, which the agency had missed.

This came about apparently because the turnover of eagle-
eyed readers for these agencies is now so rapid that they can no
longer cater for individuals apart from superstars. Nowadays
they're principally used by big organisations – 'Just send us
everything that mentions I.C.I. or I.B.M. or Shell or blood
sports.'

So I remain in blissful ignorance knowing that if I did
subscribe now I would inevitably receive – and have to pay for –
long and glowing accounts of my prowess the previous Saturday for Nottingham Forest, or whatever team my brilliant
red-haired namesake is at present delighting with his skill.

But without the prompting of these yellowing cuttings,

laboriously pasted into large books along with excerpts from *The Radio Times* and ancient theatre programmes I would have been in the same situation as an eminent musician who told me he was embarking on his autobiography at the time I was writing this.

'Did you keep a diary?' he asked.

'No,' I replied and told him about the press books.

'I've kept all my old diaries,' he said, 'but they're no damned use. There's nothing on the pages except Manchester, Birmingham, Exeter or Zurich. What the hell did I do when I got there?'

I was never methodical enough to stick the cuttings in as they arrived, but let them accumulate for a year or two – then, usually when I had a cold, I'd spend a day or so catching up, only skimming through to get them in chronological order. I've hardly looked at them since.

Why did I undertake this time-consuming task in the first place? Certainly not with the idea of providing material for a book.

During the eight years that my father represented Dunfermline Burghs in the House of Commons between the wars my mother religiously collected everything about him in *The Dunfermline Press and Journal* and *The Lochgelly Times* and pasted column after column of his reported speeches neatly into press cutting books. There is even a photograph from *The Daily Mirror* of me as babe in arms about to be carried into the Houses of Parliament to be christened in the Crypt!

I had read these books as a boy, so it was natural for me to continue the family custom. Anyway there's a fascination about seeing one's name in print and though I'm not a confirmed hoarder I've always found it difficult to throw away books, records – and press cuttings.

Looking at the entries for late 1952 and 1953 it's obvious that my willingness to take on whatever was offered led me into jobs in such absurdly contrasting fields that I can only be thankful that I survived the period without coming a cropper and being held up to ridicule.

High-brow, middle-brow and popular-brow entertainments all saw something of me but it was a brief appearance on the wireless in the latter category that was to be of more lasting significance than anything else.

85

The Radio Times shows that I appeared on a famous show called *Henry Hall's Guest Night*. Henry had conducted the BBC Dance Orchestra since the 1930s and his tuneful music and attractive, shy personality endeared him to everyone. His *Guest Night* was as much sought after then as an appearance on a top TV chat show is now. I was thrilled to be invited realising that it was probably as a result of my appearance in the Royal Command Performance.

I decided to sing *The Hippopotamus Song*. It was the first time I'd sung it on the radio, though I'd performed it on TV two months earlier from the Edinburgh Festival with a distinguished group of three German sopranos from the Hamburg Opera as chorus, with the piano accompaniment augmented by a tuba player from The BBC Scottish Symphony Orchestra. But this rather esoteric programme late at night had not had a big viewing figure.

My introduction to its writer and composer Michael Flanders and Donald Swann was another great stroke of luck in that blessed period in the late 1940s when it seemed as though the average was being put right for the rather grisly years of illness I'd had earlier. I was delighted by my unforeseen opera career but I felt trapped by it. I yearned to be able to appear in lighter entertainments as well, and Michael and Donald's humorous songs were an ideal means for me to bridge that difficult gap. The words and music had a distinction that appealed to an audience embracing lovers of both opera and revue.

A former school friend who'd at one time written me letters strongly advocating an opera career (long before it happened) had written again insisting on bringing Donald Swann to tea. During that pleasant afternoon Donald, his pale, bespectacled face glowing with enthusiasm, asserted that I was clearly the chap they'd been looking for to sing a song he and Michael had written about a hippopotamus.

'As a matter of fact,' he confided, 'Michael wrote this tune as well, I only arranged it. Thought of it in the bath!' Then for the first time I heard Donald's explosive guffaw which reveals the humour that is only just below the surface of that earnest exterior.

He was too polite to suggest that my girth and letter-box mouth had made me a good candidate for this ditty before I'd sung a note, but after we'd run it through he quickly took me to see his bearded collaborator and friend, the rest of whose life would be spent in a wheel chair as a result of polio contracted in the navy during the war. The two had met at Westminster School and more differing types it would be hard to imagine. Michael warm, extrovert with a deep voice and deeper chuckle, Donald kind, remote and tense, but both on precisely the same wavelength. It was my wavelength too. Then they had no thought of performing their own material in public, but they attacked it in private or at parties with zest. I've never reckoned up how many of their songs I've sung, but nearly thirty years later it's marvellous to embark on many of them secure in the knowledge that audiences of all ages still enjoy them.

Henry Hall's Guest Night was my first experience of singing a new popular song to a mass audience, and the reaction of the studio audience took me by surprise. They cheered and whistled as well as clapping. I can thank Henry (as well as Michael and Donald) for giving me a chance that November evening of identifying myself for the rest of my career with a robustly amorous hippopotamus inviting his mate to leave her hilltop and join him in 'mud, glorious mud.'

I had the heady experience of getting fan mail, only one letter being less than ecstatic.

'Dear Sir, Since you sang that blooming song on the radio my life hasn't been worth living. Yours faithfully, Neville Mudd.'

Curiously enough there were no recording offers, and it was several years before one came. Apparently most of the companies thought it was too highbrow! The chap who eventually decided to risk a 45 extended play record with three other Flanders and Swann animal songs entitled *Wallace's Private Zoo* was George Martin, then of Parlophone, now head of his own recording empire. He was also the first person to record The Beatles and Peter Sellers, in which reflected glory I've been basking every since.

Before the record was issued George called me to his office to discuss the design of the sleeve. He's a tall, slim thoughtful looking man with a quiet speaking voice.

'What would you like on the front?' he asked.

'What do you suggest?'

'It could either be a photograph of you or one of a hippo-potamus.'

I thought for a moment.

'I'd rather like a picture of me, but I think that perhaps a hippopotamus would sell more copies.'

He smiled faintly.

'You have a very realistic approach to our business,' he said. A hippo it was with its mouth wide open. There was a passport size one of me on the back.

George must be a wealthy man now and he's lived on the pop scene for half a lifetime where it can't be easy to remain the same modest, compassionate person I met at Parlophone in the 1950s. But he's managed it.

Two days after the *Guest Night* I was in Scotland and the more rarified end of the cultural scene to be again the Blind Harper in a new radio production of *The King of Scots* with Tom Fleming in the John McCallum part, yet in mid-December I was a bearded villain in *Babes in the Wood* at the Players Theatre in London's Villiers Street, marvelling at the capacity of Reginald Woolley to design convincing and beautiful scenery for such a postage stamp of a stage – to say nothing of Don Gemmell's direction and Michael Charnley's choreography in such a confined space.

Geoffrey Dunn – good actor as well as opera translator – was a splendidly neurotic Sir Rowland Macassar and Joan Sterndale Bennett's governess who is 'getting on instead of getting off' was a typical example of her impeccable characterisation and timing. If she had not chosen to devote most of her career to the Players she could have had great success in the commercial theatre and elsewhere.

On Christmas Day if I'd had any sense I'd have been at home with Pat. Instead I was one of a large cast anxiously putting the finishing touches to a TV production of *1066 And All That* at Lime Grove Studios (near Shepherds Bush).

The show was at 9.30 in the evening and we were rehearsing from about 10.30 in the morning. The only remotely Christ-massy atmosphere arrived fleetingly when we broke for lunch and were handed out plates of rather dried up turkey followed by lumpy Christmas pudding washed down with orange squash and coffee. The canteen was decorated with sprigs of plastic holly and a small Christmas tree bearing a few tinsel balls, a tiny Woolworth fairy and some 'presents' which were almost certainly wads of gift wrapped cotton wool. Some of the girls behind the cafeteria counter were wearing paper hats, but all of us were gloomily aware of lonely wives, husbands and families, their day ruined, saying to themselves, 'It had better be good!'

All through those sort of days – Christmas or midsummer – I was always haunted by the fear of 'drying' during the show. But Christmas made it just that little bit worse because one knew that everyone would be watching including the BBC top brass.

In *1066 And All That* – a comic potted history of England – everyone played several parts (except for Tony Britton as the Compere and Harry Locke as the Common Man). I was a Roman soldier one minute and one of the Four Georges the next. These sort of costume changes were hazardous in a live transmission in case something tore or split with no time to execute repairs. In one show – it may have been this one – I remember the wardrobe mistress crawling over to an artist on her stomach with a needle and thread to stitch up the back of his trousers while he was singing a song in close-up, so that all would be well when he had to walk away from the camera in full length shot at the end of it. What made it doubly hard for the singer was that he didn't know his pants had split and couldn't understand why someone was apparently massaging his bottom during his song.

*   *   *

One reason why I found myself in the upper reaches of high-brow musical entertainment in the spring of 1953 was that by some extraordinary administrative decision my name had been added to a BBC list of opera singers who could safely be cast to sing twelve tone music – in other words – modern works with all their complexities and discords. I've already enlarged on my inability to sight read and lack of perfect pitch, essential requirements to perform such music with any degree of comfort.

As a consequence I went through two nightmare engagements which I accepted without realising that they were far more difficult than anything I'd previously attempted.

The first was *The Trial of Lucullus* with music by Paul Dessau and a libretto by Berthold Brecht translated into English by Geoffrey Dunn. The conductor was Hermann Scherchen, a short tempered German who didn't suffer fools gladly – and so far as he was concerned that included me.

The situation wasn't made any easier by his style of conducting. He didn't use a baton. Instead his hands moved up and down no more than about six inches, his thumbs and index fingers just touching. A wag in the orchestra said that it looked as though he was milking gnats in flight.

Not only did I find his beat hard to follow, but the aptness of that description of it made me want to laugh every time I had to look at him during the performance.

There was one moment when I had to sing a top Eb and the only instrument that could help me pitch it was one of the timpani (kettle drums). I put up a prayer and I'm sure the Almighty helped me more than the percussion player.

Somehow I got through it without perpetrating a disaster but I knew perfectly well that whatever else I might take on in the future this sort of music was beyond me – the effort to learn it and the strain of performance simply weren't worth it.

But I was already contracted for another even more demanding modern work – *The Country Doctor* – a short story by Franz Kafka set as a radio opera by the German composer Hans Werner Henze.

I had accepted because the producer was Douglas Cleverdon – not only the friendliest of men but one of the great features producers of sound radio, particularly remembered for his presentation of Dylan Thomas's *Under Milkwood*. To be in one of his productions was the ambition of singers and actors alike because of his reputation for tackling adventurous works, and making the studio a happy place in the process.

When the score arrived I realised that this was going to be the kind of adventure I could do without. I was going to need a great deal of help to learn it. Thankfully it was in English but there were, to quote the fly-leaf, five different modes of utterance: ordinary speech, speech in rhythm (and what rhythm!), sung speech, spoken song and one passage of about thirty-six bars of singing, pure but not simple.

90

As well as an orchestra that included a huge percussion section (let us pray!) there was an organ and three pianos. One was untreated, another had drawing pins stuck into its hammers, while the third had paper stretched across the strings. There was also a chorus, but much of their contribution was pre-recorded and played backwards. One critic described it all as 'an extreme example of formless dissonance'.

I rang Douglas with a cry for help.

'The number of hours I'll need to employ a repetiteur to teach me this will cost more than my fee.'

'How many hours do you think it'll take?' was his breezy response.

'At least twenty.'

'OK.'

'I'll need one of the best.'

'Who do you want?'

'Bryan Balkwill.'

'Go ahead and book him, we'll pay.'

That was Douglas all over. He paid me the compliment of assuming that I wasn't making a fuss about nothing and was kind enough to persevere with me.

In the event Bryan and I worked twenty-three hours over a period of a fortnight during which he and I were appearing once a week on an afternoon TV show with the charming Jeanne Heale in which I sang little bits of rather simpler operas and urged people to go and see them if they got the chance. What housewives in Doncaster or Ipswich made of it in the midst of cooking demonstrations and flower arranging I'd no means of knowing. At any rate none of them put pen to paper.

At last I had broken the back of the wretched thing – it lasted about thirty-five minutes and I, as an elderly doctor telling the hair-raising story which included references to white maggots crawling from a stomach wound, was speaking or singing throughout.

There were several well known singers in small parts supporting me, including Marjorie Westbury, Robert Irwin and Catherine Lawson and the conductor Patrick Savill was a much more sympathetic character than Hermann Scherchen. He was perhaps the best dressed maestro I ever met and carried his score in a music case made of crocodile skin. If I was the country doctor he was certainly a well groomed surgeon with red hair and gold-rimmed spectacles.

As the day of the first rehearsal approached one part of the work still eluded me – the short passage of real singing. The intervals between the notes were so bizarre that I just couldn't get it right. Often difficult music sorts itself out in the memory during a night's sleep. Not this time. Bryan did all he could to help but to no avail.

Douglas had supplied me with a recording of a German baritone performing the work in the original language with the composer conducting. I hadn't made much use of it. Even if it had been in English it's always dangerous to copy a recorded performance. Working with a repetiteur at the piano means that every mistake is rectified and you get a solid grounding. The word they use to indicate that you really know a part well enough to rehearse it with other singers and orchestra is 'secure'.

My lack of security on this one vital passage was still acute the evening before I would have to sing it with Patrick Savill and the Philharmonia Orchestra. In desperation I put on the record and listened to the confident tones of the German baritone battling successfully with the discordant accompaniment that Bryan had so faithfully reproduced on the piano. How did he manage it? I asked myself. Perhaps he didn't, replied my alter ego. I took the needle off the disc, got out my copy of the score and opened the piano. Then I started the record again. As the baritone sang I played the notes he should have been singing. To my delight he was nowhere near some of them. He was giving the same sort of wild approximation of it that was the best I could do – going up when the music went up and down when it did likewise, getting the complicated rhythm right – but definitely only a six out of ten job.

I stopped worrying. Presumably the composer was happy or he wouldn't have released the recording.

It was amusing to watch the faces of the orchestra as they started to sight read the work. One section would look over their shoulders in amazement at the sounds coming from their colleagues and at times a hastily suppressed guffaw could be heard above the unfamiliar sounds, which by now were all too familiar to me.

When we broke for coffee Manoug Parikian the Armenian violinist who was leading the Philharmonia came over to me.

'Well,' he said, 'we're all making some weird sounds, but the orchestra are lost in admiration for the way you sang that bit in the middle. How ever did you learn it?'

I looked modestly at the carpet. 'It took me a long time,' I said.

The next day, the day of the live transmission, I woke up with bronchitis. I'd been backing a cold for some time and it had finally beaten me. Had I faced a big singing part I'd have had to cancel. As it was the voice would probably stand up for the necessary half an hour if I could only get something to ease my breathing. I saw my doctor who said he could give me a pill that would probably do so for about an hour, but it wouldn't work a second time.

I wheezed and coughed my way through the final rehearsals, took the magic tablet as instructed at 7.30 and was ungratefully surprised at the dramatic clearing of my respiratory passages a few minutes later. Sure enough within half an hour of the end of the broadcast I was once more feeling and sounding decidedly unwell. What would have happened if the decongestant hadn't worked? Well, all performers have to take decisions like this that are difficult, especially when you're about to do a part that no one else in the country knows. I suppose I must have felt that I wasn't completely dependant on the drug because the stress of performance always causes the adrenalin to flow – Sir Noel Coward once called it 'Dr Theatre' and just as it can enable middle aged ladies to leap five bar gates when pursued by a bull, it can miraculously push symptoms into the background for the duration of a performance.

Subsequently the respected music critic Scott Goddard wrote in *The News Chronicle* that I 'succeeded in making the plot clear and holding our attention.' But the frustration of such an engagement was that after so much work and such a sustained effort in performance there was virtually no feed-back, apart from a couple of mildly laudatory press notices. Any friends who'd heard *Lucullus* or *The Country Doctor* either hated them or said that it was impossible to pass judgement on one hearing.

This was perfectly fair and highlights the fact that the only people who obtain full value out of rarely heard modern works

93

are the performers who get to know them well in rehearsal. Mind you there are plenty of people around who would have mastered that work in three hours not the twenty-three I needed – except, perhaps, for those testing thirty-six bars.

From the heights of Henze and Berthold Brecht I came back to earth with a broadcast from 'Palace of Varieties' with Ernest Longstaffe, the only BBC producer I ever knew who also conducted his own show. He composed a famous ballad entitled *When the Sergeant Major's on Parade*, but he asked me on this occasion to sing *Queen of the Earth* by Ciro Pinsuti, a welcome return to tonality.

*   *   *

Just occasionally some event of great importance coincides with what would otherwise have been a routine engagement quickly forgotten and reserves for it a place among those moments in life that can be recalled in clear detail.

On Saturday at the end of January 1953 Pat took me to Kings Cross after an early lunch to get a train to Cleethorpes in Lincolnshire. I was to stay the night with the conductor of the local orchestra there and sing with them the following night, returning on the Monday morning. It was a very windy day and *The Evening Standard* I bought at the station carried dramatic headlines about an SOS call from *The Princess Victoria*, a car ferry that had been struck by a huge wave in the Irish Sea and seriously damaged. She had shipped a great deal of water on the car deck and was drifting in the gale. What was more, no one seemed to know exactly where she was.

Whenever the train stopped the force of the gale made the coaches sway. I remember John Betjeman once saying that you always knew when you were in Lincolnshire on a train journey because when it stopped you could hear the wind across the unsheltered fens sighing in the ventilators. If this had been one of those pre-war coaches he was talking about the sigh would have been a scream.

It was dark when we reached Grimsby and the station public address system, competing with the elements, announced that we were going no further.

A stout man with a toothbrush moustache and wearing an old leather flying jacket approached me.

'Ian Wallace? Good show. I'm Don, your conductor. The train can't get to Cleethorpes, the line's flooded. I've got the car here but we'll have to go inland and get home from the other side of the town. The police have closed the coast road. They hadn't much choice; the sea's gouging bits of concrete the size of bathing huts out the sea wall and hurling them across the road into shop fronts – not a pretty sight!'

He told me all this as if it were the best thing that had happened for years. On the radio that night we heard that *The Princess Victoria* had foundered with the loss of many lives and that very near us – at Mablethorpe – over twenty people caught by flood water had perished. Don remained cheerful, but it was the sort of buoyancy I remembered from the Blitz and perhaps that tattered flying jacket was the clue.

'With any luck we'll be able to do the concert,' he said. 'Admittedly the Winter Garden is on the pier and they do say that if tomorrow's high tide is an inch higher than tonight's we may have to run for it.'

I didn't sleep too well. The wind was deafening and, though we had arrived in the dark, I suspected that the sea was not very far away.

When we went next day to the Winter Garden I was amused to see that I was billed 'Ian Wallace – Ace Baritone'. Don had obviously misheard me on the phone when I said bass baritone.

Despite another fearsome day of wind we had a surprisingly good audience and though the noise of the sea was menacing it didn't rise that last dangerous inch. The only alarm was caused by some unmusical youths who threw a firecracker against a window. We were all feeling a bit jumpy anyway and I think there was probably at least six inches between me and the floor at that moment.

Don, who alas died soon after, and his wife were good, kind people determined to keep music going in this rather remote area. The size of the audience who braved that fierce night showed how much their efforts were appreciated.

I hadn't been able to contact Pat by phone, so when I arrived back at Kings Cross at lunch time on Monday she and my mother were standing at the barrier looking pale and anxious. Their relief when they spotted me was considerable. Certainly the newspaper reports they showed me made it clear that we had been very lucky in Cleethorpes that weekend to escape the worst of a great natural disaster.

*   *   *

A couple of months after my Cleethorpes adventure the English Opera Group revived *Let's Make an Opera* at Barnstaple for the Taw and Torridge Festival and the conductor was Norman Del Mar, an erudite musician who had worked in close association for a time with Sir Thomas Beecham.

We've all laughed at the comedian who sits at the piano and surprises us by the brilliance of his playing until he takes his hands off the keyboard and the recording to which he's been miming continues. It's not quite so funny the other way round.

In the first act of *Let's Make an Opera* the composer surrounded by children plays the piano on the stage – or rather in the case of a non pianist like myself pretends to do so. The keyboard is locked so that notes won't sound inadvertently and someone else, usually the conductor, plays another piano in the wings close by.

On the first night as the moment approached for me to 'play' the first piano solo I was alarmed to see Norman still seated in the orchestra pit following the play with polite attention. He was still there when I sat down on the stool. I pretended to play one or two chords. Silence.

'You know, children,' I said in a loud voice looking urgently in Norman's direction, 'I thought there was something wrong with this piano this morning when I was practising, but now I can't get a sound out of it. I'd better have a look underneath in case it's something quite simple.'

By this time Norman had left the orchestra pit at the speed of light and I only had to ad lib under the piano until I could see his not inconsiderable presence arriving on tip toe at the run beside the off-stage instrument.

'Ah, children, I've discovered what's the matter – an essential part of the mechanism was out of place. It's back now.'

On the 2nd June 1953 every leading British singer had an important engagement. They were all in Westminster Abbey to ensure the best possible vocal effect for Her Majesty Queen Elizabeth's Coronation. I was not among them, and wouldn't have expected an invitation. I had no oratorio or church music connections nor was I under contract to the well known concert agents who represented nearly every singer of note and probably provided a list for the Abbey. I joined some of them at Mornington Crescent in the late afternoon, however, to prepare for a joyous broadcast that evening.

The BBC had decided that a suitable Coronation evening entertainment would be *Merrie England* by Edward German. So back from the Abbey trooped Dennis Noble, William Herbert, Mary Jarred, Marjorie Thomas and others for a short rehearsal which took us pretty well up to transmission time. They'd been in the Abbey for hours before the long ceremony and they must have been tired. But there wasn't a hint of fatigue in the lively, happy performance which Stanford Robinson conducted that night. Always a master at interpreting English light opera he surpassed himself by our unanimous verdict.

I sang the part of Wilkins, the strolling actor who gets thrown into the Thames and then emerges unabashed to sing a vigorous song with the chorus about all the fishes in the sea and containing the lines,

'And Neptune saith.

That's Queen Elizabeth,

And she's the queen for me!'

After it was over, Pat, who'd been in the studio audience at the Camden Theatre, and I drove as far into town as possible and then ran hand in hand down the Mall just in time to see the Royal Family on a floodlit balcony of Buckingham Palace before the lights were finally extinguished and the crowds made for home.

As we walked back to the car I said, 'I don't suppose many people listened to that broadcast tonight.' I was wrong. After a day of peering into black and white TV sets folk decided in their thousands to give their eyes a rest and turn on the radio. We had, apparently, a huge listening figure on that happy Elizabethan evening.

Chapter 9

Returning to Glyndebourne in the early summer to rehearse *La Cenerentola* again with the same cast was hardly a rest cure, though it was a relief not to have a new work to learn. Coming back to an opera after nine months is to find that both your conception of your part and how to sing it have matured. You look at it with more detachment than is possible during the slog of learning and intensive rehearsal.

The press were even more enthusiastic than they had been the previous year, probably because we now had the benefit of freshness plus experience.

Later we took it to Edinburgh and I still meet people in Scotland who remember that performance nearly thirty years later. This I'm sure is partly because Oliver Messel's scenery and costumes created a fairy tale world of delicacy and lavish beauty which I can still recall in my mind's eye, a place from which so many other productions have vanished for ever.

Some time during the winter we recorded the opera for HMV in the big Number 1 studio at Maida Vale. It wasn't my first visit to these famous studios. I had appeared on a recording of *The Beggar's Opera* a year or two earlier, but there's always something awe-inspiring about arriving there knowing that the likes of Nellie Melba, Clara Butt, Caruso, Gigli, John Mc-Cormack, Peter Dawson and countless other great singers have passed through that front door to fame and fortune.

I arrived early one morning in time to hear the Royal Philharmonic Orchestra recording the overture; and when the red light on the studio wall faded at the end several of the players immediately raised their hands to indicate that they had made minor errors and would like to repeat the piece.

They played it a second time and again hands, but only one or two, were raised. This time Maestro Gui asked them in turn what they were concerned about. Then he went into the control room to listen to a play-back of the tape, which was relayed through to the orchestra in the studio.

At the end the Maestro emerged smiling. 'I am happy. Are you?' he said. Most of them nodded or murmured assent and the handful of worriers shrugged resignedly. The recording is still knocking about and was reissued not so long ago, so you may get a chance to judge what high standards that great orchestra set for themselves in a recording studio – or anywhere else for that matter.

Recording techniques are constantly being revolutionised involving such impenetrable mysteries as twenty-four channels, sound mixing and the ease of transplanting a passage from one recording into the middle of another. For the singer, who has to make do with the same old technology of brain, flesh and blood, such goings on take some of the spontaneity out of a recording session. We can only bring a certain excitement and extra quality to the first two or three 'takes' of a recording while the adrenalin is still circulating. Later efforts may be nearer musical perfection, but a faultless recording can also be boring.

Happily this recording pre-dated many of these intricacies and as we had performed the opera many times in public a number of the excerpts that we rehearsed a couple of times both for ourselves and the technicians were then pronounced satisfactory after the first 'take'.

This particularly applied to the scene where Dandini disguised as the Prince receives the ugly sisters and their father in an ante-room of the palace. The main body of the scene is a long brilliant aria with roulades one minute and caressingly sustained singing the next. Sesto Bruscantini walked into the studio to record it straight from London Airport. The rest of us had started work the previous day and at the beginning of this particular three hour session had gone through the scene without him.

He embraced us all, the Maestro included, threw his overcoat on to a chair and said,

'Maestro, ce una prova o un'incisione?' ('Are we recording or rehearsing?') Gui, sensing that Sesto wouldn't have asked the question without good reason replied,

'Faciamo un incisione!'

The red light glowed, the buzzer sounded and off we went.

Sesto was in magnificent form and recaptured in sound all the atmosphere of a performance in the opera house.

When we heard the play-back we all applauded. There was absolutely no need to do any of it again. Then, to our pained surprise, we were sent home. There was still nearly half of the session time ahead of us, but there was also a Musician's Union rule that no more than twenty minutes of music that will actually appear on the finished disc may be recorded in one three hour session. We'd done our twenty minutes in double quick time and that was that. We could have repeated the same scene ad nauseam or rehearsed something for the next day, but that was all. The rule was introduced to prevent ruthless recording companies engaging an orchestra for three hours and recording two or three symphonies straight off the reel without rehearsal, thereby depriving the players both of money and reputation if the result proved to be below standard.

In fact the orchestra for this recording had a guarantee of more paid sessions than the opera could possibly take unless there was some dire emergency – but it's difficult to bend rules that have been formulated after hard negotiation.

A fascinating aspect of Sesto's performance that day is that before an opera he is one of those singers who likes to do a long warm up with exercises and excerpts from his part for half an hour or more. On this occasion he could only have done so in the car from the airport – but then there's always adrenalin.

*　　　*　　　*

After Edinburgh Pat and I went briefly to Spey Bay in Morayshire, a favourite holiday place that my mother and I had discovered before the war and persuaded my father that it was more relaxing than St Andrews in August when a game of golf has either to be organised in advance by booking a starting time on the Old Course or trudging a quarter of a mile to the crowded first tee of one of the other three links at that golfing mecca.

Spey Bay had an old fashioned family hotel, alas destroyed by fire in the 1960s, a sporty golf course, a post office cum general store, a single track railway now defunct and the River Spey racing into the sea. The bay curving away towards Buckie is dominated by the Cullen Bin, a thousand foot hill, purple in

September. The area had been optimistically described as similar to the Bay of Naples, though I dare say any Neapolitan would be astounded at the comparison.

When Pat was a child her family used to take a holiday cottage at Lossiemouth, a few miles west along the coast, and they drove over to visit us once or twice. Those afternoons must have been our first meetings. A little early for romance when I was fifteen and she eight!

Scottish holiday hotels tend to have customers who return year after year at the same time, so they are excellent places for making friends. Though holiday fashions have changed and there are fewer such places now Pat and I made some long-standing friendships at Spey Bay. Social life in both the theatre and the music profession is restricted by the hours of work and being constantly on the move, therefore holiday time is the one opportunity to enjoy the companionship of other folk in a relaxed atmosphere.

Also at Spey Bay that year was an Aberdeen doctor who, it was said, had been captured with the 51st Division at St Valery and had been a prisoner of war for about five years. His name was Rae Duffus and he was at Spey Bay as M.O. for a nearby territorial army camp. A number of the officers had their wives and children at the hotel to make it a mixture of work and holiday. Rae's attractive wife Marjorie was there with her teenage daughter Gillian and two much younger sons John and Peter – the family having been interrupted by Rae's absence. At first I thought Dr Duffus was abrupt and forbidding. Then one evening the reserve of a whole crowd of folk in the hotel lounge was broken down by a drink or two and the full warmth of this rugged man was revealed.

He was a born raconteur, especially in the Buchan dialect (he hailed from Auchinblae) and belonged to that school of doctors who regarded themselves as on duty twenty four hours a day. Ever since that evening I have been many times to sing in Aberdeen, but I've never been allowed to stay in a hotel. If I'd tried it either Rae or Marjorie would have been round to move me to their delightful house near Queen's Cross.

That night Rae told one of several of his stories that I've been dining out on – and using professionally for thirty years. It concerned the remote village of Maud that lies about 25 miles north of Aberdeen. 'One Tuesday night in January 1878,' began the doctor, 'the village hall in Maud was packed to capacity to hear a visiting evangelist preacher. This preacher was a lady and she had been guaranteed a good turn out for two reasons. There was nothing much else happening in Maud on a Tuesday in January, and when there was a function in the hall they lit the stove, and everyone came in for a free warm. When the lady arrived she was younger and prettier than most of the folk expected.

'Dearly beloved,' she cried, 'the subject of my discourse this evening is preparedness to meet your Maker. We none of us know the year, the month, the week, the day, the hour, the minute, the second we may receive the call and we *must* be ready! For example I shall tonight be in the arms of my dear husband, yet tomorrow night I may be reposing in the bosom of my Maker.'

A voice from the back of the hall called out, 'Are ye booked for Friday?'

During that holiday, though we played golf, shopped in Elgin, climbed the Bin and made, as well as the Duffuses, other friends resident in that locality as a result of my incautiously agreeing to appear at a charity concert in the Spey Bay Hall, I also began to lay the foundations for the sort of problems that come up and hit most artists at some moment in their career.

My agent for over twenty-five years was Richard Stone, one of my contemporaries at Charterhouse who has built up one of the finest such businesses in London. Earlier that year he'd approached me to help him organise a fund-raising concert in the autumn in aid of Charterhouse in Southwark, which consists of boys' and girls' clubs supported by voluntary contributions through close ties with the school and the local parish church in Southwark. Then, as now, they did marvellous work in an under-privileged part of London; then, as now, they needed money.

Most afternoons on that holiday I sat – to Pat's despair – in a deck chair in front of the hotel, surrounded by papers, writing letters, making out running orders and generally worrying about the whole project. Because I'd been so busy for the rest of the year I'd decided the only time I could deal with it was on holiday. I was to pay the price later.

The show was quite something. We booked the Princes Theatre and the old boys of the school, known as Old Carthusians who took part were Dennis Bowen, Richard (Mole) Goolden, Colin Tilney (now a celebrated harpsichordist, then a very young and promising pianist), George Braund ('The Biggest Thing in Magic' – and probably was at eighteen and a half stone), Richard Murdoch and the great Ralph Vaughan Williams himself who gamely went into the orchestra pit and conducted his own arrangement of *Greensleeves*.

In those days, unlike now, we had no female OCs but the bill also included Florence Desmond who had a son at the school, Beryl Reid and Cicely Courtneidge who came out of the goodness of their hearts. The compere was Richard Dimbleby whose two sons were at Charterhouse and have followed in father's footsteps.

As if all that wasn't enough we had a *What's My Line* panel of OCs that included Lord Beveridge, Sir Lionel Heald, then Attorney General, cartoonist Osbert Lancaster, playwright Ben Travers and the critic Philip Hope-Wallace.

Those OCs whose occupations were to be guessed included Peter May, the England cricket captain and Wilfred Noyce, a member of the Hunt-Hillary team, not long back from their conquest of Everest.

Quite an evening – and we raised £1700 which, if you jack it up to what it would be today in 'real terms', wasn't too bad. Just in case you might think that I'd slid out of appearing on the strength of writing the letters, I opened the second half. As there were so many old friends having a reunion I thought I'd better go on then in case the audience were still in the bar. Some of them were!

The 'old school tie' network is sometimes accused of providing unfair advantages in life to its members. It certainly doesn't and couldn't in my profession – but it's quite useful when it comes to raising a few bob for a deserving cause.

*   *   *

One of the hazards of a free-lance career pursued without the benefit of second sight is the ease with which one can find oneself working a seven day week. A clear space in the diary is never gratefully accepted as a time to recharge the battery. To the perpetually insecure artist like me it looks like the first sign of a major falling off in demand for one's services. So when a couple of not very interesting jobs are offered to fill some of those free days, they are accepted with a sigh of relief.

A week or two later a more glamorous opportunity arises for the same period. The dates don't clash with the other two engagements, but now the mass of preparation for all three will be nothing short of a race against time. Then the phone rings with some heart-rending story of a charity concert on Sunday for which the invited singer has laryngitis, plans for a day out with the Stage Golfing Society are cancelled and all of a sudden I find that I've worked seventeen days on the trot.

Sitting in that deck chair working at Spey Bay I wasn't to know that Glyndebourne were about to offer me next season not one opera but four, and that other strenuous excitements were on the way. Not that it would have seriously influenced me to turn anything down that autumn to rest and prepare for what lay ahead. Why should it? I had hardly missed a performance through illness since I'd begun, and while I was apprehensive about catching cold before a show my fears were seldom realised.

Chapter 10

The first signs that I was perhaps overtaxing myself showed themselves a few months later when I was engaged to sing in a programme still popular today – *Friday Night is Music Night*. One of its features then was a game played between my friend and colleague Owen Brannigan and the BBC accompanist Ernest Lush.

It went like this. Owen was engaged to sing three songs with the BBC Mens' Chorus – they would usually be folk songs, sea shanties or plantation songs – something of that nature. In the morning Owen rehearsed using the published versions of the accompaniments. Then in the afternoon Ernest, a most accomplished arranger, changed the accompaniments to make them as unlike the original as possible introducing syncopation, key changes and disconcerting quotations from other songs. The result was witty and attractive, but difficult.

All he would guarantee was the same number of bars as in the original. Where did the game come in? There was no further rehearsal. The first time Owen heard the Lush version was in the live performance.

Owen could take this in his stride and, so far as I know, enjoyed the challenge. Then I was asked to do it for three weeks while he was otherwise engaged.

This was just the sort of situation where my lack of musical training told. I'm a quick learner, but counting bars of un-familiar music and entering in the right key was another thing altogether. I was quite literally scared stiff when I heard those strange opening bars and when, I thought, wrongly, that I'd made a bad mistake the old cliché of a red mist before my eyes became a momentary reality.

Next day the pads of my hands below the thumbs were bruised and sore. I couldn't account for it until I realised that it had been caused by gripping the metal music stand with ferocious tightness during those songs in order to control my nerves and shaking body.

I felt no better for the other two weeks though Ernest, a kind, gentle soul, was concerned that what was supposed to be a light-hearted battle of musical wits put me through such an ordeal. I think the two remaining programmes were a little less hair-raising than if Owen had been doing them. Soon after-wards Pat succeeded in dragging me off for a spring holiday to Tossa del Mar on the Costa Brava.

Tossa had yet to be fully developed, thank God, and we found warm deserted beaches and quiet cliff walks. We once happened on a football match in the local park and were the only fascinated spectators of a refereeing decision that sparked off a fight involving all twenty-two players. We never dis-covered the score but the fight was a draw. It stopped as suddenly as it began and play resumed as if nothing had happened. The sight of lemons growing in gardens, the firefly effect of the lamps on the sardine boats fishing after dark, the sound of a donkey cart passing under our bedroom window and the theme from *Limelight* on the hotel musak which always came round at that late Spanish dinner time of nine o'clock combined with an aroma of charcoal all conspired to create an atmosphere of relaxation and remoteness from any thought of work. Nevertheless every day I had to find a secluded spot and sing a few scales because the day after our return I was due to sing a song of welcome to the Queen.

A couple of months earlier I'd been invited to the home in St John's Wood of Sir Arthur Bliss, Master of the Queen's Musick. The k has since fallen into disuse. He and Cecil Day Lewis had produced a special work to mark the return of Her Majesty and Prince Philip from the first Australian tour of her reign. It was composed for an Australian soprano, a British baritone, chorus and orchestra.

Anyone less like the popular conception of a composer or musician than Bliss it would be hard to imagine. If he'd been an actor he'd have played generals or directors of merchant banks. Brusque, moustached, well groomed and wearing the sort of suit that is a discreet advertisement for its tailor, it was only a certain intensity in his manner that revealed the artist.

He took me through my part on the piano and with characteristic modesty asked if there was anything I'd like altered. He told me that the conductor would be Sir Malcolm Sargent and the Australian soprano Joan Sutherland. At that time I'd just about heard of her. The operatic roles that would deploy the full majesty of her vocal powers were still in the future. She was a jolly plumpish girl with an excellent voice but at the afternoon rehearsal on the day of the performance Sir Malcolm, who could radiate quiet menace if he suspected you hadn't done your homework, sharply told her off once or twice for minor lapses. It's easy to forget that famous conductors are as nervous as soloists about big occasions and the slim figure in the black alpaca jacket, his black hair brushed straight back from his furrowed brow, prominent eyebrows and mildly mephistophelean countenance was probably noticing the occasional butterfly in the region of his diaphragm as he faced a new work on a royal occasion with two singers he didn't know very well.

We were never told whether Her Majesty actually heard *A Song of Welcome*. It was broadcast at 9.30 p.m. Considering the trip she'd just completed no one could have blamed her if she'd decided on an early night. It was a dignified, impressive work that has not survived the occasion it commemorated. After it was over Sir Arthur who'd joined the studio audience (once again the Camden Theatre was the chosen venue) drew me into a corner. He had a secretive air about him and glanced over his shoulder before softly asking me if I was free on the 29th July. I was.

'Good. I want you to sing it again at a Promenade Concert, but keep it to yourself.' I was delighted. I'd never sung at the Proms.

I defy anyone not to feel some misgiving the first time they step on to the platform of the Royal Albert Hall and look across that vast arena and up to the highest gallery. If you watch a tennis match from there on TV, sooner or later a player will mishit a ball high into the air. As it soars away, just think of making your unamplified voice carry even higher to that top gallery. In fact a correctly projected voice travels well to the seven thousand people and more who jam the place for a popular Promenade Concert, but it's hard not to be panicked into singing too loud, which takes all the beauty out of the voice and leads to quick exhaustion.

It was also something of a shock on arriving at the hall to discover that my partner was Elsie Morison, another Australian soprano. No one ever volunteered why the change had been made and I never asked. Joan had got a good notice in *The Times* when we'd done it the first time and maybe she just wasn't free for the Prom; but I've always hugged to my bosom the fascinating notion that the first occasion that I sang with one of the most celebrated singers of all time she got the sack and I didn't!

*   *   *

Of the four roles that I was to sing for Glyndebourne at various places that summer two were old friends: Dr Bartolo in *Il Barbiere di Siviglia* and Don Magnifico in *La Cenerentola*. The latter we were to take to the Berlin Festival for two performances in September.

The two strangers were Busoni's *Arlecchino*, a one act opera in which I was to be Ser Matteo, a humble tailor whose wife runs off with someone else and *Le Comte Ory* by Rossini. My role here was more predictable, the young count's long suffering tutor who finds himself embroiled in all his master's follies. Looking at the score I could see that I was also embroiled in some very arduous singing.

Yes, you've spotted it as quickly as I did – *Le Comte Ory* is in French, which poses all sorts of problems for non-French singers. Though some of it has to sound nasal, until you get the knack the sound is apt to disappear up your nose giving an unpleasing sinusitis effect. What you won't have realised unless you're a mad opera buff is that *Arlecchino*, despite its Italian ending and Italian sounding composer, is in German! Four operas, three languages.

I laid siege to Ellen Morgenthau, a German girl who worked in Glyndebourne's London office in Baker Street to which the management used to retreat out of season and begged her help with pronunciation and meanings of words. I had no German at all. She was a great help because, like most Germans, she was absolutely meticulous.

Preparing for such a formidable season has to be completed before rehearsals begin. Not long ago my old friend and colleague Edmund Bohan, a fine tenor from New Zealand, told me that after a concert in the north of England a man put his head round the dressing room door and said to him, 'If I had a voice like yours I'd never work again.' As the late Professor Joad used to say on a famous radio programme called *The Brains Trust*, it depends what you mean by work. For a singer with four operas to perform in quickish succession it meant firstly learning the new ones and revising the old with repetiteurs like Valda Plucknett and Christopher Shaw who lived the other side of London so that often one hour's coaching involved two hours' travel. But the benefit of their skill was worth the journeys and expense. Then there were the hours of memorising – pacing up and down the room or the garden mouthing the words and checking the pronunciation.

There were the hours with the dictionary making sure of the meaning of every word. Often the English translation (if any) in the vocal score would be no more than a paraphrase – a useless guide for putting the correct emphasis on the words in the original language.

There were the hours with Rodolfo being coaxed and encouraged through the difficult passages by a mixture of technique and low cunning, both of us arguing about French and German pronunciation from shaky positions of authority. Though an hour in his studio sent me away elated at the sounds I was making he was reluctant to give me – or any of his pupils – exercises to do at home.

'Everyone doa them wrong. I mova da voice for you.' He would too, first sending his pianist (nearly always a young student) out of the room. 'I don'ta want them to learna my secrets and then go and givea lessons themselves.' It was a groundless fear – he had a genius for teaching which no accompanist could possibly have stolen from him even if they'd wanted to. But then as an artist he was entitled to his share of insecurity.

When it was time to pack my cases into the car and drive down to Sussex I was music and word perfect which is Glyndebourne's contractual requirement before you set foot in the place to start five weeks of rehearsal. I took up residence in dear Mrs Bradbury's little house in Ringmer near the turn-off for the opera house. She was the widow of a member of the Glyndebourne estate staff who let rooms to the likes of me. In fact she didn't just let accommodation, she welcomed you into her home which she shared with her daughter Pat and it was very difficult to get her to accept any payment in return.

I could come and go as I pleased and there was always bacon and egg for breakfast. I'm jolly sure she'd have provided lunch and supper as well if I'd given her half a chance. She was a quiet bird-like lady who loved to hear all the opera house and village gossip, enjoyed a good story and never said an unkind thing about anyone in my hearing, and I was her lodger many, many times during the 1950s and early 60s.

The famous comedy actress Athene Seyler once wrote that a young actress needed the courage of a lion, the hide of a rhinoceros and a nice home to go back to at night. I certainly had the latter at Mrs Bradbury's. Often I would decide quite at the last moment to go home to London. She was never put out.

'Have a nice time, dear, and give my love to Pat.' *Her* Pat, by the way, is a moving spirit in the village and a dear friend.

Driving up the narrow road over the beginning of the Downs past the field with the two white horses then down the steep incline to the imposing Elizabethan house in the trees on the left hand side was a bit like returning to school. The early days of driving through the arch and leaving the car anywhere had gone for ever. Now it was a case of walking from the artists' park past the tennis court and the yew hedges towards one's rehearsal.

For the first few days we were in the organ room with the sun streaming in through the windows tempting us to look out over the beautifully kept lawns to a tantalising glimpse of water-lilies on the lake, or the cows in the field beyond the ha-ha, or invisible moat, which gave the false impression that they could wander over the lawns to the window. At one end of the oak panelled room with huge oil paintings is the organ with its massive pipes, at the other the grand piano round which we would gather for a musical rehearsal either with the conductor or the irrepressible Jani Strasser, his horn-rimmed spectacles dangling round his neck on a piece of cord as he vainly searched for a pencil and notebook in his satchel and called for silence in the most frequently imitated voice in the establishment. For three hours at a time we would go over ensembles, from duets to those involving every principal, again and again until he considered the balance was correct and all the musical dynamics were being observed. Jani was prepared to drive us all slowly and inexorably to screaming point with his demands, criticisms and suggestions – but he got results.

A few days later that morning walk would be to the theatre, cold at ten o'clock in the morning even on a summer's day, but with plenty going on backstage – scene builders sawing and hammering, seizing the chance before stage rehearsals would halt their activities or take them to work elsewhere. There was always the aroma from the huge glue pot bubbling away on a gas-ring, the repetiteur's piano in the orchestra pit tinkling already as young men like Raymond Leppard or Bryan Balkwill limbered up in preparation for a three hour stint of the constant stopping and re-starting which is the lot of an opera rehearsal pianist. His music light was the only illumination from the dark depths beyond the edge of the stage, itself economically lit for rehearsals by a few work lights. If Professor Ebert had got there early he might well be standing in a grey flannel suit ambushed by Jock Gough, the stage carpenter who, like Ebert, was a pre-war Glyndebourne original, and apt to harangue him about the impossibility of having Act Two scenery ready until next week. A formidable figure with gimlet eyes, a shock of grizzled hair, and a shabby apron, Jock would stab the air with his empty pipe as he made his points loudly and with force. Ebert would listen and nod abstractedly, but his restless pouched eyes under his mane of silver hair were far away contemplating some picture in his imagination which he would be communicating to us during the morning.

And communicating is the best way to describe Ebert's production methods. I have tried at various times both in this book and elsewhere to give the reader some sort of insight. What one can never impart is the spark that enables the Eberts, the Beechams and, yes, the Rodolfo Meles of this world to bring out of others performances and skills which they never believed they possessed. A morning on *Il Barbiere* meant seeing him portray all our parts as only a former leading actor could, from Rosina to Figaro himself. It was not only stimulating, it was often entertaining as well, but woe betide you if fooled around or let your concentration wander.

Arlecchino is a strange haunting piece with a strong element of *commedia del arte* as the title suggests. For me it was a welcome change to be a genuinely sad character with a scene of touching pathos near the end. I was more thrilled with one or two good notices for this departure from my usual sort of part than I was about the excellent press for *Il Barbiere*, which just shows what a perverse sort of chap I am. Singing alongside me in the cast of *Arlecchino* were Murray Dickie and a promising young fellow called Geraint Evans.

Le Comte Ory once again brought together Bruscantini, Oncina and Wallace as well as Fernanda Cadoni, who had been an ugly sister in *La Cenerentola* – but the star turn was the Hungarian soprano Sari Barabas, from the world of operetta, just about the most glamorous opera singer I've ever encountered. We rehearsed at Glyndebourne for Edinburgh Festival.

The story is of the young Count Ory who in mediaeval times is in amorous pursuit of a Countess, the chatelaine of a castle. He decides that he will gain entry to the castle disguised as the mother superior of a group of nuns who are on a journey. The travelling 'nuns' are his male companions in disguise. They include his reluctant tutor. Once into the castle the 'nuns' discover the wine cellar and a bout of heavy drinking is followed by a hopelessly inadequate attempt on their part to make a dignified and holy exit.

After Ebert had given us the moves and his general conception of the opera he went down with a bad attack of influenza. For his son Peter who was assistant producer it was an embarrassing situation. He didn't know when his father would be able to return and was therefore unwilling to put his own stamp on the production. We kept on running through it and gradually developed our own business and ideas. This continued for several days and when the Professor returned he seemed pleased with what we had done. Probably it was something to do with our having worked with him for years – he could trust us out of his sight for a bit. The finished article was more inspired by Carl Ebert than produced. Be that as it may the distinguished critic Ernest Newman in *The Sunday Times* described it as one of the best productions Ebert had ever done. It took Edinburgh by storm – and once again the decor was by Oliver Messel who gave all the men tights and cod-pieces. At the dress parade mine, which was laughably enormous, was concealed beneath my cloak.

Bruscantini's was small in comparison and when I removed my cloak and the highly exaggerated evidence of my virility was revealed he crossed the stage and solemnly shook my hand.

'Magnifico!' was his comment.

While we were still rehearsing *Le Comte Ory* at Glyndebourne Moran Caplat came and sat beside me in the staff canteen at tea time one day.

'Next year at Edinburgh we're going to do Verdi's *Falstaff*. We've no doubt you could act it, but we do appreciate that it's a high baritone part. Will you have a look at it and let us know as soon as possible. I do hope you can say yes.' He smiled, gave me a pat on the shoulder and was gone.

I sat on in a daze. What a great opportunity had just been mentioned, almost casually, over a cup of tea. Many times at the Cambridge Theatre I had watched the inimitable Mariano Stabile play and sing the part, which he had learned from Toscanini and made his own for a generation. This was a role in a different class from the buffo parts I'd attempted up to now. It was one of the classic roles of Italian opera on which a big career could be based.

I rang Rodolfo with the news and added that I could be in London two days later.

'Very good, Ian, I havea the score, you getta the records and we'll have a good look at it, eh?'

At about one o'clock in the morning two days later after four hours and quite a few glasses of Chianti he shut the score and looked across the table at me. I knew what he was going to say.

'Ian, ifa we do this we make a fool of ourselves. Look, you can singa alla the notes; you can sing a top G, but not in a rough way, you understand, likea this drunken man. You can singa ninety percent of it very well butta for ten percent we'da be bluffin'. For Edinburgh Festival eesa not enough.'

His use of the first person plural was correct because learning such a role would have been a joint effort. It was a great disappointment but I had known all along. I'm not a high baritone and there was no getting round it. I think that if I'd disagreed with Rodolfo he'd probably have made an effort to pull my voice up but if he had I wouldn't still be singing now – except in the bath.

The Swiss baritone Fernando Corena got the job at Edinburgh and then Geraint Evans made such a success of it at Glyndebourne that it took him to the Scala Milan, the Metropolitan New York and many other international opera houses. He's not a high baritone either, but has just that little extra bit of height on the voice that matters – a couple of millimetres difference in the larynx perhaps. He's also got everything else it takes to be a superb artist.

The villain of the piece was Verdi. If ever there was a character whose music should have been composed in the comic bass range it was surely the fat Shakespearean knight Sir John Falstaff. I hope there's a musicians' club in the next world. If so, I'll be having a word with Giuseppe Verdi about it – though it'll be hard to get a word in edgeways with Geraint, Fernando and Mariano all rabbiting on about what a marvellous part he wrote for them!

Before we went to Edinburgh I had received another exciting offer. The theatrical impresario Laurier Lister who had had great success with revues like *Penny Plain*, *Tuppence Coloured* and

Airs on a Shoestring had decided to mount another starring those two lovable sisters from the world of radio and music hall, Elsie and Doris Waters. To support them he invited Elizabeth Welch, Desmond Walter Ellis and me. We were to start rehearsals in September, the day after *Le Comte Ory* finished in Edinburgh.

I was intrigued with this offer particularly as I was to sing numbers by Flanders and Swann, as well as other excellent material.

There was one big problem. After the first few days of rehearsal I would have to fly off to Berlin for nearly a week to sing the two performances of *La Cenerentola*. To my delight Laurier was prepared to do without me for those few days.

When we got to Edinburgh I decided to lash out and buy a new car – in fact Sesto and I both did. We invested in identical metallic light blue Humber Hawks. Mine bore the licence plate letters LWS which someone suggested stood for 'Let Wallace Sing'. Indeed there was no stopping him!

Pat and I had come to Edinburgh in her dinky Hillman Minx soft top coupé, her mother's twenty-first present which I often told friends was what I'd married her for. I still possessed the six year old Austin 12 that was perfectly serviceable but unprestigious. Not the public's idea of an opera singer's car, some folk said to me and they included my accountant, so I was an enthusiastic sitting duck for any salesman who knew his job. I can't remember if I found him or he found me.

But how to get it back to London in time for a mid day rehearsal of the revue when the last performance of *Le Comte Ory* only finished at ten o'clock the previous evening? Not only that, I couldn't exceed 50 m.p.h. as it was still being run in – and there was the Minx to get home as well.

Pat and I packed up everything by lunch time and went to bed, setting the alarm for 6 p.m. I never closed an eye and I don't think Pat did either. We were on our way in convoy by 10.30 and to make it more interesting the rain was lashing down.

All through the night we made our way sedately south going by Carter Bar, Scotch Corner, Boroughbridge, Doncaster, Retford, Newark, Grantham – none of them by-passed in 1954. We sucked glucose tablets and kept opening the window. As we neared Stamford about 8.30 in the morning I saw the Minx ahead of me wander towards the middle of the road a couple of times. Pat is a super driver so there was only one explanation. I tooted the horn, passed her and waved her down.

'You're nearly asleep – we must stop.'

'You look awful,' was her reply. We went to the George Hotel at Stamford and ordered a mammoth breakfast. As we began the bacon, egg and sausage part of it a man came over from a nearby table and put his hand on my shoulder.

'Excuse me,' he said in a strong Glasgow accent. 'Would you be good enough to settle a bet between me and my friend as to who you are?' I was so tired and hungry that I didn't even look up.

'You've won your bet,' I said. (A more arrogant remark could hardly be imagined.) He returned triumphant to his table and I heard him say to his friend. 'There ye are. I told ye he was the manager of Partick Thistle.'

We reached London safely, but I'd never do such a foolhardy thing again. The risk of falling asleep at the wheel on such a journey is very great and was almost certainly what killed the great horn player Dennis Brain who collided with a tree near London on a similar overnight journey from Edinburgh three years later.

Chapter 11

A Soho rehearsal room is a far cry from the elegance of Glyndebourne. An old upright piano with cigarette burns etched on the notes, ballet bars screwed to the wall and elderly bentwood chairs with their backs to it. Throw in a few metal ash trays and a heavily worn stripwood floor and you've got the picture. In size it might be about the same as the ballroom in a medium sized hotel.

The title of the revue was *Pay the Piper* and we had a twelve week tour lined up prior to opening in London just before

Christmas. Except for a few sketches all the numbers were musical.

I'd never met Elsie and Doris Waters, though I'd heard them many times on radio in their cockney characters of Gert and Daisy; when I was at Glyndebourne in June I'd noticed that they were doing a Sunday concert at Eastbourne and I'd gone to see it. It gave me a talking point when I was introduced to these two tall, delightful ladies who dressed beautifully, had a merry twinkle in the eye and drove everywhere in a stately Daimler.

'I did enjoy you at Eastbourne,' I said, 'especially that joke about Wally and the garage.'

They both blushed and Doris said, 'Oh dear, we felt as soon as we'd cracked it that it was too rude for our act. We're rather ashamed of ourselves – and to think you were there!'

The joke was in a part of their act where Gert always asked Daisy about her husband Wally.

' 'ow's 'e getting on with the garage business, Daisy?'

'Oh, Gert, I think it's a bit too much for 'im.'

'Why do you think that, Daisy?'

'Well last night 'e was talkin' in his sleep, strokin' my bottom and sayin' "My God, only five thousand miles and the tread's gorn!" '

Even in that rehearsal room where we'd all assembled for a first meeting and were looking one another up and down, I sensed that they felt a little out of their element, but were determined to do their damnedest to make a success of it. Our boss Laurier Lister was there to make the introductions – a slim sandy haired man with a sad expression in repose, his sensitive features partly concealed by a moustache. He gave the impression that his successes as a theatrical producer came from scrupulous attention to detail and a great affection for the people he worked with. A quiet, good man, and one could only hope he'd got the mix for this concoction right.

I met for the first time the warm, vivacious Elizabeth Welch and the reserved, slightly distraught Desmond Walter Ellis as well as three young artists whose contribution to this show gave each of their careers something of a fillip: April Olrich, a ballet dancer of striking appearance, large eyes, corn coloured hair and the sort of expressive personality that most ballet schools frown on; Fenella Fielding, a comedienne with raven hair, seductive low voice and a relish for the outrageous; lastly Julian Orchard, tall, angular, his kindly equine face frequently creased with mirth as a low chuckle emerged from behind the hand that he would clap to his mouth on hearing something that amused him. He had as highly developed a sense of the ridiculous as I've ever encountered. We drew to one another within five minutes and remained close friends for the rest of his all too short life. He kindly agreed to keep notes for me of what was happening at rehearsal while I was away.

Though the thought of singing in Berlin was exciting I realised as the day of departure approached that I was scared of flying. Pat was, I felt, no more than normally apprehensive, nothing to compare with my dread of this, our first time in the air. I had tried to find a way of going by train, but it was impossible to get to West Berlin from Britain except by air.

We solemnly made our wills though, apart from my mother, I had no one to whom I could leave my modest possessions in the event of Pat joining me at the bottom of the North Sea. I put in some pompous clause about a scholarship for a young singer and wondered lugubriously whether somebody would be reaping the benefit of it this time next year.

When we walked out to board the plane I was horrified to see that it only had two propellors, which was half the number it should have had so far as I was concerned. It was an Elizabethan of what was then called BEA, British European Airways. Pat and I sat facing John Pritchard who was to conduct *La Cenerentola* in the absence of Maestro Gui who was otherwise engaged. John was an experienced flyer and kept me in close conversation as we roared at break-neck speed down the runway and finally took off, banking steeply over the reservoirs near Heathrow.

'You did well to keep talking, Ian, on your first take-off,' he said with an understanding smile. I was still trying to work out why the air hostess had offered us boiled sweets just before we started. It was a little too reminiscent of the sweetie one had got as a child with nasty medicine. Someone explained that it was to make you swallow and pop your ears as the plane climbed and pressure changed at the higher altitude.

Pat was next to one of the tiny oval windows which had a

good view of the port engine. After a while she said to me, 'There's something that looks like oil trickling slowly across the wing.' My worst fears were immediately confirmed. Ships spring a leak, but the water comes in from outside. We were losing our precious life-blood the other way round.

'I've memorised a rivet,' she added, 'and if it gets past that I think we ought to tell someone.' Shortly afterwards the door that led to the flight deck opened and the captain appeared.

'Oh God,' I thought, 'he's come to tell us to prepare for an emergency landing.' He nodded to us calmly as he walked up the aisle and disappeared into the toilet. On his return his attention was caught by some knob on the ceiling near where we were sitting. If we were going to report the oil leak this was the moment. I gave Pat a nudge. She looked out of the window and shook her head.

'It's not reached the rivet,' she said. The captain examined the knob intently for two or three minutes, twiddling it backwards and forewards. I glanced round my fellow passengers to discover that every single one of them was following his every move. I've no idea what was amiss, but anything not a hundred per cent in an aircraft and even those who love flying stop talking and reading the paper. Eventually he shrugged his shoulders and returned to the job of getting us to Tempelhof.

Meanwhile in London Julian Orchard came out of the morning rehearsal to see lunch edition placards for *The Evening Standard* that read 'Plane Crash – Famous Singer Killed.'

'I went weak at the knees,' he told me on my return. When he bought the paper he found that the two sentences on the placards were unconnected. A troop carrier had crashed on take off at an RAF air-field but everyone had instantly carried out escape drill and no one had perished. The famous singer was an American pop star who'd had a car crash.

That same lunch time my mother had turned on the radio to hear the words 'a plane has crashed.' She experienced the same symptoms as Julian, but enjoyed a reviving gin and French when she realised that we weren't involved.

About the same time as these dramatic events we were bumping down through heavy cloud, one of the more disagreeable parts of flying, and a young man across the aisle from me was lying in his seat, body rigid, eyes tight shut, arms above his head and hands clutching the back of his seat.

'At least,' I said to myself, 'I'm not as badly affected by it as that poor chap.'

There was an unmistakable thud just below my feet. My face must have betrayed sudden anxiety for John Pritchard casually and tactfully remarked that as they'd just let down the under-carriage we would be landing very soon.

When we arrived at Tempelhof I walked down the gangway feeling as exhilarated as Alcock and Brown. We'd had a much more comfortable journey than Moran Caplat and Jock Gough who had accompanied the scenery in a cargo plane. Moran, who had served with destroyers during the war, declared that he'd seldom been so stiff and cold. 'Once or twice I felt like asking the pilot if we could stop somewhere and have a cup of tea,' was his typically cheerful response to a long, bumpy flight.

West Berlin in 1954 was a bustling, prosperous city. New buildings of imaginative design had sprung from the rubble of the bombing, neon lights glittered for the length of the Kurfur-stendamm, the cars were new, smartly dressed crowds thronged the streets and we all of us marvelled how it could have been done so quickly after such a crushing defeat. Carl Ebert had returned to Berlin as Intendant of the Opera House, but the famous Charlottenberg Theatre had not yet reopened and the operas were being temporarily housed in an old auditorium known by Berliners as the Zoo Theatre. Old it might be but what a splendid acoustic.

The familiarity of our own scenery and costumes made the first night feel just like doing it at Glyndebourne, save for the German orchestra and the tall, dark John Pritchard conducting it.

The first sign that this was a different sort of audience from those in Britain came at the end of my aria in the first act, usually the first applause point in the evening except for the end of the overture. At Glyndebourne I could reckon on a reason-able round of applause, but so early in the evening it wasn't anything more – it's a comic patter song and very few of the audience in Britain understand all the words in Italian. The applause comes because it is strenuous and the allegro vivace at the end goes at a good lick.

Whether the audience in the Zoo Theatre understood the words or not their applause literally exploded. I stood in my pose for the last note as we were taught to do at Glyndebourne. We were forbidden to acknowledge applause during an act. It was a case of waiting in character till it stopped. The applause went on and on. I felt foolish standing there with my arms outstretched to my two daughters, and discourteous as well. Very slowly I inclined my head and then, equally slowly, my trunk. I must have resembled a melting snowman.

Eventually this incredible ovation subsided and I was able to sing the couple of lines of recitative and make my exit. Standing in the wings were two Scottish members of the chorus David Kelly (now Director of vocal studies at the Royal Scottish Academy of Music and Drama) and Daniel McCoshan. David, pointing towards my dressing room whispered, 'One more applause like that and ye'll no get through that door – big head!' Then they both gave me the sort of hug associated with scoring a winning goal at Wembley.

Whenever I hear any artist getting a really big applause it always brings a lump to my throat and I think it dates from that evening in Berlin. At the end we had the sort of reception that happens once in a lifetime. One London paper said we took over twenty curtain calls. That must have been when they lowered the safety curtain and the correspondent went to file his report. We went to our dressing rooms and were starting to change when we were told to come back on stage. Behind the iron which is what we call the safety curtain we could hear muffled cries of 'Kommen sie! Kommen sie!' Up went the iron to reveal the crowded auditorium, but now many of the audience had moved to the front and stood cheering and waving handkerchiefs, scarves, even raincoats. The stage manager stated categorically that in all we took thirty-seven calls.

The cast would be the last people to take any particular credit. In was an accident of history that we were the first company associated with the Western Alliance to visit the city since before the war and everyone was determined to make us welcome. Also the older opera goers were glad once more to be able to salute an Ebert production. He had left Germany when the Nazis gained power and they must have missed him.

'When did you last hear a reception like that?' I asked one of the theatre staff.

He thought for a moment. 'I think it was when Toscanini brought *Il Barbiere di Siviglia* in the 1930s,' he replied. 'But of course it doesn't happen very often because we don't really care for Rossini.'

We had to refuse impassioned invitations to go to a party given by the supporters club of the Opera House. I wanted to go very much, but Pat and I were previously invited, along with other British members of the company, to supper with the British High Commissioner to meet – wait for it – the Lord Mayor of London.

I felt strongly that we would be acting as useful ambassadors by going to the German party, but Moran pointed out that our other invitation had the status of a royal command – so we went to a function so English and so remote from the excitement and emotion of the earlier part of the evening that it was hard to believe where we were and why. We'd only been away a few days, yet the copies of *The Tatler* and *The Times* on the drawing room coffee table, normally such reassuring sights, seemed incongruous.

The next day – a rest day – many of us had enquired if we could go beyond the Brandenberg Gate and have a look at East Berlin. The famous wall hadn't yet been built. We were told that it might be possible in a bus vouched for by the British High Commission and agreed to by the Russians. This was forthcoming and we were warned to do exactly as we were told. We would leave the bus at our peril except where permitted to do so by our guide. The peril wasn't death or anything like that, but the Festival management was mortally afraid that the Russians might think it amusing to detain a few singers long enough to prevent a repeat of our cultural success the following night.

We set off with a Union Jack fluttering on the bonnet and as we entered the East Zone the contrast with what we had just left was complete. Streets virtually deserted, very few cars and those mostly old and black. We drove down a wide boulevard with identical blocks of workers' flats on each side and a marked absence of shops. Here and there were huge photographs of leaders, including Stalin who had died the year before. The few people about were drably dressed, but several, seeing the flag on the bus, waved to us rather listlessly, like shy hitch hikers.

The first stop was at a music shop in a side street, which surprised me as we had seen so few other shops, but the others knew of it because it was one of Eastern Europe's excursions into cultural propaganda. You could buy a great selection of German music there at fantastically low prices. Not being much of a student of German music I hadn't heard of it, hadn't made a list and hadn't brought any cash, so Pat and I sat in the bus while the Glyndebourne chorus took a splendid opportunity to add to their music libraries. This was why so many of them had been keen to come on this trip, which for me was merely a fascinating glimpse behind the Iron Curtain. As we waited and watched the few passers-by we were depressed by the general air of poverty and cheerlessness of our surroundings on a grey, late September afternoon.

Next we were taken to the newly erected Russian war memorial. My mind picture is of an avenue flanked on either side by large blocks of marble commemorating the great battles of the war between Russia and Germany. At the far end of the avenue is a grassy hillock with stone steps up to a circular mausoleum built on the top. Inside is a huge mosaic frieze depicting Russian soldiers, sailors, airmen, factory workers, farmers, miners, nurses, women workers, surgeons, scientists and many others. At the western end of this enormous semi-circular work of art the figures have slavonic faces, but as the eye moves east the features become more and more oriental. It has a certain magnificence and the stone floor was covered with wreaths from trades union and governments from all over Eastern Europe. Yet it left me unmoved and one or two of our company who had fought in the war either stayed in the bus or were repelled by the sight of it.

We owe our freedom in part to the heroic Russian resistance in battles like Stalingrad, but this memorial on foreign soil had the whiff of propaganda about it – and a touch of Sam Goldwyn as well.

'They think that's a hill they built it on,' observed our German guide sardonically, 'but it was a pile of German bodies. As they rot it'll sink.' None of us believed him – but it was good guide patter. I don't suppose his successors say it now.

1. Even in 1920 I'd have had a job
   to make the weight for the 2.30.
   My sporty companion at North
   Berwick is my father.

2. Grandad and auntie Peggy —
   two of the 'talented Temples' in
   the early 1950s.

3. Friar Tuck at Heathmount
   School c. 1931. Extreme left is
   Robert Hudson of the BBC.

4. As the Charity Commissioner in *The Government Inspector* by Gogol for the Glasgow Citizens' Theatre, May 1945, before returning south to seek my fortune. L. to r. Molly Urquhart, self, Helen Lacey, Frith Banbury and Denis Carey.

5. Schaunard in *La Bohème* at the Cambridge Theatre, London, 1946. My operatic debut.

6. An engagement picture of Pat and me in early 1948.

7. A scene from *Le Pauvre Matelot* at Chester Festival, 1950 − when the incident with the oil lamp occurred on the first night. L. to r. the old sailor, Jennifer Vyvyan, Francis Loring and Arthur Servent.

8. *The Four Men* in Sussex, 1951 − John Leather, a younger sailor, Robert Speaight and W.E. Holloway.

9. Don Magnifico and his daughters Clorinda and Tisbe (Alda Noni and Fernanda Cadoni) being horribly contemptuous of Cinderella in *La Cenerentola* at Glyndebourne, 1952. Note superb Messel decor.

10. A 'Soldier of the Queen' in the Royal Command Performance at the London Palladium, 1952.

11. Sergeant Swilly in *The Highland Fair* at Edinburgh Festival 1952.

12. Rodolfo Mele, my teacher, who made possible so much of what happened in the 1950s and later.

13. Professor Carl Ebert in the Organ Room at Glyndebourne with his son Peter.

14. A still of my test for *Ben Hur*, 1956 — no wonder I didn't get it!

15. Don Magnifico being even more beastly to Cinderella — *La Cenerentola* at the Opera House, Rome, in 1955. I'm threatening Giulietta Simionato and Sesto Bruscantini is disapproving in the background.

16. Singing at the Old Carthusian charity concert at the Princes' (now the Shaftesbury) Theatre, London, 1953.

17. Sesto Bruscantini and I admiring our identical new Humber Hawks at Edinburgh, 1954.

18. Moran Caplat, C.B.E., who retired in 1981 after being General Administrator of Glyndebourne since 1949. My association — and friendship — with him began just one year earlier, in 1948.

19. Maestro Vittorio Gui with a spectacular variation on the bifocal theme.

20. *Le Nozze di Figaro* at Glyndebourne, 1956. Hugues Cuenod and Monica Sinclair whom I leaned on so heavily are the other singers. The picture of a Messel set is by his nephew Anthony Armstrong-Jones, now Lord Snowdon.

21. The scene outside Holyrood Palace during the serenade concert for Her Majesty the Queen during her summer visit to Edinburgh, 1956.

22. My debut with Scottish Opera, 1964 – Leporello in *Don Giovanni* in 1964 with Peter van der Bilt in the title role.

23. Cesar in *Fanny*, Theatre Royal Drury Lane in November 1956.

24. 'Toad' on trial. *Toad of Toad Hall*, Queen's Theatre, London, 1964.

25. Pooh Bah in *The Mikado*, BBC TV 1973, with Sara de Javelin (left) as Peep-Bo and Valerie Masterson (right) as Yum-Yum.

26. The *My Music* team some time in the middle 70s. Back row: Denis Norden, Steve Race, John Amis. Seated: Frank Muir and self.

27. Talking to Michael Flanders during his *This Is Your Life*.

28. Eamonn 'picks me up' to my obvious surprise at Capital Radio before I've even got my coat off. 1978.

29. David Money and Donald Swann ready to play me in with 'Mud' for *This Is Your Life*.

30. The one consistent thread running through it all has been sound radio. This is a picture of a live broadcast on BBC Radio 2 from the Theatre Royal, Norwich — *Around Midnight* with Brian Matthew, 1st April 1981.

31. Perhaps the shape of things to come? A scene with Paula Wilcox in a farce by John Graham called *Consider My Position* at the Yvonne Arnaud Theatre, Guildford, 1980.

32. Pat and I with Peter and Silvia Ebert before the Annual Dinner of the Incorporated Society of Musicians at Peebles Hydro at the end of my presidency.

33. John with my mother, Christmas 1981.

34. Rosie caught by the *This Is Your Life* still cameraman.

After the second performance Ebert came to my dressing room. 'My boy, I have to tell you frankly that my board of directors want you to join our company. I would like it very much, but you and Pat would have to live here in Berlin.' It was a tremendous compliment and certainly the leading Berlin music critic had said very nice things about my performance, but the thought of living for months at a time in this to some extent beleaguered city, giving up friends and language, and abandoning my mother in London all seemed a high price to pay, even to become the principal comic bass in Berlin. I asked time to think it over.

'My boy, they want you to start almost at once.' I had to tell him that I was under contract at least until Christmas in England. He shrugged. 'I knew it would be so, and though I would love to have you here, I am not sure you would be very happy.' I knew he was right. I wouldn't make a good exile, unless a Scot born in London falls into that category.

The flight back was early in the morning, a sparkling day with not a cloud in the sky. We were calling at Düsseldorf and several of our fellow passengers were business men, mostly stout with brief cases to match.

Sitting next to me was a small, bald headed man who appeared to be unwell. He sat with his head in his hands for half an hour but when they brought the breakfast he looked up and partook with the rest of us. I realised he'd been praying. Pat was opposite me and on other side, nearest the window, my old friend Hervey Alan who was ex-RAF. As we began to let down for Düsseldorf I noticed an effect like large wads of cotton wool over the fields. When I pointed them out to Hervey he said, 'It looks a bit misty down there.' The next moment we were in it, and an impenetrable greyness swirled past the window – thicker than clouds. Soon we broke out into brilliant sunshine, but factory chimneys and church steeples were flashing past not all that far below us and we heard the engines roaring up to full throttle as we tilted upwards and the undercarriage clunked back into retraction.

'Was is das?' asked a fat business man of no one in particular.

'Mist on the runway,' answered Hervey with all the bravura of a Lancaster pilot announcing the arrival of flak or a Messerschmitt on bearing one four zero. My little bald headed friend who had resumed his attitude of prayer spoke for the first time.

'What does this mean, sir?'

'Oh I suppose we'll stooge around for a bit until it clears,' I said with what I hoped was a reasonable degree of nonchalance.

'What if it doesn't?'

'Well, they'll send us somewhere else.'

'It could be misty by the time we get there.'

'True, but they carry quite a bit of fuel for emergencies like this.' I didn't know whether they did or not, but I was as anxious to reassure myself as anyone else.

'Eventually, though, the petrol will run out.'

'Well, I don't know much about these things but I do know we have to come down then,' I said with a weak smile.

'You cannot get away from it, sir, there is an element of risk in this form of travel.'

I didn't like the turn this conversation was taking. 'Of course, but there's an element of risk in crossing Piccadilly Circus.'

He looked at me sadly and shook his head. 'Are you all right with God?'

Now there's a difficult question.

'I hope so,' I replied.

'You hope so? Don't you *know*?'

'No. I suppose it depends how He feels about my record.'

That stopped him for a moment. Then he said, 'I hope it won't be my record He'll look at for I know the answer – eternal judgment.'

I could only look in the general direction of my navel and slowly shake my head.

Our second attempt to land at Düsseldorf was successful, and as my friend rose to leave he handed me a card. 'I hold religious meetings in an upper room near Leicester Square tube station every Friday evening – except this month for I'm on my way to Rio di Janeiro. I hope I may see you?'

'I hope so too,' I lied in my teeth, 'but I fear all my Friday evenings are booked for some time ahead.' It was no more than the truth.

When we crossed the Kent coast in the clear autumn sunshine Hervey grabbed my arm and pointed to a vast area of south east England.

'Look, Ian, that's the house where I was born!' he cried.

Already I was starting to go over the *Pay the Piper* numbers in my head as the bus took us to Cromwell Road Terminal. I was due at rehearsal that afternoon. Our taxi home was in the charge of an ancient driver and his vehicle also had seen a great deal of service. It rattled and clanked across London, but going up West Hill to Highgate it all but stopped and Pat said, 'I think we'll have to get out and push.' As we edged to the summit at a steady eight miles per hour I noticed an advert on one of its folding seats.

'This cab is powered by Regent. It packs punch!'

Chapter 12

The tour of *Pay the Piper* was the only one of such length I ever took part in. I did it all by car, which meant a longish journey every Sunday (usually with Julian for company) and therefore never a proper day off in three months. We opened in Bournemouth and at once I was faced with the fact that touring a revue containing approximately thirty-five numbers destined for the West End of London was back-breaking work. There were constant extra rehearsals to make cuts, put in new numbers, change the running order, polish, polish, polish the performances as Laurier Lister strove to get the best possible value from the material at his disposal.

We all had about fourteen quick changes and I remember Desmond Walter Ellis saying that the first thing he did before embarking on a revue was to buy a dozen pair of braces and a similar quantity of studs and cuff-links.

I had one difference of opinion with Laurier. For the first few weeks he had insisted on including *The Hippopotamus Song*, though I felt that it was *déjà vu* and wanted instead to sing *The Elephant Song*, the only one that Michael and Donald had written especially for me some time before this show had been mooted. Eventually he agreed and asked me what I would like in the way of costume and musical arrangement.

'I'd like you to get someone at Chappells to do an orchestration exactly like the piano part Donald composed – no tricks, no brilliant arrangement – and I'll go and hire a grey morning coat like they wear at Ascot with a grey top hat, grey gloves and a grey cravat. I'll build up my nose a bit with putty to give just the hint of a trunk.'

Laurier looked doubtful. 'What about the set?'

'We don't need one. I'll do it on an empty stage in front of the half stage tabs (curtains).'

He thought for a while and then said, 'Well frankly we can't afford to spend much more on the show, so we might as well try it like that – but I'm not happy about it.' I knew why. All the other numbers were lavishly designed and costumed while the brilliant orchestrations must have cost a fortune; but I had a suspicion that some of the excellent material – both words and music – had a job to fight their way through all the colour and musical fireworks to the audience.

The Elephant made his debut in Glasgow and stopped the show, as they say. It's a marvellous song in which a cunning pachyderm realises that if he loses his memory life will be much easier.

'I'm an introverted, elephacentric hypochondriac,' he chortles,

'And I'll stick in the elephant's nursing home till I get my memory back!'

All I had to do was to make sure that they heard every word. One night in Edinburgh after the show I was sitting in my hotel bedroom writing a letter. I had been over to Glasgow earlier in the day doing a broadcast. I was smoking and drinking coffee. Suddenly for no apparent reason my heart started pounding. The beats got heavier and faster till I feared it would batter its way through my ribs. I lay on my bed terrified. It was late at night and there was no phone in the room. Gradually it subsided and I gingerly undressed and lay down again wondering if I'd had a heart attack. It took me a long time to get to sleep.

Next day I had recovered. It had been another sign, I suppose, that I was asking a good deal of myself one way and another. I decided not to consult a doctor. When a big London chance is only weeks away most artists (however stupidly) shy away from the possibility of being told to lay off.

The welcome extended by theatres to our company varied. I recall two extremes. His Majesty's Theatre, Aberdeen where James Donald, the tall, courteous owner came to the dressing rooms on Monday evening before the show. After saying how glad he was to see us he said, 'What would you like to find in your dressing room after the show?'

Thinking he was joking I replied, 'A whisky and water.' And so it was – every night, and a tea tray between the shows on matinee days as well.

When we thanked him he waved us aside. 'You are guests in my theatre and you've been good enough to come a long way.' So much for Aberdeen's reputation for thrifty Scots.

It was rather different at the Grand Theatre, Blackpool. About the same time on the Monday night there was a knock on my door. It was the manager.

'Mr Wallace?'

'That's me.'

'Aye, well we've bin dreadin' you coomin'.'

'Me? Why?' I felt slightly sick.

'Oh not joost you, the whole bloody show. Ye see it's winter time and the locals don't want this sophisticated roobish. Noon of them'll bother to coom, I'm tellin' yer'.

He did, and he was absolutely right.

Alas, *Pay the Piper*, despite all the excellent numbers by Flanders and Swann and others, the superb decor and the tremendous efforts on the tour to get it right for London, quietly died at the Saville Theatre in two and a half weeks. There's never any point in post mortems, though possibly if we'd arrived in London at almost any other time than December 21st – a traditionally dead theatrical time except for pantomimes – we might have had a fighting chance. The press had reservations but not lethal ones and I took comfort from the fact that several critics welcomed me as a recruit from opera to the lighter theatre. They all seemed to like the Elephant and another Flanders and Swann song about a sadistic member of the Inland Revenue, both of which I sing to this day.

It wasn't the right vehicle for Elsie and Doris, though they had some splendid moments and their indestructible niceness shone through everything they did. It wasn't their fault that it didn't quite work and Laurier could say that bigger theatrical gambles had been known to pay off. Our brightest star was undoubtedly Elisabeth Welch.

One compensation for the collapse of the revue was that I could accept an invitation from Maestro Gui to sing Don Magnifico in *La Cenerentola* at the Opera House, Rome. Sesto Bruscantini and Juan Oncina would be in the cast joining the celebrated Giulietta Simionato who was to be our Cenerentola. Peter Ebert was producing so I would be among friends. Nevertheless to sing a major buffo role in Rome was very different from singing a small one at Parma.

I decided to see if Rodolfo would come with me and he and Meg jumped at the chance to visit relations in Naples at the same time. Pat completed the party. Shortly before we left I appeared in a TV variety show with Jack Hulbert and Cicely Courtneidge, in which I was to sing *The Income Tax Collector* from *Pay the Piper*. The song wasn't published at that time, so I sent Donald's manuscript copy of the music. The first line of the last verse goes:

'My stalwart pen is never lax when I'm assessing income tax.'

For TV all the lyrics of songs and the dialogue are typed up for the scripts which are not only for the artists but camera men, sound operators and other technical staff.

The first time I ran through the song in the studio for the camera rehearsal there was a yell of laughter from everyone when I reached that line, and I could hear Cicely Courtneidge's well known chuckle above the rest. They were all pointing at their scripts and some had tears rolling down their faces.

When Donald had added the lyric to his manuscript it had been necessary to write the word 'pen' very close to the following word 'is', and an exceptionally naive or unaware script typist had made them into one word. It took several runs at the verse before order was restored.

*   *   *

The chorus master at the Teatro Reale in Rome, to give it its proper title, was Maestro Ricci – tall, grey haired and a friend of

Rodolfo. The morning after our arrival there was to be a chorus rehearsal on the stage of the wine tasting scene in the cellar of Prince Ramiro's palace.

When I arrived on the vast stage and looked out over the auditorium I realised that it was a good deal bigger than any other I'd seen – except when I'd sung a brief scale in the empty Scala, Milan. Covent Garden was cosy in comparison. The orchestra pit was a sizeable chasm between stage and the nearest members of the public, capable of accommodating a hundred musicians. The men of the chorus – and there seemed to be a great many of them – were standing about in groups chatting and hardly glanced in my direction. Maestro Ricci announced that I would sing through the scene with them before the production rehearsal began.

'Geeva them hell, Ian, don't mark it!' whispered Rodolfo. Marking is what singers do in rehearsal, singing quietly to save the voice. He sounded so urgent that I gave it all I had even though I hadn't warmed up and it was early in the day for such an effort. At the end some of the chorus shouted 'Brava!' and a few briefly clapped.

As we walked through the warm spring sunshine after the production rehearsal in search of lunch Rodolfo explained.

'Ian, Maestro Ricci tolda me this morning that the management could not believe that a Scotsman like you could do a buffo parta like this. They letta you come because they respect Maestro Gui, butta eef this morning they thoughta you were no good they would have paida the money and saida goodbye. That's why I tella you to sing out.'

'Well?' I said, feeling suddenly cold despite a shade temperature of seventy-five.

'Issa quite all right. You hearda what the chorus thought – and they don'ta like foreigners too much anyway.'

A feeling of enormous gratitude to Maestro Gui for his faith in me and his courage in taking such a risk on my behalf swept over me. Now it was up to me not to let him down.

Rodolfo was a tower of strength – always out before breakfast on performance days looking for a hunchback. He had a deep superstition that if he found one and touched his shoulder all would go well that night. He invariably did – or so he said. He scouted for reasonably priced restaurants and shops, though always embarking on a noisy altercation about the bill, whatever it was. At the end of taxi rides during which Pat and I were forbidden to speak English, the drivers always accelerated away shouting and shaking their fists at my indefatigable teacher, who would smile broadly and say, 'You know, Ian, that driver issa very nice man.' I shudder to think how a taxi ride with Rodolfo in London would have ended. I never experienced it.

I felt very nervous on the first night but it was made much easier for me being surrounded by familiar faces in the cast – to say nothing of the Maestro on the podium. It was good to hear the audience react and laugh at the comedy of the words – not just at the business as they tended to do at home.

The critics gave me a rather muted welcome, which was only to be expected as the opera had been given the previous season and Don Magnifico had been sung by the highly accomplished Italian buffo Italo Tajo. Comparisons were inevitable.

Working with Giulietta Simionato was a joy; a much more experienced singer and actress than Marina de Gabarain, she was most touching in the scenes when I was being the cruel step-father. With a pleading look in her eye she would murmur 'No, papa, pieta (pity)' as I was singing. It was all I could do not to stop and say 'It's all right, love, I'm only acting.'

We did a matinee at cheap prices when many of the audience for this fairy tale opera were children. Near the end when Don Magnifico realises that his ambitions for himself and his ugly daughters have been thwarted and that Cinderella has won the Prince he taps his head and sings 'Addio, cervello!' ('Goodbye, brain!'). The yell of children's laughter that greeted it took me right back to Bert Montague's pantomimes at the Princes' Theatre. It's often hard to believe that you really are communicating to an audience in a foreign tongue. At that moment I knew I was and it was a moving revelation.

The performances were either side of Holy Week so we joined the vast throng in St Peter's Square for the Pope's Easter blessing. I was unprepared for the cheers and applause that greeted his words and the shouts of 'Viva Papa!'

Sesto was our self-appointed guide while Rodolfo and Meg went to Naples, but soon decided that someone with a better command of English should be enlisted. He introduced us to his friend Manfred Pedicini Whittaker. Manfred had the bearing of an English regular army officer, including moustache, yet his gestures and brown eyes were Sicilian. The Italian side of his family made the famous drink Marsala, the English side had had army and diplomatic connections. He had a beautiful house in the Via Savoia and an estate in Sicily. He was a regular visitor to Glyndebourne, a fine water colour artist and a generous, exuberant host. His sudden switches from Italian to impeccable upper class English were fascinating.

He saw to it that we missed nothing that could be squeezed into our comparatively short working visit to the Eternal City. Unfortunately at that time of the year many of the art treasures are covered up as part of the Easter observance, but there was still plenty on which to feast our eyes. My profession was rewarding me in more ways than one. We were to see Manfred often in London in the future and over our living room mantelpiece is his painting of a Sicilian windmill, which I managed to buy at an exhibition before any of his English relations got the chance – much to Manfred's delight. He died three years ago.

Italy was deep in a financial crisis while we were there and I consulted Manfred about the best way to get my fees back to London. I'd been told that there was a freeze on lire leaving the country.

'My dear chap it's easy. Do like me and have a hernia.' I looked suitably mystified. 'Oh no, I haven't really got one, but I travel all over Europe wearing a truss stuffed with Canadian dollars.' I decided that wasn't quite my style and consulted the British Consul, who turned out to be Greek.

'Well, it makes a change from the usual enquiries at this time of year,' he said. 'Because it's so hot during the day the British tourists go out in thin clothes. Then at five o'clock the temperature drops suddenly about twenty degrees and they go down with pneumonia. Their relations come to me for money to get them home and pay the doctor. You just want to get some money home?'

'That's right.'

'It's quite easy,' he assured me. 'Get a declaration signed by the theatre stating the full amount they've paid you – then add up all you've spent and a day or two before you leave take it to a bank. They'll subtract one sum from the other and credit your bank in London with the balance. They do it through the exchange control of the Banca d'Italia.'

I did as he suggested and when I presented myself at a bank near our hotel a few days before we were leaving and explained the position the clerk seemed quite happy. 'Come back the day before you leave and it will be all arranged, Mr Wallace,' he said, only he didn't say Wallace – like most Italians he pronounced it Valachay.

When I returned a few days later he looked uncomfortable.

'Mr Valachay, there are difficulties. I must ask you two, three questions. First one – while you are in Rome you stay at a very expensive hotel, no?'

'No,' I said.

'Where you stay then?'

'At the Albergo Regno in this street.'

He raised his eyebrows a fraction. 'Yes it's nice, but I agree with you, it's modest. Next question – while you are here you buy very expensive present for your wife, no?'

'No.' She was standing beside me to prove it.

'Well then, you spend a lot on entertaining the conductor, the agent, the manager, many people, no?'

'No. As a matter of fact many people here have insisted on entertaining us and refuse to accept hospitality in return. They say very kindly that I am here to earn my living not to give parties. Now it's my turn. What's all this about?'

He looked even more embarrassed. 'Mr Valachay, the Banca d'Italia exchange control say that no one singing a big part at the opera house could spend in three weeks as little as you do.'

'I've spent a hell of a lot!' I protested. 'Why I've even brought over my teacher from London.'

He shook his head. 'Not enough.' He was quite adamant and I suddenly realised that they thought I was trying to take money out fraudulently for some Italian. Then I had an inspiration. 'Listen,' I said, 'I'm not an American, I'm a Scotsman.'

His expression changed. 'Scotsman – I see, just a moment.' He picked up a phone and dialled a number. When the voice answered he said, 'Controlo? Ah, buon giorno ce Banca di Lavoro via del Corso, si. Signor Valachay e arrivato, senti (listen) lui non e Americano, no, e Scozese; si (he laughed)

Aberdeen (he laughed even more and I could hear metallic mirth from his earpiece as well) grazie tanto, ciao!' He put the phone down and gave me a flashing smile. 'Mr Valachay, it is all arranged.'

Standing on the stage at the last performance singing the big sextet that comes towards the end, I looked out over the huge, elegant auditorium. Even in the midst of the intricacies of Rossini's ensemble I was able to think to myself, 'Savour this moment, Ian, it doesn't happen to many folk.'

When my little party came down the dressing room staircase for the last time a line of people stood waiting. 'Get out your money,' whispered Rodolfo. Some I recognised. There was my dresser and the boy who brought the Campari sodas in the interval. One explained his presence with the one word 'Scarpe' (shoes) another by 'Perruche' (wigs). As I shook hands with each Rodolfo whispered the number of lire to be handed over. Halfway down the line I said to him, 'I've never seen half these people and I'm sure they didn't do anything for me.'

'I know, but eesa necessary to make a big impression for when you come back.' I was making a hell of an impression on my wallet.

Outside the stage door stood an old man. He was frail and leant on a stick. His coat was almost in rags but it had obviously come from a good tailor many years ago.

'Let 'eem carry something to the taxi for you, Ian,' then as I did so he added quietly, 'Give 'eem something. He's an old singer and this is his only way of making a few lire.' As we got into the taxi I saw Giulietta Simionato come out carrying a tiny parcel. She immediately handed it to him for the same purpose and took his arm as they crossed the pavement to her car. Rodolfo said, 'Eet helps his pride to do a little something for the money.'

Chapter 13

Glyndebourne bombarded me with work that summer. A new production of *Le Nozze di Figaro* as well as revivals of *Le Comte Ory* and *Il Barbiere di Siviglia* in Sussex and *Il Barbiere* and *La Forza del Destino* at Edinburgh, my first time playing the harassed and bitter monk Fra Melitone, who despite the complexities of his character provides some comic relief. I enjoyed the switch to Verdi, but when the last night at Edinburgh was over I'd rehearsed four operas, two of them new productions, and given thirty-seven performances, the last twelve in nineteen days.

Pat and I had a short battery charging spell at Spey Bay before I plunged into my usual morass of broadcasts and concerts which were interspersed with a few novelties. I acted as presenter for some televised symphony concerts from Scotland, always with the script in my pocket and knowing that if I had to produce it I was unlikely to be asked back. Then I unwisely accepted an offer to be link man for a TV documentary about the famous knitting mills in Hawick and was confronted in the live transmission with the sort of situation that is an interviewer's nightmare, particularly when the interviewer is new to the game. A decent, honest man as unaccustomed to the ordeal as I was, he answered every question either 'yes' or 'no', and nothing I could do would make him elaborate. He was followed by a splendid talker whom I failed to restrain so that we entered the last section of the programme behind the clock. This was a parade of top models specially flown from London to Edinburgh for the day wearing the sweaters and twin-sets that firms like Pringle sell all over the world.

At the last rehearsal the producer decided to change the order in which the models would appear and the manufacturers of the garments who had supplied the descriptions for the script also decided on some alterations. I was to read it out of shot in the form of a running commentary and there was no way that the cut and altered version could make sense without being retyped. No BBC secretary was available so it was rushed off to a typing agency.

It didn't arrive back until we were on the air and was only handed to me just as the fashion parade was about to begin. No one had checked it. There wasn't time. As the first girl appeared I grasped my lip-mike and looked at the first line.

'This is Risemary. She's wearing a ponk gulf cordigan . . . Next we meet Munica in a navy blue knotted twon sut . . .' etc.

Fighting a mixture of outrage and an overwhelming desire to shake with laughter I managed to translate this gibberish into a fashion parade commentary; somehow it was the *correct* words that seemed so incongruous and they threw me even more than the wrong ones. Translation could only be done at a measured pace and I committed the ultimate sin of over-running and was faded. While still talking into camera, I noticed out the tail of my eye that the monitor television screen in the studio was showing a close-up of the comedian Fred Emney smoking an enormous cigar. The next programme had already begun.

Not long afterwards at a public dinner in London where I was to reply for the guests I began to experience a feeling of unease and tenseness unlike anything I'd felt before. It wasn't anxiety about my speech which I managed to deliver though when I got to my feet I felt dizzy instead of nervous. Over the next few weeks these feelings attacked me more frequently – not always when I was near a performance – and my heart developed a talent for syncopation.

Though I had every faith in our local G.P. I found myself dialling the number of John Partridge, one of the doctors who'd looked after me when I was on my back during the war. He'd been best man at our wedding and a close friend ever since.

'John?'

'Hullo, Wal.'

'I don't think I'm very well.'

'Oh yes?'

'The odd thing is I could have described it to you before I picked up the phone, now all I can tell you is that I'm shaking like a leaf.'

He laughed and it was a reassuring sound. 'I've been expecting this call for at least three months.'

'What?'

'Your name, Wal, it's all over the place for so many different things. Look, come down on Sunday, bring Pat and we'll talk about it.' John practises in Surrey.

After he'd looked me over he said, 'When did you last have a holiday?'

'That's what's worrying me,' I replied. 'We had one in late September and this is only December.'

'Did you take any music with you?'

'Only a couple of songs.'

'Did you talk to your agent?'

'Twice at the most.'

'The BBC?

'Just once.'

'Now don't muck about, when did you last have a holiday?'

'Yes, I see what you mean. On that basis about ten years ago.'

'Exactly. How often do you play golf?'

'I don't have the time.'

'Make time.'

'I feel as though I'd have a heart attack going up the first fairway.'

'You will feel like that, but you'll be a lot better by the fourteenth.'

'Shall I cancel everything and go on a cruise?'

'Don't you dare. The way you are at present you'd worry because you were feeling better! No, you've got to fight this where you live and work. What you've got is rather like those air raid warnings in the blitz. You've had a yellow and we must avoid the purple. That would be if you actually keeled over in front of a camera or on the stage, and it would be very hard to fight back after that.'

'What about the red?' I asked.

'That's the "no flowers or letters" bit,' he said cheerfully. 'If you do what I say there's no fear of that, but you must learn to relax. I can give you something for a few weeks to help you, but until you realise that life's for living there's not much I or anyone else can do to help. Do you know, Wal, the more my patients earn the more often I see them sitting in that chair.'

It took me a long time to unravel those tensions and learn to relax, but I was lucky indeed to get such candid and timely advice. I think that very few people in show business get through a career without something of the sort happening, and obviously some of the symptoms are well known to folk in other walks of life who are under pressure.

In January we went to Venice, again at Gui's invitation, for *Il Barbiere di Siviglia* produced by his step son Franco Enriquez. As the train slid out of Calais I found myself scared by the different architecture from England, and that in turn made me apprehensive about what such irrational fears boded for my future. I believe it's known as a panic reaction and I found that accompanying it was a feeling that despite all John had told me, I was suffering from some new illness that no one had ever had before.

Venice was a great help – even though in January it is not at its best. Parts of the canals had been drained for maintenance and the odours were unsavoury. One day the Piazza San Marco was carpeted in snow, to the bewilderment of the pigeons, and the Lido looked as if it had been packed away for the winter – even the trees were wrapped up against the wind. Most Venetians seemed perpetually wracked by paroxysms of bronchial coughing, but the little Fenice Opera House with its chandeliers must be one of the most beautiful in the world and the production was well received and supported.

One of the lines in *The Gondolier*, among my favourite Flanders and Swann songs, is 'On board my gondola I serve Coca Cola in flagons which once held Chianti.' One day we saw a yellow gondola stacked high with cases of that invigorating American beverage. I sent Michael a card. His reaction was typical – 'Art ahead of reality yet again!'

On our way home Pat and I decided to take John's advice about life being for living. We had a few idyllic days at Andermatt in the Swiss Alps – not ski-ing, one of the things absolutely forbidden by the doctors after my wartime spinal illness, but watching Olympic ski jumpers practising, enjoying the crisp mountain air and the picture post card world of snow covered mountains and blue skies.

I was much better but still had the benefit of a mild sedative and I resolved to play golf whenever I could that spring and to throw away my pills and potions as soon as possible.

There was only one opera for me at Glyndebourne in 1956, a revival of *Le Nozze di Figaro*, and the company wasn't going to Edinburgh.

At an early *Figaro* rehearsal some of my British colleagues were noticeably off-hand with me, and so were several of the staff, which was most unusual. The reason turned out to be a letter in that morning's *Daily Telegraph* written by the paper's chief music critic, Martin Cooper, taking the Royal Opera House to task for, among other things, neglecting to employ a number of British singers who had established themselves at international level. I was one of them and I think that some of my friends thought that I had inspired the letter. In view of the considerable rivalry existing at that time between Covent Garden and Glyndebourne (now a thing of the past) they thought it rather bad form on my part. In fact the letter was a complete surprise to me and I wasn't too pleased about it. I rang Mr Cooper and suggested that I'd have liked to be consulted before publication.

'Do you mind it?' he asked.

'Not really, but I can't help thinking that as you've pointed out they haven't used me in ten years you've probably made certain that I won't get a job there in the next ten.'

'I'm afraid you may be right,' was his reply.

In fact it's been a bit longer because I've yet to sing at Covent Garden and it's a bit late now. To be fair they did ask me if I'd like to do Fra Melitone in *La Forza del Destino*, but when I told them that, like most comic basses, I sang the 'Predica' aria a tone down they said that Mr Solti (as he was then) wanted it in the original key. If I'd had any sense I'd have kept my mouth shut about keys till I'd signed the contract!

One of the happiest moments in *Figaro* is the scene in the third act when it is revealed that Dr Bartolo and the house-keeper Marcellina are Figaro's father and mother. The sextet which imparts this information is a brilliant combination of beauty and humour. On the first night it became a nightmare. I had a sudden return of the tension symptoms. It wasn't anxiety about remembering words or music, just a fear of collapsing in a heap! I was shaking from head to foot. The Marcellina was Monica Sinclair, a big strong girl. As in a few minutes our youthful indiscretion would be revealed to the audience I decided to move to where she was standing and take her arm. I also leaned on her fairly heavily throughout the scene.

About a year later we met at a party. 'You know, Ian,' she said, 'I've always wanted to thank you for something. On the first night of *Figaro* last year I was feeling very unwell – I was pregnant, and in the sextet I thought I was going to faint. You obviously noticed how I was and came over and held me up.'

At the time neither of us had wanted to admit to being ill. But how easily we might both have slumped to the floor – a dramatic development that had never occurred to Mozart's librettist Da Ponte.

Walking to my dressing room to prepare for a subsequent performance I glanced at the list of guests invited to Mr Christie's private box that evening. They were always on a handwritten card pinned to the door leading to the boxes in the part of the foyer open to the gardens and known as the covered way. At the top of the list was H.M. The Queen followed by H.R.H. Princess Margaret.

When we were presented in costume in the organ room during one of the intervals the Queen, to my surprise, said, 'You and I will be meeting again soon, Mr Wallace, I'll be listening at a window of Holyrood Palace while you'll be singing on a high windy platform.'

I don't know what got into me but I replied 'Yes, Ma'am and I'll be wearing the kilt.'

'But not that wig,' put in Moran Caplat, pointing to the full bottomed affair that Oliver Messel had designed for my character, and Moran and I were treated to that radiant smile which illuminates Her Majesty when she's amused.

The Holyrood serenade concert is watched by thousands, not only in the courtyard of the Palace, but perched on the nearby hill known as Arthur's Seat. On this occasion it was also to be televised live. I had been engaged to sing with massed bands led by the Band of the Royal Corps of Signals conducted by Major John Judd. When I had enquired about the time of rehearsal I was told that there couldn't be one as the bands would only be arriving in time for the concert, having rehearsed their numbers elsewhere. Consternation!

By a piece of luck the Royal Signals band were playing on the front at Eastbourne while I was at Glyndebourne, so I got in touch with John Judd a cheery, red-faced character and asked if we could rehearse somewhere in Eastbourne during the week. He suggested that I meet him at the bandstand at four o'clock one afternoon when they'd finished playing. I arrived in time to enjoy a selection from *The Arcadians* along with about two thousand holiday makers in deck chairs basking in the June sunshine. I imagined that we'd go back to the band room to run through the songs and I was casually dressed in a sweater, open necked shirt and grey flannels.

As the strains of *The merry, merry pipes of Pan* rose to its climax and the audience applauded, Major Judd picked up his public address microphone and held up his hand for silence.

'Don't go away, ladies and gentlemen, I've got a great surprise for you.' Then he told them all about Edinburgh and finished by saying, 'and now Ian's going to sing to you the songs we're going to perform for Her Majesty.'

I don't know if it was a great surprise for the audience, but it was a hell of a shock for me. 'But Major Judd,' I said, 'we'll have to stop and redo some of the songs.'

'Never mind, lad, but don't stop unless you have to.'

There was nothing for it, I had to rehearse in front of two thousand people who thought it was all part of the act when I *did* stop and argued the toss about the tempo of *Wi' a Hundred Pipers*.

Poor Major Judd got it in the neck from the local council. By keeping all those folk sitting there for another half an hour or so a number of other planned entertainments lost money that afternoon.

The floodlit palace looking like something from Grimms' Fairy Tales, a sea of faces in the twilight, tiny red lights glowing on the TV cameras and what looked like hundreds of bandsmen playing the introduction to J. Airlie Dix's old song *The Trumpeter* affected me less than I expected as I stood kilted and carrying a rather splendid stick until it was time to draw breath and sing, picked out by the floodlights like an enemy aircraft in war time. I'd decided on the stick in case the size of the occasion produced the dreaded symptoms – for there would be no Monica Sinclair to lean on this time.

Afterwards I had the signal honour of being presented to the Queen for the second time in a month. Very graciously she recalled her visit to Glyndebourne and told the Lord Provost at her side how much she had enjoyed it. In view of the fact that Glyndebourne's long reign as the provider of operas at the Edinburgh Festival had ended the previous year and that I was their sole representative there that night it was a kind gesture which was warmly appreciated.

Though the company didn't go to Edinburgh there was a visit instead in September to Liverpool. The fortnight at the Royal Court Theatre with *Figaro*, *La Cenerentola* and *Don Giovanni* was hardly as sensational as Berlin, but the Liverpudlian opera lovers turned out in force and on the last night we were given a dinner in the Town Hall. During the meal the police band played a selection of operatic airs and we all sang at the tops of our voices providing added percussion with forks on wine glasses. Our management were embarrassed at our uninhibited behaviour, but the councillors were enchanted and a police car was dispatched across the city to get another opera selection from the band's music library. Unfortunately the moment had passed before it arrived.

Among the councillors was the celebrated and outspoken Liverpool M.P. Bessie Braddock who attracted the attention of cartoonists by being short and stout. Before dinner she asked me if – 'for a bit of a laugh' – I'd serenade her with *The Hippopotamus Song* later in the proceedings.

'I'll be up in the musicians' gallery when you're being shown the ballroom. I'm so like a hippo that we'll have some fun. It'll be a sort of cod Romeo and Juliet balcony scene.' Sure enough, she appeared on cue and it was a great success. I came away from that unstuffy civic ceremony a Bessie Braddock fan.

Chapter 14

One of Rodolfo's great friends was Ezio Pinza, a world class bass singer. They had been students together and Rodolfo told me that this tall, handsome Italian had once been a racing cyclist, which had done a good deal for his breath control. I was often told that his glorious voice had the sort of sound that I should strive to produce. I think Rodolfo always hoped that one day I'd be able to progress from comic to lyric bass.

Pinza in his sixties had deserted the operatic stage and made a triumphant debut in *South Pacific* on Broadway co-starring with Mary Martin. More recently he had had another success with *Fanny* a musical based on a film trilogy by Marcel Pagnol which had starred the French film actor Raimu in the part of César which Pinza played in the musical. The music was by Harold Rome and the book by S. N. Behrman and Joshua Logan.

The Hungarian impresario Sander Gorlinsky had bought the London rights and was to present it at Drury Lane in November starring Robert Morley in the part of Panisse played in America by Walter Slezak.

Pat and I were at Spey Bay when Richard Stone telephoned to say that the Gorlinsky management wanted to audition me for the part of César the following morning. I knew none of the *Fanny* music so, after rumbling down from Aberdeen on the sleeper train and a quick dash home for some songs, I stepped on to the famous stage of the Theatre Royal and sang *Some Enchanted Evening* from *South Pacific*.

'Have you anything else?' asked William Hammerstein, who was to direct it.

'I've got a song about an amorous hippopotamus.'

'Let's hear it.'

I embarked on this most familiar of territories and then read some dialogue without knowing anything about the character or the situation. Afterwards I met Robert Morley in the corridor as I was making my way towards the stage door.

'Let's face it,' he said, 'you may not be the greatest actor in the world, but I don't think we'll find a singer who can do any better.' It only dawned on me as I walked to the Garrick Club for lunch that I'd probably got the job. I returned to Scotland enveloped in euphoria.

Auntie Peggy was living at that time in a bungalow in Prestwick on the Ayrshire coast. Pat and I had stayed a night with her on our way south from Spey Bay at the end of that dramatically interrupted holiday and she'd taken us to see the summer show at the Gaiety Theatre at Ayr, a mere couple of miles down the road. I'd been so impressed with a waif-like, very winning young singer in the show that I'd gone round afterwards to congratulate her on her performance.

Billy Hammerstein belonged to the third generation of that famous family to enter show business. In his thirties, he was tall and broad shouldered, with a crewcut and the reputation for being able to do great things with crowds on TV. He wasn't perhaps quite so happy directing individuals. At the first read-through there was no one there in the title role of *Fanny*. 'We just can't find a suitable girl in England,' explained Billy apologetically.

'I know one,' I said.

'Well why didn't she audition?'

'Because she's in a summer show in Scotland.'

'Get her here,' said Billy.

'I'll try. It depends on the Popplewell brothers who own the Gaiety Theatre, but as the show only has a week or two to run maybe they'll agree.' I had no idea whether they would or not but I was sure after hearing the music and seeing the script that she was just right for the part.

'What's her name?'

'Patricia Bredin.' Billy pointed to the phone on the table.

'Give my office the details and they'll fix it.'

The Popplewells co-operated a hundred per cent and Pat Bredin sang and read for Billy. He offered her the understudy, which understandably and bravely she turned down.

'What was the matter with her?' I asked him.

'Oh she was great but . . . well, we decided to get a girl from America and she'll be here tomorrow.' In other words they were only going through the motions of looking for a British girl. While Pat Bredin was flying to London Janet Pavek was already airborne from New York with the part in her pocket. So far as I could gather she had been in the chorus of the New York production and had understudied. She was dark, pretty, but gentle and appealing were not the adjectives to describe her. She was a product of the tough school of American musicals, hard working, efficient and brash. There were plenty of roles in musicals that Janet could have done splendidly but she was hardly what M. Pagnol had in mind when he wrote the films in which Fanny was the heroine.

Coming as I did from the world of opera and Carl Ebert who told us exactly what he wanted, I waited in vain at the first rehearsal for Billy to give me a lead. My first entrance was from the Marseilles waterfront cafe of which I was the proprietor.

'When I come out where do I go?

'I don't know,' he said with a slightly mocking smile. 'Let's just muss it around a little – y'know, see what gives – and for Christ sake hold your head up and try to look like a star!'

At the end of a week I was in despair. To make matters worse the play was to be done without French accents which might have inspired the sort of gestures and mannerisms that help to build up a character. With my operatic background and auntie Peggy's imitative genes I had been looking forward to that part of it. But Robert made no bones about his determination to play it Anglo-Saxon, so that was that. 'Think of us as a couple of motor mechanics from Lewisham, dear, and just roughen your voice a little.' That sounded even more beyond my scope than what we were supposed to be doing.

Indeed the only part of me that was making any progress was the beard which I'd decided to grow and trim into some suitably gallic shape. It was also to help me age twenty years though that wasn't going to be too hard as I weighed all of fifteen and a half stone at the time.

Billy was not the director for such an inexperienced top of the bill in a musical as me, and though Robert was sympathetic he had his own problems with the tricky musical numbers and was realising why Rex Harrison had spent so many months before the New York run of *My Fair Lady* getting those marvellous songs firmly under his belt. After one particularly frustrating day I told Pat that if something didn't happen soon it would be a race between me and the management – resignation or the sack.

At one rehearsal Billy had said, 'I know this is based on the Marcel Pagnol film trilogy but I don't want anyone to see those films. This is a musical and we wanna fresh angle.'

I called Richard Stone and asked him to arrange as soon as possible a private showing of the middle film of the trilogy in one of the Wardour Street cellars where they have little viewing theatres for just such contingencies. It cost about twenty pounds and I invited Julian Orchard, who was playing a small part as well as being my understudy, and Mona Washbourne, one of the best actresses on the English stage, who was playing the important part of Honorine, to come along for the ride.

The film was in French with English sub-titles. As we watched I quickly realised why I had been having such problems making sense of some of my lines and understanding César. We saw long stretches of the film which seemed to have nothing to do with our show. Then a familiar scene would arrive and one of my lines of dialogue, word for word the same, would appear on the sub-titles. But the reply to it was quite different and there might be another twenty or thirty lines before my next line in our version of the scene emerged. It was like finding missing pieces of a jigsaw puzzle. Of course three films into one musical needed savage cutting, but now I had a far better idea of what I was supposed to be doing. Incidentally, watching the great Raimu play César was partly an inspiration, partly a depressing view of the unattainable.

One other thing was painfully obvious. The Fanny of the film was a great deal more reminiscent of Pat Bredin than Janet Pavek.

After a quarter of an hour of rehearsal the next day Billy stopped me. 'What's happened to you overnight? Suddenly you're giving me a performance. Did you get your hair cut or something?'

I owned up.

'Gee, why did you pay out for that? I'd have fixed it.'

I didn't remind him of his strict instructions, but Robert did. 'Now then, bossikins, you did say you wanted a fresh angle,' and he gave me that impish smile that one schoolboy gives another who's had the courage to cock a snook at the teacher.

Robert's wit and wicked enjoyment of things going wrong kept rehearsals lively. When the stage director Gerry Phillips dashed in one afternoon and announced, 'It's marvellous, they're all booking to come in parties!' Robert's jowls descended in mock apprehension.

'Dear God!' he exclaimed, 'are they afraid to come on their own?' He was also a generous host, every now and then bearing a few of us off to the Savoy Grill for lunch and an equally stimulating feast of good conversation. Before we knew it the dress rehearsal had arrived. Less hopeful for our well being was the advent of petrol rationing in the wake of the Suez Affair.

In a scene change done in a black-out towards the end of the dress rehearsal I had a nasty fall and lay momentarily over-come with tiredness and pain in a knee. Within seconds Robert was bending over me. 'I know exactly how you feel. It's like when we were in the nursery and got tired just before bed-time. That's when you trip over your toy train and the whole world seems to be against you. Come on, César, only half an hour and we can go home.' I was in need of that sympathetic encourage-ment and I remember it still with gratitude.

There was no question of a pre-London tour but we had several public previews – now taken for granted, but then something of an innovation. At the first one I was anxious to hear the audience reaction to my big number *Welcome Home*, which was César's attempt in song late at night to dissuade his son Marius from going to sea. They responded well and, very relieved, I ran up the little staircase from the café to my bedroom door only to find that I couldn't open it.

I kept pushing it frantically. The orchestra had run out of music but our greatly experienced musical director Michael Collins soon had them repeating my exit theme over and over again. Eventually I forced the door open a few inches and inserted my hand. It snapped back on my wrist and I was trapped. The audience were enjoying my predicament but I was thanking my stars that it wasn't the first night.

After I'd been standing there for what seemed like five years trying to release my hand I heard someone coming up the stairs behind me. It was Billy Hammerstein all the way from his seat in the stalls. He pushed the door hard until I could get my hand out and then, to the delight of the public, he pulled the door open towards us demonstrating that the chap with his name in lights outside the theatre didn't know which way his bedroom door was hinged. Billy bowed to me. I returned the compli-ment. Then he ran down the stairs and off the set while I disappeared through the door to the biggest round of applause of the evening.

On the first night *Welcome Home* stopped the show and it was the last thing Billy and his wife heard before they had to leave Drury Lane and fly home as a result of a family bereavement. I bear him no animosity. He needed a more experienced principal and I was a little too dependent on father figure directors at that stage in my career. The reception at the end of the show was good but the critics were not much impressed and though we played for ten months to moderate business, it was as much a matter of keeping Drury Lane warm for the next show as anything else.

Robert's ebullience survived it all. Every Saturday he entertained the principals to a superb dinner in his dressing room between the matinee and the evening performance, as well as giving the whole company two or three splendid parties in the course of the run. I was depressed by some of my notices and once again he gave me badly needed comfort. Before the second performance I went into his room and told him I thought it was a bit tough of Milton Shulman to say that if Robert was a whale I was a sardine.

'Never mind, dear, you've got the courage to quote it. When I went to New York years ago to do a play about Oscar Wilde one of the top critics wrote "Robert Morley played Oscar Wilde like Winnie the Pooh!"'

As the weeks passed I did what I could to improve my performance, experimenting with different ways of saying lines until I got a more positive reaction from the audience. But the rake (slight incline from back to front) on the stage and the dazzling arc light that followed me wherever I went meant that my tension symptoms were never far away and certainly on that vital first night I had not been as relaxed or in command of myself as I had managed on similar occasions in opera.

I also had Robert's fairly outrageous ad libbing to contend with. In the long run it did me a great deal of good, teaching me to keep things fluid on the stage and not get too set in a performance – but at the time I often felt embarrassingly at a loss when what he said forced me off the script. To have replied with my next line would have been meaningless. I never expected to win one of those ad lib encounters, but one Saturday night I emerged with the spoils.

On my first entrance Robert seized my panama hat, folded it into the shape of a matador's headgear, put it on, plucked my handkerchief from my breast pocket and started to flourish it like a bull-fighter's cloak. I let him make a few passes until he ran out of ideas and shouted 'olé!'

I looked at the audience, looked at Robert and shook my head. 'It would have to be a very old bull,' I declared.

We never referred to such encounters afterwards and they did nothing to alter my affection for him. On one occasion he probably saved me from giving up my career and pointed me in the right direction to overcome the problems with nerves and lack of confidence which had dogged me for more than a year.

In the interval on another Saturday night with a full house I felt the dressing room revolving round me and heard myself say the words that should only occur in fictional stories about show business. 'I can't go on – you'd better tell Julian.'

My dresser, Frank Small, flew out of the room for help which arrived swiftly in the form of an unlikely double act, the diminutive Gerry Phillips and Robert who cried, 'Do you feel dizzy, that you're about to have a stroke, a heart attack or both?'

'Yes,' I replied faintly.

'Good. I know what it is – the French call it a *crise de nerfs*; I get it often and cure it by lying flat on my stomach for half an hour. No time for that, so come on the stage with me, dear boy, and if you *are* going to faint, try and do it early in the act then we might just catch *The Sunday Express*. We can do with a bit of publicity.'

It was a turning point. From then on I never had another bad attack. The reasons for it all, apart from those discussed with John Partridge, probably had something to do with having climbed up the ladder rather too fast and attempting things for which I wasn't ready – like twelve-tone music and starring at Drury Lane. But a chance remark by Robert casually thrown out in the wings before a scene also went to the heart of the matter. 'You and Pat really ought to have a family – why not do it the hard way and adopt a mentally handicapped Hungarian baby?' The Hungarian uprising was very much in all our minds at the time.

Although we didn't feel quite equal to that sort of challenge he was only echoing a sense of emptiness in our life and a lack of purpose. For ten years I had experienced much of the glamour as well as the drudgery of a musical and theatrical career. Pat had played the supporting role of looking after me to perfection, but for her in particular there was little to look forward to except perhaps being able to afford a new car or a better record player, poor substitutes for the joys and agonies of bringing up a family. Robert's remark was the spur I needed and about that time we set things in motion with the National Adoption Society. Pat needed no spur at all, but had quietly decided not to rush me into anything even though I was approaching the upper age limit to be an adoptive father.

Before *Fanny* ended in September 1957 there was a matinee when Robert and I between us nearly lost Drury Lane its licence. Kevin Scott, the young American who played Marius, brought his baby to the theatre that afternoon because his wife was unwell. There was a scene where Robert wheeled a pram across the stage containing his wife Fanny's baby (whose father was Marius). Instead of the usual doll we decided to give Kevin's six month old infant a walk in the pram across the stage. When the procession reached the centre Kevin junior proved that he was already following in father's footsteps by crying so loudly that he threatened to drown the dialogue. The audience became hostile and there were a few outraged mothers besieging the manager's office at the end with dark threats of reporting us all to the NSPCC. But as Kevin said afterwards very few people can claim to have made their Drury Lane debut before the age of one – and to have created such an impression.

Another oddity during the run was when Michael Flanders and Donald Swann opened at the Fortune Theatre on the opposite side of the street with their two man show *At the Drop of A Hat*. On the first night it was arranged that I would cross the street still in one of my César costumes and step on stage to join them in the final chorus of *Mud, Mud, Glorious Mud* which ended their show. The audience were bewildered and some even embarrassed because they hadn't the slightest idea who I was and by what right this fat, bearded interloper was trying to claim some kudos for a wildly successful evening in which he'd played no part. Ah well, publicity agents, like everyone else in show business, have their resoundingly bad ideas. Michael and Donald needed no boost, but had gladly agreed to my coming and, in their moment of triumph, introduced me to the audience with tact and enthusiasm.

When the curtain fell on the last performance of *Fanny* I shaved off my beard before going to the end of term party. Close friends and colleagues walked straight past me. Those who laugh at the idea of spies using false beards would have been amazed. A last night celebration has inevitably something about it of putting on a brave face. There are always the few who have lined up a new job, the few who say they have and haven't, and the many who are hoping for the best. We had all been shocked that a tiny number of the chorus had collected their money for the whole week on Friday and hadn't turned up for the last two performances on Saturday – and that *isn't* show business. Though I was very tired and looking forward to a rest I was sad to say goodbye to Robert, Mona Washbourne, Michael Gough, Kevin Scott and, despite my reservations on casting, to Janet Pavek who had left the cast some weeks before we closed and who wrote nice letters from America over the next few years; and of course to Julian, who did have one spell of playing César when I was laid low for ten days with flu and laryngitis. In the middle of it I rang Robert in his dressing room during a performance to report progress.

'Hallo, dear boy, how are you? Just a moment. Davey! (his dresser) would you mind reducing the volume on the tannoy from the stage, I can't hear Mr Wallace on the phone, the applause for Mr Orchard is absolutely deafening!'

Perhaps saddest of all was to say goodbye to the theatre itself. There isn't another quite like it and the same could be said for the stage staff. Maybe in the 1980s they call artists by their first names, but they never did so then, managing to make the use of 'Mr' friendly and informal. The carpenter made a beautiful mahogany chest for my dressing room and indeed it would be no exaggeration to say that the Theatre Royal treated us like royalty. When my dresser Frank Small went to the wardrobe department of BBC TV he was succeeded by Tom Davis from Southern Ireland who had played Davis Cup tennis for his country and once showed me the fire that playing at such a level requires.

I had ventured to criticise the Centre Court antics of Lew Hoad, winner of the men's singles at Wimbledon that summer.

'You don't know what you're talking about – the tension out there's terrific.' Tom was a small diffident man and it was the first time he'd raised his voice to me. In response to my look of astonishment he apologised and confessed to having played tennis on that Centre Court himself. It was like suddenly discovering that your milkman was Caruso.

The end of *Fanny* was also the levelling out of a fairly steep ascent in my fortunes, though after a six week holiday, mostly in the south of France, we got home to find that after starring in a musical – even a not very successful one – things will never be quite the same. A little cluster of good offers waited: the singing chairman in an Edwardian music hall series on commercial TV entitled *The Jubilee Show*, Pooh Bah on a recording of *The Mikado* for HMV with Sir Malcolm Sargent and a nice part in *Tom Thumb*, a film for children directed by George Pal. The star studded cast included Russ Tamblyn, Peter Sellers, Terry-Thomas, Bernard Miles and Jessie Matthews, but the real star was Pal himself with his repertoire of camera tricks to create the illusion of the tiny Tom Thumb dancing through a normal sized world.

Our studio at Pinewood was a fascinating world of pencils the size of telegraph poles, cotton reels like cable drums and many other giant sized household objects to make Tom Thumb look tiny in comparison. Russ leaped and danced among them with an acrobatic dexterity that had to be seen to be believed. There is a sequence where all the toys come to life and when I saw the film on TV last Christmas it was good to realise that Pal's magic works just as well today.

I am an old shoemaker whose tiny 'talented shoes' enable Tom to do all sorts of miraculous things. My stall is at a fairground where to the accompaniment of the town band I sing a sort of 'Roll up!' song to attract customers. I had recorded it on a previous day with an orchestra conducted by Muir Mathieson, whose name on film credits was like a hallmark for so many years. For the filming itself I had to mime to my own recording over and over again as they shot the elaborate scene involving many people dancing and milling about from every angle. Miming is not as easy as it sounds and if your lip movements don't exactly match the sound recording that whole piece of film is wasted.

Round about this time I had an encounter in a film studio with one of my boyhood heroes, Buster Keaton. He had come over to try and sell a comedy series to one of the commercial television companies in London. I'd been booked to take part in the pilot. The scene was an opera sequence where everything goes wrong. I was a slave who entered dragging what looked like a heavy ball and chain fastened round my ankles. In fact the ball was made of rubber and bounced at a critical moment. In the end the scenery collapsed on top of us. I think the plans for the series collapsed too, for though everyone who saw our pilot (I didn't alas) said it was very funny, I got the feeling that there was only Buster Keaton's marvellous comic invention behind it – no money.

When I arrived at the studio for the one day allocated to our scene I was introduced to the great man and told him I was one of his millions of fans. He looked at me with that mournful unsmiling look that was unchanged by the passing years.

'Did you ever see that movie where I was leanin' against the house and when I walk away the wall falls outwards on top of me but where I am there's an open window and there I am standing up because I've been saved by the empty space in the wall?'

'Yes,' I said, 'it was incredible.'

'You know, everybody figures that I had a double do that or that maybe there was some kinda camera trick. No, sir. I just stood there on the spot they marked out and prayed. The set designer said look, Buster, it's a matter of trigonometry. That empty square has to pass through that angle and if you're on that spot Godammit it can't hit you! Well I guess he was right, but I'll never forget it and hopin' I wouldn't prove him wrong!'

It was revealing that he felt impelled to tell me, a total stranger, about it within a few moments of our meeting. The filming must have been more than thirty years earlier and yet the agony of waiting for that trigonometry to preserve his life had obviously haunted him ever since.

Chapter 15

It's easy to explain why my memory is much more selective from now on. Artists thrive on new experiences and challenges. There are still some to come but, inevitably – for a singer more than an actor – repeating one's repertoire is part of the pattern. So now as I look at the press books the images that flicker in my mind's eye more often remind me of an incident or a performance without providing any background and fail to pinpoint the preparation or the backstage anguish immediately before stepping into the lighted arena.

I see the balding, Germanic figure of Gerard Hoffnung in white tie and tails, gallantly fighting a duel with conductors' batons up and down the auditorium stairs at the Royal Festival Hall – in defiance of his doctor's advice – as part of his first triumphant Hoffnung Concert. I can hear again the enormously loud chord in Donald Swann's version of Haydn's *Surprise Symphony*, and the roar of laughter as I used the rail of the conductor's rostrum as a harp to serenade April Cantelo in a TV jingle for Bournvita in the style of Verdi written by Joseph Horovitz.

Gerard, whose brave but faulty heart failed him in his thirties, was a cartoonist extraordinary, a raconteur without peer and a tuba player by conviction. Though a serious musician he believed that a concert to make music lovers laugh would be an enormous success. He recruited Malcolm Arnold to write a *Grand, Grand Overture*, Franz Reisenstein to compose a *Concerto Popolari* with quotations from all the famous piano concertos and he prevailed upon the Dolmetsch Ensemble to perform the *1812 Overture* with recorders and children's pop-guns with the corks tied on with string. Vacuum cleaners and a road rammer were in the percussion section of the orchestra and the evening culminated in an extravaganza called *Let's Fake an Opera*.

It was the first of many Hoffnung Concerts. Something of their flavour can be recaptured from the records which must be rare collectors' items these days, but to savour them fully you needed to be there – or, even better, to take part.

Over the page in my scrapbook there's a photograph of me in flowing robes and a burnous looking every other inch an Arab. MGM had called me in to do a test for the Sheikh in *Ben Hur* and I played a scene extolling the virtues of my beautiful horses. For a day or two delicious rumours circulated that the film had been flown to Hollywood with a good report, but Hugh Griffith got the job. If they were making it today I feel sure they'd only be testing Arabs – there wouldn't be a Scot or a Welshman in sight – not even Windsor Davies.

Nearby is a newspaper article announcing that I'd lost two stones and was now a mere thirteen and a half. Medical knowledge had reached the point where people who had suffered from a TB spine could safely lose weight. Up to then the fear had been that dieting lowered resistance and you ran a risk of recurrence. All of which explains why I had no chance of playing anything except character roles till I was nearly forty. By then it was too late to do anything else! Despite endless starch-free rolls that sounded as if you were rustling a newspaper as you ate and diabetic jam to cut as much sugar as possible I had no trouble from my old complaint but contracted a new one instead – hepatitis, better known as jaundice, which laid me low for weeks and prevented me from accepting an offer from Sir Thomas Beecham to record Handel's *Acis and Galatea* – one of my greatest regrets because I had no other opportunity to work with the great man.

But all these snippets from a year's work were of no importance in comparison with the day in late August when we went to the offices of the National Adoption Society and collected a six week old baby girl. This was the start of a probationary period of three months during which the adoptive parents are subject to the scrutiny of the health visitor who has to report on the suitability of the home background and the care provided for the baby – as opposed to the suitability of the prospective parents which is thoroughly checked by the society before a baby is handed over.

'You see, Mr Wallace, we are only concerned with the

well-being of the child. We wish you and your wife much joy in parenthood but if we don't think you are the sort of people to make a happy home and a stable background for one of our babies we will tell you so and that will be the end of the matter.' So said the gentle voiced but very firm Miss Helen Blackburne at our first interview.

Fortunately we managed that hurdle all right, but there is a day hanging over all adoptive parents at the end of the three months when they take their baby to court to have the adoption made official before a judge. I believe there have been some changes in the law in the last twenty years which may have altered the situation, but in 1958 the natural mother could turn up at the court having changed her mind and claim the baby back. The book we bought about adoption contained the sentence 'Do not give your heart to the child for the first three months.' Excellent advice – and like so much wise counsel totally impractical. Three hours is more like it.

I soon made the discovery that, while other babies crying irritate you, your own is quite easy on the ear except, perhaps, at three in the morning. I'm not going to kid you that I was much of a nappy changer and later on I made the fatal mistake of reading bed-time stories with far too many histrionics causing tears and a head disappearing under the bed-clothes. My sole success in baby care was on the first evening after a pretty solid period of crying. Ever since we'd taken delivery in fact.

'It must be the food,' I said.

'Nonsense. I'm going to give her exactly what it says on this bit of paper that came with her,' replied the baffled probationary mother. 'They must know what they're talking about.'

'Wait, where's that baby book?' I demanded.

'In the kitchen.'

I left the room of tears without a word, returning in triumph a few minutes later. 'They've been driving her with the choke out,' I announced. My merry quip was not too well received.

'What are you talking about?'

'Too rich a mixture for her age – look.' We diluted it accordingly and within half an hour, after a few burps and a sigh of contentment, a very tired young lady was asleep. Having shown the way I left all subsequent decisions on family feeding to Pat for the ensuing twenty-four years.

In the middle of that night I was awakened by Pat leaping out of bed. 'What's the matter?'

'She's so quiet I think she must have stopped breathing.'

I lay anxiously awaiting her return or a cry of anguish. Soon she was back.

'It's all right, she's sound asleep. It's silly but I thought something awful might have happened.' It was silly really, but I'd thought so too.

About six weeks later Pat was sitting on the edge of the bed as I returned from a teeth brushing session. 'Surely we could apply to the court now. Nothing could happen to stop it going through, could it?'

I knew exactly how she was feeling. The thought of having our baby snatched away was too awful to contemplate. Admittedly it was only a very slim possibility. Part of the adoption society's job is to make sure that the natural mother of the baby has absolutely made up her mind before it is placed for adoption at all, in order to avoid such a heartbreaking situation. But always at the back of our minds was the outside chance that waiting at the court would be someone with a greater legal right than us. A day of great joy or unbearable sadness lay ahead and there was no certainty in advance which it would be.

When we arrived at the court buildings three months to the day and carried in our small bundle, there were at least three young women in the hallway who were the right age to be the mother of a four and a half month old baby girl. We looked at them with murder in our hearts, which was reprehensible and totally understandable to anyone who's been through this particular experience. But none of them were there on the mission that we had secretly dreaded.

When we were called into the judge's room he was sitting alone behind his desk, his wig reposing on a small stand.

'I never put it on for adoption orders,' he said with a smile. 'Now then, all the papers seem to be in order and I have only two questions to ask you. First, are you going to tell her she's adopted?'

'Yes.'

'When?'

'As soon as she's old enough to understand.'

'Good. Is it your intention to adopt a second child?'

'Yes,' we replied in unison.

'Splendid. I am happy to sign this order and I very much hope you will carry out your intention to provide a companion for this very sweet little girl.'

I think if he'd told us we had to adopt another ten before he'd sign we would have agreed to it. It was over and we were a family at last after being married for ten and a half years.

Now we could plan a christening. We'd already decided on names, but until this day they had only been what are called in film and TV studios 'working titles'. They were Rosemary Ann Gordon, but she's usually called Rosie.

Chapter 16

I really could hardly believe it when I found myself in a boys' club in London's Holland Park face to face with a heroine of my schooldays, Ginger Rogers. She had flown from America to take part in a BBC TV production of *Carissima*, a musical by Hans May and Eric Maschwitz that had enjoyed a fair success in the West End. Persuading this great star to head the cast was a coup for Francis Essex the producer of the show. Her co-stars were David Hughes – the Welsh pop singer who had made a courageous, completely justified decision to 'go straight' and enchanted both public and critics with his fine tenor voice until his tragically early death soon after an opera performance in London some years later, and Lizbeth Webb who made her name in the Vivian Ellis – A. P. Herbert musical *Bless the Bride*.

Ginger, tall, trousered and completely without make-up, gave the impression at that first rehearsal of being an unglamorous, slightly leathery lady from the country. She announced that we ought to have a production conference. This was before Francis could get a word in.

We sat round a table with our scripts and began to read. Almost at once Ginger said, 'Hey, this scene leaves me with egg on my face.'

Francis smiled politely. 'What does that mean, Ginger?' It was a new expression to us all then.

'Well – kinda out on a limb – embarrassed. Tellya what, let's leave it and I'll have a look at it tonight OK?' We passed on to the next scene. After a few lines Ginger stopped once more.

'Gee! This is like opening a can of peas.' Francis with a winning smile asked for enlightenment.

'We-e-ell, it sorta gives the game away and nobody knows quite where they're going. I guess I'll have a little look at that one too.'

We had quite a number of these sessions and Francis's rehearsal time was shrinking by the hour. After each Ginger's part was a little bigger and Lizbeth Webb's a little smaller. Liz was remarkably forebearing.

'I don't mind at all, it's probably better that way,' she said more than once with a tight smile.

Francis was in a cleft stick. He didn't want these re-writes but he knew Ginger wasn't here for the money and could easily decide to take the next plane home at any time. I don't think she would have done. Such a professional lady wouldn't have treated her fellow artists like that and wouldn't have wanted the bad publicity. On the other hand she was obviously very accustomed to having her own way.

Though the performance was live there was one scene, filmed a week in advance, of Ginger at Idlewild Airport in America crossing the tarmac late at night to board a plane. The location for this scene was Gatwick. Among those seeing her off were Warren Mitchell (long before Alf Garnett) and myself, two middle aged characters in a story I've quite forgotten.

We went down to Gatwick in the dusk and were told that the scene would be shot as soon as Ginger emerged from the make-up room. An hour passed and then another. Two hours in make-up, that's what you'd expect if you were going to play the phantom of the opera!

We'd pretty well given up hope of getting home before the early hours of the morning when we were called out on to the tarmac, taking up our positions for a rehearsal; the flood lights cut through the darkness and there, walking towards the aircraft in a superbly cut mink coat was the Ginger Rogers I remembered dancing *Cheek to Cheek* with Fred Astaire, beautiful and twenty years younger at least than the charming but somewhat steely lady we'd been working with for the last couple of weeks. In that moment of nostalgia we found ourselves applauding. Later the make-up staff said she'd done it all herself as they watched in admiration what amounted to a demonstration.

The way the story was written when we filmed that Gatwick sequence Warren Mitchell and I were happy about seeing her off. We waved, smiled and embraced one another. By transmission day the script had been changed yet again; the departure now was a sad one, making Warren and me look like a couple of insensitive boors or else two lousy actors. We settled for the former. There was no time or money to trail back to Gatwick and do it again.

On the big day Ginger gave another demonstration – this time of stamina. She had a hell of a part and at the morning run-through in a studio that included a canal in Venice complete with gondola she said at one point, 'I don't know why the hell you don't film this now while I'm fresh. By tonight – oh brother, will I be bushed!'

She wasn't of course. Not only did she find time to send us all telegrams – mine read 'Best of everything this day' – she also gave us signed photographs, each with a different message and dated. She was busy at it in her dressing room when I looked in to wish her luck. Then she went on and played a blinder, as they say, proving that star quality always goes with great reserves of vitality.

1959 was certainly my year for meeting Hollywood stars. I did a variety broadcast with Chico Marx – the one who played the piano with that marvellous stabbing finger in those immortal Marx Brothers films.

'I tell ya,' he said, 'radio's fightin back. It's real big in the States right now – sump'n to do with transistors, I guess.' It's still fighting, thank God.

A tiny part of the fight that year was *Monday Night at Home* – a miscellany of contributions by people from gamekeepers to High Court Judges who leavened the showbusiness lump of Peter Ustinov, Joyce Grenfell, Peter Sellers, Gerard Hoffnung, Jonathan Miller, Peter Bull, Rene Cutforth and many others, not forgetting Ivor Cutler, whose brand of self-effacing, sinister humour is like an eccentric one-man show in a bed-sitter and always enlivened the programme. There were also short, exquisite musical interludes on disc chosen by the Irish singer, Robert Irwin.

It was my job to link the items and the producer, John Bridges, who had begun his adult life in the Brigade of Guards and possessed a sharp ear for real quality in the English language would often spring a new item on me at the recording session saying, 'Listen to this, then write me a twenty second link as dry as a martini.' He had an acute sensitivity for the length of pauses between items. Silence on the air is regarded by many broadcasters as a dangerous switch-off opportunity always to be avoided. After a moving item John would leave several seconds for the listener to reflect; after something in a different mood he would go straight on, playing the cue-light button like the conductor of an orchestra.

Walter Flesher and Lord Birkett were the gamekeeper and the judge and unashamedly my favourites. Birkett, who had been one of the great advocates of his day, discoursed in his friendly, precise manner on such varied topics as the mid-wicket conversation between Peter May and Colin Cowdrey during a famous Test Match stand at Edgbaston and the eccentricities of legal colleagues. I recall the pithy exchange between a prisoner and one of his brother judges.

'As God is my judge, m'lud, I am not guilty,' cried the man in the dock. To which the judge replied, 'He's not, I am, you are, six months.'

Walter Flesher brought the rugged beauty of the Yorkshire Dales and the entertaining details of village life to the listener without a superfluous word. He'd lost an arm in World War One which, John Bridges told me, robbed him of the chance of playing cricket for Yorkshire. His wealth of country lore and his talent for imparting it were perhaps some consolation to this gifted and humble man.

Though the programme was usually recorded it was sometimes necessary to do it live when a recording studio was unavailable. One of those occasions was the evening after the worst of the Notting Hill race riots of that year. 'It's not our job to comment,' said John Bridges, 'but let's slip in a record of Paul Robeson to show how we feel.'

160

In the same live programme a studio attendant, unaware that we were on the air, appeared at my side with a jug of water. John signed to me through the glass that separated the studio and the control panel that I should have a word with him for the benefit of our listeners – it was that sort of show.

'Hallo,' I said, 'what can I do for you?'

'I've come to change your water,' he replied, indicating the jug and glasses on the table beside the microphone.

'Thank you very much, but I'm not a goldfish,' I said. At that moment he noticed the red light on the wall, clapped a hand over his mouth and fled.

*　　*　　*

Glyndebourne had decided that my defection to the world of musicals was a temporary aberration and asked me back for a revival of *La Cenerentola* with my two old friends and the gorgeous Teresa Berganza whose pregnancy was so far advanced that she could only do the first few performances. This was a matter of worry to those of us who knew the rumour if not the fact that in a previous era Concita Supervia had died as a result of singing this role while expecting a child. Each evening, I and the ugly sisters kneeling round her as she embarked on the strenuous rondo at the end of the opera, *Non piu mesta*, put up prayers that it wouldn't be too much for her. Far from it. She sang with such relaxed ease that she could probably have managed the rest of the season if Cinders in a maternity ball gown had fitted in with the plot. Designed by Oliver Messel it probably would have done.

The decade ended for me as it had begun with a pantomime – *Aladdin* at the London Coliseum with music by Cole Porter and directed by Robert Helpmann, the only person in my career so far who has ever succeeded in getting me to dance on the stage. If he couldn't who else could? Though most Emperors of China would have considered my routine with a lift at the end grossly beneath their dignity.

The Widow Twankey was the cockney actor Ronald Shiner and Aladdin, following the trend away from female principal boys, was Bob Monkhouse. One night I was sitting in my dressing room listening to the show unfolding through the tannoy. Aladdin was in a vast cave and Abanazer, a wondrously villainous Alan Wheatley, was addressing him in a sepulchral ehoing voice made possible by our sophisticated sound system. There was a sudden sharp bang, a gasping cry from the audience and then Bob's voice saying, 'Oh uncle, you *have* dropped a clanger.' This was greeted by an explosion of laughter and sustained applause.

One of the weights that counterbalance pieces of scenery lowered from the flies had somehow become detached and fallen from high above the stage. It had missed Bob's head by inches – in fact he said afterwards that he felt the wind of it as it brushed his shoulder before crashing at his feet. His instant reaction to reassure the audience was quick thinking and control at its best. When he left the stage at the end of the scene he nearly fainted with reaction. He had missed being killed by a hairsbreadth.

Such incidents in the theatre are rare, but heavy lights and scenery are often secured by cables and balanced by counter weights, so there is always the thousand to one chance of something heavy making a rapid and unscheduled descent despite all the care and stringent precautions that are taken.

At another performance of this pantomime the second half was held up for about twenty minutes because the enormously heavy safety curtain – or iron – which had been lowered in the interval and which worked hydraulically refused to rise. Firemen were called who winched it up manually but then said that they weren't prepared to guarantee that it would hold.

It was decided to go ahead with the second half though we were warned not to go down stage beyond the pagodas – two elaborate pieces of scenery level with the proscenium arch. If the iron did crash down then we would all be on the safe side of its line of descent. Having a vivid imagination I'd decided that even so we'd be in trouble. The Coliseum has a revolving stage like an enormous gramophone turn-table and I reckoned that if the iron hit the edge, that would snap it from its axle, tipping us all into the basement!

Widow Twankey and the Emperor of China had a romantic scene in part two in which he waltzed her round the stage singing a love song *Trust your destiny to a star*. Ronnie Shiner and I knew that to do the number justice we had to risk that massive guillotine. As we waltzed beyond the pagodas he whispered in my ear, 'Who's yer next of kin, mate?'

* * *

Like most wives Pat will only ring me at work if it's a matter of life and death, so when Eddie Fraser, who was producing a Kenneth McKellar TV show in which I was the guest, came into the studio where the orchestra rehearsal was taking place in Glasgow and said that my wife was calling from London my heart missed a beat. Something must have happened to Rosie or my mother.

'Sorry to bother you, darling, but I felt I had to ring you. I've just had a call from the National Adoption Society, they've got a baby boy and do we want him?'

'Of course we do, when?'

'On Tuesday.'

'Good heavens – can you get everything ready?'

'I'll have to, won't I?'

We'd applied for a second child, but never thought we'd be so lucky so soon. Adoption societies don't operate a queue system. Babies are placed where there is likely to be some common ground with the adoptive parents. Colouring of eyes and hair as well as the possibility of inherited interests are carefully considered. Apparently there was music in the background of this baby boy which made them think of us.

Pat had a great race around to collect all the necessary things. In one baby shop they were out of stock of some vital item.

'We'll have them in in about six weeks, madam.'

'That'll be too late,' said Pat, almost in tears with frustration.

The assistant regarded her completely flat tummy and observed, 'Aren't you panicking a little early, madam?'

When John arrived he looked rather scrawny and ugly – as opposed to the delicately elfin creature we'd collected on our first visit to Manchester Square. As I was writing that sentence the tall, handsome devil he's now become put his head round the door asking me to give various messages to the members of his band who await with cautious optimism the impact of their first record on a CBS contract – I mentioned there was music in his background. Rosie, who's recently graduated from Sussex

University in Social Administration, had spent the morning typing impeccably a list of the band's equipment for a gig in France – but I'm getting a long way ahead of myself.

Perhaps it was no accident that the completion of our family coincided with maybe the high point of my opera career. It was to be the last time I would sing *La Cenerentola* at Glyndebourne, but if the notices are to be believed, the understanding between Sesto Bruscantini, Juan Oncina and myself had burgeoned into something a little out of the common. A couple of press quotes may be forgiven: Frank Howes in *The Times*: ' . . . The orchestral playing was a delight and all the singing, even in those broader episodes which it is Mr Ian Wallace's business to bring off without transgressing Latin refinement, was admirably stylish. Mr Juan Oncina and Mr Sesto Bruscantini, both Glyndebourne favourites of long standing, who were prince and valet by turns in this version of the Cinderella story, know to the lifting of an eyebrow and the turn of a semi-quaver what operatic acting is and can achieve in the way of comedy.'

Ernest Bradbury in *The Yorkshire Post* ' . . . Mr Pritchard gets a dazzling display from the Royal Philharmonic Orchestra. The two comic men, Bruscantini with the rolling eyes, singing asides from the corner of his mouth more powerfully and clearly than some artists can with the whole of it, and Ian Wallace, testing the sherries in the cellar as though they were a mixture of arsenic and ambrosia – these two never put a foot wrong, or make an unecessary gesture; their timing is a marvel.'

The Cinderella was a lovely quiet Italian girl, Anna Maria Rota, who also delighted the critics with a voice of exceptional quality. At one time it was hard to cast this opera as so few singers could manage this role. She was the third we'd had at Glyndebourne, and in the autumn I did some guest performances at Sadlers Wells in English with another, the Scots soprano Catherine Wilson, who though not a mezzo scored a notable triumph. It was my one and only engagement with the Wells and it was good to be playing the comedy in Arthur Jacobs' excellent translation, though I had a fatal tendency to lapse into Italian in moments of stress.

My opera career wasn't over by a very long chalk but I was within a year of my last performance at Glyndebourne. There remained a revival of *Arlecchino* at Edinburgh Festival, a revival of *Il Barbiere* in the summer of 1961, then in 1962 we recorded it for the HMV Angel label. The record company insisted on using Victoria de los Angeles and Luigi Alva instead of Alberta Valentini and Juan Oncina. The first of these changes was understandable. Valentini was young and inexperienced, but the loss of Juan cast a shadow over it for Sesto and me. It was like the beginning of the break-up of a football team – except that none of us in football terms was more than about twenty-eight. At forty-two a singer should have years of good vocal life ahead.

Luigi was a most friendly, co-operative colleague and both he and Victoria were at the height of their powers. The recording remained on the catalogue for many years and is still played occasionally on the air. When it was over I'd no idea that I'd never sing at Glyndebourne again. As a freelance you never know these things. You get offers, you accept them and hope to be asked back. If you're not – well . . .

It was inevitable that Glyndebourne would have to say goodbye to some of us. The essence of festival opera is change of cast and discovering young singers of promise. My career there spanned thirteen years and very few people have been as lucky as that. I had received from Carl Ebert a sort of extended post-graduate course in operatic acting, I'd worked with his son Peter who, in his less demonstrative way was a thoughtful and imaginative director, and I'd enjoyed the help and encouragement of Vittorio Gui as well as his invitations to sing in Italy.

I'd also been privileged to enjoy the friendship of John and Audrey Christie. The romantic story of the wealthy, aristocratic eccentric landowner who wore shapeless canvas suits and tennis shoes and looked like a sharp and intelligent John Bull with massive brow and chin and shrewd blue eyes twinkling through gold-rimmed spectacles, and who married the beautiful and equally aristocratic opera singer Audrey Mildmay is well known to opera lovers the world over. Nevertheless, when a man builds an opera house in his garden for his wife, has the vision to engage Fritz Busch and Carl Ebert to watch over its artistic development, and when that wife, having enchanted the early audiences, stands aside and helps to make it a house of

165

international standard and reputation, there are going to be beneficiaries other than a grateful public. I was one of them and am proud still to be thought of as a friend and welcome guest whenever I go there. John's son George and his wife, Mary have maintained the atmosphere of hospitality and the tradition of excellence which, in such a changing world, is an admirable achievement.

I've already mentioned briefly Moran Caplat who, at the time of writing, has just retired as general administrator. It would be easy to underestimate his influence and control of affairs because of an outward impression of the light touch and a tendency to remain in the background. But a glance at the formidable personalities he had to deal with during the thirty odd years he was responsible for the administration of this world famous artistic enterprise speaks for itself. Like many singers I can count this bearded ex-naval officer and actor with his cherubic countenance and quiet humour among my oldest friends – not every boss can say that about the people who worked for them.

If I'd known I was giving my last performance one other person I, or anyone else singing at Glyndebourne would have wanted to thank publicly was Moran's assistant, Janet Moores, daughter of the proprietor of Ringmer's grocer's shop and a tower of strength. This tall, red haired girl took to the rarefied amosphere of opera as if she'd been trained to it. She was a confidante and a source of information. Nothing was too much trouble and thank goodness even in retirement she's still got a part-time job there – a kind, familiar face that makes my last performance seem so much more recent than it actually was.

*   *   *

There had been a great deal of talk at the 1960 Edinburgh Festival – my last of those for a long time – of an opera house for Scotland's capital city. I got fairly hefty press coverage for suggesting that such a project would be putting the cart before the horse. What Scotland wanted first, I suggested, was an opera company of such a standard that the public would soon demand a suitable house for it. I'm not a one for making public pronouncements but this one came to fruition much sooner than many of us had dared to hope – no doubt because many folk in the arts in Scotland felt exactly the same.

I suppose 1960 would have been an ideal time to capitalise on my Glyndebourne publicity and develop that side of my career. With hindsight I'd have needed to change my agent from a theatrical one with a penchant for comedians to one in the musical field. I didn't because I knew that for my type of voice and the parts I played any chance of a bigger career inevitably lay abroad and we've been through all that already.

So after those Sadlers Wells Cinderellas I went off to do a more down to earth pantomime – *Babes in the Wood* at the Leeds Empire sharing the top of the bill with Nat Jackley, one of the great visual comedians whose drill routine with his troupe of assistants was a classic. He could move around the stage in jerky eccentric rhythm as if he hadn't a bone in his body. I was in Leeds for nine weeks living in a rather run-down hotel and spent Christmas Day wandering disconsolately through a deserted city looking a trifle wistfully through lighted windows at happy family scenes – knowing that Pat was battling alone to entertain two tiny children at home. It was all rather Dickensian.

Why on earth did I do it? There was nothing else on offer and it was the best paid job I'd ever had. It was also the first time I'd been billed 'above the title', as they say, since *Fanny*. But I had been very ill-advised. Anyone coming to a provincial pantomime in a star spot (I was the Sheriff of Nottingham) was expected to bring some comic material – or an act. I was sent a basic script and learned it – all I had by way of an act was *Mud*. I ought to have known, but that was one of the penalties of working in so (I nearly said too) many fields.

Nat took pity on me and allowed me to 'feed' him in one or two scenes as well as reading out the post cards asking us to greet the parties in the audience. One night he handed me one which said 'We'll all be in the dress circle and in the middle will be Mrs Higgins who is only four feet ten. Ask her to stand up and she'll say "I am standing up."' Nat had gone to the trouble of asking the electrician to turn one of the spotlights round so that it could pick up the front row of the circle. Out I went, greeted the party and asked Mrs Higgins to stand up. The spotlight came on and hovered uncertainly along the row of people, none of whom reacted in any way. 'Come on, Mrs Higgins,' I pleaded. Nothing, but an uneasy stir of embarrassment from everyone else. 'Oh well,' I said lamely, 'what about the party from Yeadon?'

When I got off, Nat was standing in the wings wringing his hands. 'I'm terribly sorry, Ian, I gave you the wrong card. They're coming *next* Thursday.' By the end of the run I was doing a little more to jusify my salary, but it was one of the very few engagements that I really hated from start to finish.

Almost before the curtain was down on the last performance workmen moved in to demolish the theatre. Quite a few people staged a sit-in as a protest. 'Pity they didn't sit there more often in the past,' observed the manager lugubriously, 'then we might have had a dog's chance of saving it.'

Two nice things happened while I was in Leeds – the nearest I ever got to a pop disc was released and the titles found their way into my entry in the *Classical* record catalogue. Side by side with Handel's *Sosarme, Arlecchino, Le Nozze di Figaro, The Mikado* and *Iolanthe* were *In other Words* (a George Robey song) and *I Can't Do My Bally Bottom Button Up*.

The other was a telegram from Arthur Lucas – secretary of the Stage Golfing Society – telling me that I'd been elected their captain for 1961. I'd really taken John Partridge's advice to heart and played for the stage team whenever possible. The matches were the most congenial therapy ever prescribed and the treatment took me to courses all round London. No need to be a good golfer for every contest was played on handicap. Kenneth Horne, Richard Murdoch, Robertson ('Bunny') Hare, Jeremy Hawke, Michael Medwin, Kenneth More, Garry Marsh, Gerald Case, Sean Connery, Bruce Forsyth, Eric Sykes and the late Sir Stanley Baker were the sort of names available to Arthur Lucas or his worthy successor Frederick Bradshaw when selecting a jolly crew to sally forth for Walton Heath and do battle with the Bar Golfing Society – a battle of words as well as golf shots – on a June Sunday. We played the County Cricketers (and Brian Close would come all the way from Yorkshire for the day), Lloyds, the Stock Exchange, the Vaudeville Golfing Society (our colleagues from the world of music hall and pantomime), the Civil Engineering Contractors who arrived in Rolls Royces, Range Rovers or helicopters, and various clubs like Wentworth and Sudbrook Park, Richmond. Richmond has been our tolerant host for a great many years. Mind you, we are paying guests.

Pat became something of a golfing widow, more than once, on my suggestion, pursuing us in her own car and providing a 'gallery' of a loaded push-chair.

In those happy days we had a club room and a billiard table on upper floors of the Salisbury – a famous actors' pub in St Martin's Lane. A simple lunch and good company was on offer every weekday and a lunch regular was Peter Saunders – the 'Mousetrap Man'. That cheerful spot is no more, nor is the annual function which filled all captains and presidents of the society with apprehension, the dinner in November at the Savoy Hotel, attended by approximately five hundred members and their guests – a stag party with four speeches and a cabaret. The dinner enjoyed a reputation for good and witty speeches and the committee, regrettably, selected the captain and the president more for their ability to give a good performance in this department than on the golf course for the good reason that, after the subscriptions, a successful dinner was our only source of revenue.

The list of guest speakers included the Duke of Edinburgh, Anthony Eden when Prime Minister, Reginald Maudling when Chancellor, Edward Heath when Leader of the Oppositiion, Douglas Fairbanks Junior and Bob Hope.

Most people imagine that a theatrical stag party could be no more than a festival of blue jokes. No one would deny that the humour was intermittently robust, but a showbusiness audience expected better of this dinner than unrelieved schoolboy vulgarity.

'Bunny' Hare as President: 'I played against the President of Wentworth and after a ding dong struggle I finally had to admit defeat – on the tenth green. They call that course the Burmah Road. It may be all right for the Burmese, but I come from Tooting!'

G. D. ('Khaki') Roberts Q. C. (a prosecutor at the Nuremberg War Trials): 'The Bar and the Stage have this in common, we take our job very seriously, ourselves never.'

Naunton Wayne: 'This is a very precarious profession. Take me. Two weeks ago an uncle died and left me twenty thousand;

last week an old aunt died and left me ten thousand; this week – nothing!'

Kenneth Horne proposing the toast 'Our Guests': 'And I know you'd all want me to welcome on your behalf that great old friend of the Stage Golfing Society, Walter Birch. (Applause). Well, that just shows the sort of people you are because there's no such person!'

Lord Burghley (later 6th Marquess of Exeter): 'A friend of mine at university received a sharp letter from his tailor demanding payment of an outstanding bill. He wrote back. "I have today received your communication and would inform you that I have a way of settling accounts. As they come in I put them in a drawer. On the first of each month I take them out of the drawer, shuffle them and pay the top three. Any more letters from you couched in similar terms and you won't even be in the bloody shuffle." '

One of the great secrets of after-dinner speaking is to pay the audience the compliment of having done some homework specially for the occasion, as opposed to trotting out a set speech that has stood the test of time. After a few touches of originality it is usually safe to rely on any sure-fire gags you're lucky enough to have gathered into your repertoire over the years.

Having said that, inspiration can be alarmingly elusive. It certainly was prior to the dinner when I had to be on my feet as captain. I had to pay some tribute to the man who would be proposing the health of the Society, the Welsh golfer Dai Rees, who had performed the rare feat of captaining a British Ryder Cup Team to victory. I cudgelled my brains to depressingly little effect. At such moments the *Oxford Dictionary of Quotations* can sometimes get one out of the mulligatawny. No use looking up Dai, so what about die? There it was, staring me in the face from *Henry V*.

'There can be little doubt, gentlemen, that when the American team made their way to the notice board to discover their British opponents, a line from *Henry V* was ringing doom laden in their ears: 'If we are marked to Dai we are enow to do our country loss.' The laughter and applause was out of all proportion to the effort involved. For me it was a case of 'saved by the Bard'.

Chapter 17

The word impresario crops up frequently in this book and its meaning is stretched by the English beginning rather than the Italian end. A dictionary will tell you it means the manager of an opera company and originates from an Italian word meaning enterprise. In my mind an impresario is someone who is impressed by a talent and prepared to back his judgment by presenting that talent be it a playwright, a ballet company or a comedian to the public.

I'd briefly met Charles Ross some time in the 1950s when he and I had played a villain and a monk in an episode of *William Tell*, an ITV series that attempted to follow *Robin Hood*. Charles had since abandoned acting to become a producer – or impresario – and rang me one day asking if I'd ever considered doing a one man show. It wasn't something I'd thought about, and my first reaction was that I couldn't possibly sustain an evening on my own. One man shows were for gigantic talents like Noel Coward, Victor Borge or Joyce Grenfell. As a boy I'd been taken to see another who did it with less humour and more drama, Ruth Draper.

'All right,' said Charles when I paraded my objections, 'what about a four handed musical revue?' I couldn't argue against that and a few nights later Pat and I were at the Blue Angel – our first visit to a night club in thirteen years of married life. To our astonishment Pat's aunt Nancie and her son who live in Scotland were at a nearby table. 'Lucky you're with the right girl, Ian,' she said with a laugh. She had a point. One would not expect a clandestine assignation at the Blue Angel to be observed by a middle aged aunt from Fife.

We'd come to see a cabaret act that was drawing the town. Written by Bryan Blackburn and Peter Reeves, it was based on the simple idea of updating the words of medleys of popular songs. Bryan had temporarily added the role of performer to his script-writing talent and teamed up with Peter whose musical knowledge gave a further witty edge to the act. Charles wanted me to join them and former opera singer Rose Hill (now a stalwart of the Royal Shakespeare Company) – in a musical revue *4 to the Bar*.

I enjoyed Bryan and Peter's act from start to finish and told Charles to count me in on the project. After a careful search we found the right accompaniment, Anthony Bowles who would arrange the music and play the piano plus John Jobson on double bass, both of them up on the stage with the rest of us.

I was to write my own linking material and Rose would be introduced after the interval to lift the proceedings with one or two Edwardian ballads like *Mother Knows* and a hilarious number with a recorder. We got permission from Jo Horovitz to use the Bournvita commercials in the style of Bach, Mozart and Verdi which I'd first performed with April Cantelo in a Hoffnung Concert.

Three numbers by Vivian Ellis (words and music) set the seal on my having a happy evening. *Uproarious Devon* and *I Remember Venice* – both very funny – and *When a Woman Smiles* – one of the rew romantic numbers I've ever dared to sing in public. Vivian's talent for humorous lyrics to match his music is unique. *Uproarious Devon* even went well in Exeter:

> 'So come to the Golden West,
> But bring an extra vest.
> You can see Clovelly much better on your telly
> And you won't feel so depressed.'

The search for a West End theatre was a long one. We went on tour and were briefly at London's Arts Theatre Club, before going to Dublin and the old, friendly Olympia Theatre, by far our biggest venue for this intimate entertainment.

Until a certain moment arrived on that Dublin first night I hadn't really thought about its potential danger. By then it was too late. After Bryan and Peter's first triumphant assault on the audience it was my job to change the mood. Alone on the stage in the light of a single spot I sang unaccompanied the Irish folk song *She moved through the Fair* – with my idea of an Irish accent.

The next day I was having lunch in Jury's Hotel when two hands were put over my eyes and a richly Irish voice I knew well said, 'It's bad enough havin' a Scots bass baritone singin' an Irish tenor song in Dublin – but gettin' good notices for it, that's disgraceful. What are you drinkin'?'

It was dear Dermot Troy, a young Irish tenor of great promise with whom I'd sung at Glyndebourne and who died only a year or two later.

Eventually we got into the Criterion Theatre, but not before we'd been back to Dublin for another week, when again a warm public took us to their hearts. The only hazard about playing a successful show there is the need to fight your way through the chairs in the wings where the priests sit for an evening's innocent enjoyment out of the sight of their parishioners.

After the last night we were invited to the house of an Abbey Theatre actor for a party. It wasn't far and I decided to walk through a typical Celtic wetting drizzle that made the big square by Trinity College gleam in the light of the street lamps. Ahead of me was staggering a man whose party must have started much earlier in the day. He swayed from side to side apparently relying on support from the large brolly he was grasping with both hands.

Without warning he veered into the road his pace quickening in an effort to retain his balance. The taxi driver had no chance, his locked wheels sliding on the wet road. The reveller shot into the air and descended in a grisly parabola, crashing in a heap several yards ahead of the cab, which just managed to stop before hitting the crumpled body a second time.

I seemed to see it all in slow motion and for the first time experienced the sensation of the phrase 'rooted to the spot'. The driver got down from the cab, his face in the dim light the colour of ashes. We both approached the motionless figure lying in the road. Before we reached him he sat up, shook his head, staggered to his feet and, holding out a mass of black fabric pierced by mangled spokes muttered 'Ye've bust me fockin' umbrella.' Before we could say anything he'd staggered off into the night. The driver lit a cigarette with shaking hands and so did I, then he shrugged and returned to his cab. He didn't even ask for my name and address.

At the Criterion we struck the worst theatrical season in years; shows closed all round us yet we managed to run for six months which in the circumstances was like going round St

Andrews in seventy-seven in a force ten gale and a thunder-storm.

The first act finale was a send up pop sequence by 'Rich Clifford and the Shudders'. No prizes for guessing whom Bryan and Peter were gently ribbing. I interrupted them as an Indian pop singer wearing a turban and trying to slip a plug for his carpet selling business into the act.

One night when the curtain rose for the opening of the show which I did on my own for some twenty minutes, I noticed in the middle of the front row a large Indian gentleman wearing a turban. A butterfly stirred in the pit of my stomach.

All through part one he was enjoying himself and as he laughed his gold fillings twinkled merrily. But how would he take my Indian impression? Racist jokes were not such a controversial issue in 1962, but I had no wish to cause offence to anyone. To my relief when I uttered my first line in the sketch, 'Oh good evening all you beautiful, loverlee people!' he once more displayed his lavish dental work.

The following evening Bryan and Peter came to my dressing room to tell me that when they got to the Blue Angel, where they were still doing cabaret after the show, the previous night the same Indian gentleman was ensconced at a table near the front. After their act he'd sought them out.

'Where is your friend?' he asked.

'Oh, he doesn't do cabaret, he goes home to bed.'

'What a pity, I wanted to congratulate him.'

'Don't worry, we'll pass on the message,' said Bryan,

'Good, and please tell him that I particularly liked the scene where he tried to sell the carpets – it was a perfect take-off of the rapacious commercialism of the Pakistani!'

We did one Sunday performance of *4 to the Bar* but it wasn't at the Criterion. We made a minor bit of theatrical history by taking the show, costumes and all to Wandsworth Gaol. There's nothing unusual about entertainment in prisons, but we were the first West End Show to penetrate the huge forbidding doors. Behind them was an audience that was not only enthusiastic but far quicker on the draw than some of those we'd encountered in Piccadilly Circus.

I got the biggest laugh – not only of the evening, but of my career, and I stood there wondering what on earth I'd said to provoke it. It came in the early stages of a story I was telling about my Italian debut at Parma. 'I went to Parma once,' I said. 'Oh, not to sample the cheese or to sniff the violets.' That was it. They laughed uproariously and went on laughing, then they applauded and stamped the floor with their feet. I stood wondering what I'd said. I even stole a glance over my shoulder in case something was happening behind me. Nothing. At last I was able to go on, trying to look as if I'd intended all along to cause such hilarity. I know now why they were laughing and, if you're familiar with prison slang, probably you do too.

The following evening when Bryan and Peter arrived at the back door of the Blue Angel a man detached himself from the shadows and made that international signal – 'psssst'. Thinking it was a 'touch' the boys tried to hurry past.

'Just a moment, guv, I've got a message for yer – from the lads.'

'What lads?'

'The lads inside. They wanted to let yer know how much they enjoyed the show. You see I got me release this mornin'.' It was a disconcerting example of the efficiency of the underworld grapevine that he knew where to find them late at night in a back street. Still, we appreciated the message, as we did the copy of the prison house magazine which was forwarded later with a most discerning notice and some lifelike cartoons of the cast despite the pitch darkness that enveloped the auditorium the whole time we were in view. We were all left with the impression that some of the brain power 'inside' could have been brilliantly successful on the right side of the law.

Noel Coward was kind enough to come round after a performance and tell us all how much he'd enjoyed it. He added that I had good command of an audience. I was greatly encouraged by this word of praise from 'the master', as he was affectionately known by theatre people, and it made me think that as I'd talked and sung my way through the first twenty minutes of a West End show on my own perhaps a one man entertainment was something I ought to try to put together.

With opera and classical songs as ingredients it could hardly be a commercial proposition, but maybe a niche for it could be found at the lighter end of the concert market.

My collaborator and companion in this enterprise for more

than fifteen years was David Money whom I'd first met, shortly after Pat and I were married, at a party given by Bruce Boyce with whom I'd sung both at the Cambridge Theatre and in *The Night Bell.*

'This is David Money,' he said, 'who's related to half England and knows the other half.' It was only a partial exaggeration. The son of General, he'd been at Charterhouse some years earlier than me and, after studying at the Royal College of Music and privately with George Reeves and Louis Kentner he'd become an accompanist, a teacher and a music critic.

A congenial companion, it is amazing how at any party or gathering in any corner of the United Kingdom he can find someone who knows either a friend or a relative. So often in the midst of a conversation he will, with a diffident shrug, declare that so and so was his second cousin or the son of a great friend of his father. All this is helped by an uncanny gift for never forgetting names or faces, which is in contrast to my distressing habit of failing to recognise people who've lived in our road for twenty years.

My first steps towards such an entertainment were hesitant. If I was offered a recital I would send a list of songs to the music club or other concert giver and introduce them on the platform off the cuff. I did this in the Scottish lowland town of Biggar where the enterprising and likeable Tom Laing, who ran a recording company in Edinburgh called Waverley, offered to record the concert. I was only too glad to have his help and he issued an LP with my extempore comments between the songs. The audience included sheep farmers and a number of retired ministers from a nearby home; the only thing that left something to be desired was the piano.

'We got it for forty pounds and spent another forty pounds on it, but since then John Ogden's been here and beaten the hell out of it,' the club chairman informed me on arrival.

Not only was the record well received, a music critic from an Edinburgh evening paper happened to be on holiday in the neighbourhood and wrote a glowing account of the concert. With all this encouragement David and I set to work to make the evening less extempore. I wrote a script including some of the stories and songs I'd used in *4 to the Bar.* We decided that most of the linking material must be light hearted and some of it, hopefully, downright funny. Nevertheless the singing would have to be the best that I could achieve. To maintain an element of surprise I did not disclose the items in a printed programme.

When the Cheltenham Town Hall reopened in the early 1960s resplendently refurbished, David and I were among the first artists to appear there and give our more polished offering one of its early airings. After that the two of us must have travelled scores of thousands of miles – mostly by car – to venues as widely spread as Inverness, Elgin, Aberdeen, the Channel Islands (by air), Exeter, Ipswich, Birmingham, Liverpool and Brighton. As well as most of the major cities there were literally hundreds of smaller places where either the local music club was our host or we were touring sponsored by the Arts Council. We appeared twice at London's Queen Elizabeth Hall and HMV recorded the first visit giving us for a time an album to sell at other concerts.

Music Clubs have tended to book *An Evening with Ian Wallace*, as it's usually described, to give a serious season of music a light hearted beginning or end, and another source of engagements has been the arts festivals that have continued to proliferate since 1951. In the last year or two we've added the end of one or two piers in the summer on a Sunday night to the list of customers.

At one time there were three completely different versions of the show so that we didn't repeat ourselves on return dates and a further check on the mileage can be gathered from the fact that getting to locations took the best years of the life of one Daimler Sovereign and two 4.2 Jaguars. I've gone a little down market since then!

David was the perfect partner for the long journeys, ready to talk or to sit silent beside me, sensing the varying moods to which all solo artists are a prey on performance days – particularly in my case when new songs or stories were being introduced for the first time or the memory test loomed of two different versions of the show on successive nights. In rehearsal he was a wise music counsellor and suggested all sorts of improvements to my renditions. These rehearsals mostly took place at my home – Pat and I had moved a mere four hundred yards from my mother's house to our own when John completed our family in 1960 – and invariably afterwards we adjourned to a couple of chairs adjacent to the drink cupboard for refreshment and relaxed conversation. The secret of any performance's success is in the preparation and David was a visitor to our house for that purpose almost every other day for a great many years.

On the platform he contributed more than just accompanying the songs with style and sympathy: he listened to the jokes and laughed at every performance as if he'd never heard them before – an invaluable asset to the success of the evening; and at any social gathering afterwards – whether in a village hall or one of our charity galas in a stately home – his mastery of the art of conversation took some of the weight of such occasions from my rather weary shoulders. He must have been exhausted too, coping with Handel, Rossini and all stations to Flanders and Swann.

I use the past tense about my old friend only because most artistic associations have a limited life and ours was no exception. I felt I needed a fresh approach and with great reluctance told David a part of this meant experimenting with a new collaborator. He accepted it with grace and understanding, as I knew he would. There often comes a time when artists feel a need to go their separate ways, Flanders and Swann in later years and Frank Muir and Denis Norden are examples of the same sort of decision, and of the continuance of friendship in their wake.

Now three accompanists share performances of the show: Keith Swallow, an excellent solo pianist as well as an accompanist much in demand who used to play for the late Owen Brannigan; Mary Nash, one of the best opera repetiteurs in the country, a niece of Heddle Nash, the great lyric tenor and a cousin of his son, baritone John Heddle Nash; and Colin Brown who plays for me in Scotland when he can be spared from his duties as head of music at a Stirling school.

The subtle differences in interpretation of the same songs by these three excellent musicians helps to keep me on my toes as I get older – and because they are all younger than me they keep me in contact with younger age groups in the audience. I hope none of them will have to tap me on the shoulder one day and tell me to pack it in. That's my job and I'll try and quit before my vocal cords have to attempt the no longer possible.

It's disappointing – from my point of view as well as yours – that this part of my career has not provided, so far, any chapter of accidents, humorous or otherwise worthy of mention, even though much of the show's dialogue describes various mishaps in my opera career and elsewhere. We've always managed to turn up at the right time at the right place with the right music and to get through the evening – two hours including an interval of about twenty minutes – without falling off the platform, forgetting more than the odd line, having a piano leg crunch through a flimsy board, or getting the bird. There's always a first time and maybe between writing this and publication I shall have been run over by a concert grand with brake failure on a raked stage, left my music two hundred miles away, arrived at Newcastle-under-Lyme instead of -upon-Tyne or at an empty hall on the wrong night.

In the last twenty years I've probably averaged around twenty-five performances per annum which means roughly five hundred, mostly in different places though I've been back to some as many as four times. My 'props' never vary: a decent piano, preferably a concert grand (I'm a perpetual optimist), tuned on the day, a comfortable chair for when I'm talking to the audience, a small table to carry a jug of water and a glass, and lastly some sort of lighting that enables the customers to see me. It helps any artist to establish a rapport with the audience and I confess that I'm happiest doing the show in theatres where the lighting on stage and the auditorium in darkness makes it more of a show than a concert. In the last year or two I've found myself in the vast Roman Catholic Cathedral in Bristol and a church near Teignmouth in Devon. That's perhaps the best answer to the reverend gentleman the other day who came to see me about doing it for charity. 'This may be embarrassing, Mr Wallace,' he said, 'but is it dirty?' Nevertheless there are one or two sentences that are better expunged from the text on hallowed ground.

Chapter 18

When the Angel recording of *Il Barbiere* was issued in 1963 the press used words like definitive, brilliant, sparkling – which was a good way to bring down the curtain on the international parts of my operatic career (except for a couple of Austrian curtain calls). As with Glyndebourne, of course, you only find out it was the end years later!

Those curtain calls were invitations from Maestro Gui to sing at the Bregenz Festival in the summers of 1964 and '65. The little town on the shores of Lake Constance stages a summer festival with a huge auditorium on the shore and a stage on the lake itself which ballet dancers or operetta performers reach by boat. The opera was in a theatre on dry land. The first visit was a reunion with Sesto and Juan for *La Cenerentola*. Part of the time Pat, Rosie and John, now six and four, came out to join me in the little gasthof near the theatre where I was staying. Returning to our bedroom after a rehearsal I found Pat struggling to remove her wedding ring.

'Hallo, have you decided you've had enough?' I enquired.

'No, you idiot,' was the fond reply, 'but my hands are swelling and I'd better get it off while I can.'

The poor girl had German measles. It was a mild attack, and as all the other women in the gasthof looked beyond the age of pregnancy we just pretended all was well. Our marvellous mother's help, Carol Bell, looked after the children till Pat felt better in a few days. This was an unremarkable domestic incident, but perhaps highlights the problems of families on tour, as opposed to being on holiday. A hint of the illness to the opera company or the hotel management and all sorts of complications could have arisen.

The opera was sponsored by Austrian Television who transmitted one performance live and recorded it for later transmission to many other countries on the Eurovision link. The next year it was *Il Barbiere* again, which also got wide TV coverage.

This time I was on my own in Bregenz and felt again the great loneliness I always experienced working abroad.

I walked along the lakeside or drove the little car I'd hired up the hairpin bended roads to the top of one of the Vorarlberg mountains to eat my picnic lunch where the sunlight was so strong that I could read the airmail *Daily Telegraph* without my glasses. The view, whether by the lake or in the Alps, was superb, yet I yearned for company and even began considering whether I wasn't tired of being so much on the move. Perhaps the time had come to abandon my career altogether and do something entirely different, but – and I can recall the very moment of the decision – in a lakeside park with an orchestra playing in the open air and an advertisement for a show jumping (springen) championship on a placard beside the path – I said to myself that I'd be a fool to entertain any idea of leaving show business and an even bigger one to swop performing for management, an idea with which I'd been toying for a mile or two.

If I could reach that conclusion when lonely, depressed and far from home there was no point in taking the matter any further. If I'd known then that in the next two decades I'd travel at least half a million miles by car, train, boat and plane in pursuit of opera, all manner of concerts over and above the one man show, broadcasts, TV appearances, lectures and speeches it might have taken me a little longer to make up my mind.

On that second visit to Bregenz I could look back on my usual crop of unlikely jobs – the part of Tanenui, the Tahitian first mate of a Pacific trading schooner skippered by Bill Kerr, the Australian actor-comedian, with Scots radio actor Duncan McIntyre in the engine room and Christina Gray, the girl who'd inherited the boat, on board to relieve monotony. It was a radio series called *Pride of the Pacific* by Rex Rienits. In each episode I had to sing a Tahitian song in Tahitian, and play the speaking part with my voice in my boots.

Bill Kerr, who provided so many laughs in *Hancock's Half Hour*, gave us many more during rehearsals. Indeed we were often hard put to it to pull ourselves together for the recording. Vernon Harris our producer was remarkably forbearing and forgave the moments when a normally dignified citizen like

Duncan McIntyre actually lay on the studio floor helpless with mirth after Bill had blown down the engine room voice pipe and asked for 'two more knots and a porridge sandwich, you Highland bastard!' None of which was in the script.

Bill had some difficulty with the names of our ports of call and one afternoon had wrestled with hilarious unsuccess to pronounce one of them each time it occurred in the script. The following morning there was no sign of him until he walked in an hour and a quarter late; holding out his arms to our long suffering producer he said, full of contrition, 'Vern, what can I say?'

Duncan McIntyre supplied the answer, 'Well, you can't say Nukualofa for a start!'

* * *

1964 was the year that the Tory Prime Minister Sir Alec Douglas-Home lost a General Election and Harold Wilson came to power with a majority of six. For the only time in my life I played a small part in the Conservative campaign which may have been enough to nudge Sir Alec so narrowly out of Number Ten.

The Central Office approached me some months before the Election about writing and making a record of light hearted songs to cheer Tory hearts and cause alarm and despondency in the Labour ranks. This arose because during the early 1960s I'd developed a sideline of appearing at private functions with a cabaret act which always included something I'd written specially for the occasion.

When I was engaged to appear at the Tory Winter Ball I sang my own version of a well known nursery song:

'Little man kneels at the foot of the bed
Quizzical smile and patrician head,
Hush, hush, whisper who dares
A Knight of the Thistle is saying his prayers.
If I open my fingers a little bit more
I can see Reggie Maudling keeping the score.
A vital election lies ahead
So I'll find a good book and I'll go to bed.
I'll shut my eyes and I'll curl up small

Till I can't see the Liberal Party at all.
Thank you, God, for Robin Day
And what was the other I had to say?
I've said bless Reggie, now who can it be?
It certainly isn't the TUC.

Hush, hush, whisper who dares
The favourite game in the City is bears.'

Next day, not only was it quoted in several papers but I was hauled in to do it on TV in an early evening show called *Tonight*, hence my call to Central Office.

I've always preferred to keep politics and my professional life separate, though with a childhood spent in a political atmosphere an interest in political events and even at one time thoughts of entering politics are natural enough. There are many artists who feel so strongly about achieving political objectives that they are happy to devote their talents to that end, others who have gifts and a relish for working in the field of satire, but I feel that I'm best suited to being a musical entertainer whose material is mostly escapist. In that case there's no point in dividing the audience down the middle rather in the way politically minded vicars do with their congregation by giving the impression that the only true Christians in it belong to the party of their choice.

Why in the face of all that I took on the job is easily explained. There were to be no artists' names on the label, it was the first time I'd been asked to write lyrics for anyone and when your father has fought four General Elections, the chance to take part in one yourself is hard to resist.

I am no composer, so I adopted shamelessly Bryan Blackburn and Peter Reeves' technique of putting new words to old tunes. *Phil the Fluter's Ball* became *One Man Band*:

'Have you heard of Harold Wilson?
He's the one that waves the stick,
And all the others follow him,
He's beating like old Nick.
If you look round the orchestra
It isn't hard to tell,

The trumpet and the saxophone
He's playing them as well!' etc.

In those days the Liberal Party leader was Jo Grimond, which made an old plantation song seem appropriate.

'Gone are the days when my heart was young and gay,
Gone are the hopes that, like Gladstone, I'll hold sway.
Two armies march but to both of them I'm foe.
I hear the Liberal fainthearts murmur poor old Jo.'

I had qualms about that one as I like and admire Jo – to say nothing of the fact that he is Pat's aunt Nancie's brother. Typically, neither bears me any grudge, though they can't have enjoyed it much at the time.

250,000 copies were made on the sort of lightweight plastic the *Reader's Digest* use to advertise their albums of LPs and with a true blue label bearing the title *Songs for Swinging Voters* it was pushed through letter boxes. I quickly realised the consequences of entering the political arena. Though the record was anonymous the press release named me as the author and solo singer. The abusive and in some cases obscene letters I received from political opponents didn't reach flood proportions, but were enough to warn me that I would either have to become a much more committed political animal – or resume my former policy of keeping politics out of my professional life.

The press publicity included a cartoon in the London Evening Standard which was scarcely flattering to Sir Alec and members of his cabinet, portraying them as a pop group, and elsewhere the comment was either enthusiastic or savagely critical, as it was bound to be. When one or two subsequent invitations to do similar things arrived I always found an excuse for a polite refusal.

There was a much less controversial end to 1964 when I became a member of the honourable company of Toads, joining Mole, Badger and Ratty in the persons of Richard Goolden, John Justin and Martin Friend at the Queen's Theatre for a Christmas season of *Toad of Toad Hall*. Leo McKern, who'd played Toad on a previous occasion, once remarked that it was a more strenuous part than King Lear. Not having received any offers to play that tragic role I can't comment – but Toad twice through in a day is demanding. The wretched fellow is so bumptious and extrovert that playing him is the equivalent of driving a police car flat out with the siren wailing, blue light flashing, headlights undipped down a one-way street against on-coming traffic.

Even so it was impossible to make any impression on the young audience when Mole was on the stage. That crafty old animal who, alas, died last year at the age of eighty-six had a magic touch with children of all ages and because of it his fellow actors forgave some shameless upstaging which in any other circumstances would have earned him acid dressing room rebukes.

'Dicky' Goolden, then in his seventies, had a disconcerting habit of lying down in the wings for a little snooze between appearances. Until the rest of us became accustomed to finding his recumbent figure in dark corners we were apt to think he'd died; but, like Napoleon who used to refresh himself in mid battle by a ten minute sleep, he always awoke in time for his next encounter.

Chapter 19

What might be called my domestic opera career ended up in just the way I would have wanted. Three different companies in the second half of the trendy sixties gave me the chance to play roles in the buffo repertoire that had previously eluded me. The first was Leporello, the Don's servant in Mozart's *Don Giovanni*. I'd sung the minor role of Masetto in the opera, as already mentioned, nearly twenty years earlier at the Cambridge Theatre and at Parma in 1950. Now Scottish Opera, the company I'd always hoped would somehow arise, had been founded and become a going concern in record time under the administration of a fair haired young Englishman from Sadlers Wells called Peter Hemmings.

Very wisely he adopted the policy – fully supported by his

musical director, Alexander Gibson, and the board of management – that where a Scot was up to singing a role he or she would be invited to do so. Where this was not the case, someone from elsewhere in Britain or abroad would be preferred. Such a policy was bound to provoke controversy from time to time and be plagued by borderline cases, but it effectively prevented the company from being parochial in outlook and indeed gave it from the outset an international flavour and reputation.

The title role in *Don Giovanni* was sung by Peter van der Bilt from Holland, the production by Peter Ebert in a fascinating abstract set by Ralph Koltai was in English, and one critic was kind enough to say that it was incredible that this was my first Leporello. We played it in Edinburgh, Aberdeen and Glasgow and one moment from the first night in Glasgow remains with me.

In those days Scottish Opera had an excellent amateur chorus as opposed to the excellent professional one it has now. Of course it is in the nature of things that amateurs can be more relaxed on first nights than their professional counterparts whose reputation at such times is on the line.

There's a rustic scene in the first act where a group of peasants are celebrating the wedding of two of their number – Zerlina and Masetto. The Don and Leporello enter and the latter approaches a boy and girl. He distracts the boy's attention getting him to move away. He then puts his arm round the girl and pinches her bottom. She screams and the Don, tongue in cheek, rebukes his servant for unseemly behaviour.

On the first night – still very tense as it was early in the evening – I entered to see the girl standing on her own – no boy near her. Now without the build up of getting rid of the boy I knew that the pinch would look tasteless and contrived. She was standing, as instructed, with her back to the audience and when I got close to her, a hopeless look on my face, she smiled and said quietly, 'He's no here.' I could see that all too clearly. Then she added, 'He's got food poisoning.'

There was nothing for it. I pinched her and we got on with the opera.

After that performance there was a party at Robert Ponsonby's flat in Glasgow where he was presiding over the fortunes of the Scottish National Orchestra. It was an excellent affair and when it was over Michael Maurel (the Masetto) and I returned to Green's Hotel in Woodland's Terrace where we were both staying. It had been a frequent staging post for me since 1944, and would be still if Ronald Sinclair hadn't sold it to be converted to flats.

We neither of us were drunk, but Robert is a generous host. The hour was approximately one thirty in the morning and the hostelry was silent as the grave. My room key was lying on a table beside the locked reception office, Michael's was not. Mine was a single room with only the one bed. There was another entrance to reception. The counter where arriving guests signed the register was shut off from the inside when the office was closed by two folding glass windows.

'Wait here, Mike,' I said, disappearing into the dining room and returning with a fish knife from someone's breakfast table. I slipped it between the two windows and raised the little sneck (Scots word for bolt) that held them in position.

'Well done!' said Michael moving forward to climb into the office and retrieve his key.

'Oh no. I thought of the fish knife and what I start I finish.' (I did mention we'd had one or two). I climbed over the counter into the pitch dark office and the dim light in the hall did nothing to improve visibility. I felt my way round the wall looking for the light switch. At last I found it. When I depressed it no lights came on, but all hell was let loose. I'd switched on the fire alarm and in the dark I couldn't find where to put it off again.

To our amazement no one appeared – except the old porter who came down the stairs humming a merry tune.

'Oh it's you,' he exclaimed, 'I was shoe cleaning upstairs and when I heard the bell I thought I'd gone crackers.'

Obviously the other guests were either deaf or had been to the same sort of party we'd enjoyed.

The next year I sang Pistola in *Falstaff* – not one of the buffo parts I referred to at the start of this chapter – which gave me a chance to watch at close quarters the performance in the title role of Sir Geraint Evans. It proved what I'd always thought, that had he not been gifted with such a fine singing voice a distinguished career as an actor would have brought him equal success.

The Ford was the Australian baritone John Shaw, a huge, severe-looking man who was a fanatical golfer and an inveterate backer of horses. I had the pleasure of introducing him to a number of Scottish links including – on Derby Day – the Old Course at St Andrews. On our way from Edinburgh we had to stop at various betting shops to add to the substantial sums he had already wagered on Charlottown to win the big race.

We started our game late and after a typical Shaw round including some magnificent shots and others where a club hurled down the fairway in a rage had exceeded the distance of the ball, the only place open for lunch was the Victoria Cafe where nice waitresses of a certain age agreed to accept our late order for fish and chips and a transistor portable radio from the kitchen so that we could listen to the race.

'There's some delay,' said the commentator just as we were expecting to hear that they were under starter's orders. 'Yes, the farrier has been called so one of the runners must have cast a plate.' John stiffened. 'I can't quite see which it is but I'm pretty sure it's Charlottown.'

Chips flew in every direction as John's fist crashed on the table and his chair did a back somersault. He began to pace up and down the empty cafe with a face as black as his hair. Scared, elderly waitresses peered fearfully round the service door. After a great deal of fill-in commentary we heard the reassuring words,

'Everything seems to be sorted out and Charlottown is being led to the start . . . They're under orders – They're off!' As so often happens in a race commentary the winner wasn't mentioned for the first half of the race and poor John looked like a man waiting for the hangman. Goodness knows how much he had risked on that newly shod thoroughbred.

When Charlottown was first past the post he was beside himself with joy and whirled each of the waitresses in turn round the tables in a victory waltz, singing at the top of his considerable voice. Then we set off back to Edinburgh pausing only at the betting shops in Cupar and Cowdenbeath to relieve them of his winnings.

Between these two 'Scottish operas' Francis Essex, who'd become Programme Controller of Scottish Television (ITV), seized on me as about the only Scot he knew and offered me a fascinating job in an ingenious programme he'd devised entitled *The Man Behind the Star*. The stars included Bruce Forsyth, Andy Stewart, Roy Castle, Frankie Vaughan and Tony Hancock. Each did a one man show to a studio audience and on another day I interviewed them at length. The two programmes were cross cut so that their show was interspersed with parts of the interview to give added piquancy.

The interview with Tony Hancock was the most difficult. We had lunched in London to discuss it and though he was friendly and remembered me from broadcasts we had done together it was an uncomfortable hour and a half. On the day itself he was too tense to say a word to me before the recording, sitting mournfully alone in a corner of the canteen with a cup of coffee cold beside him and smoking endless cigarettes.

When the red light went on he was watchful and suspicious, assuming that look of baleful arrogance which was so funny on TV in the seedy East Cheam digs with Hattie Jacques and Sid James; only now he wasn't acting. Gradually he relaxed and when it was over he got up from his chair and hugged me.

'Oh, mate,' he said, 'you made it so easy.'

I didn't think I had. I'd asked some unavoidable questions about the decline of his career at that time. Perhaps because I was a fellow pro with my own feelings of insecurity I managed to find the right words. That interview came painfully back to me when I read of his lonely death in a hotel bedroom in Australia.

The Man Behind The Star was never shown outside Scotland, though Francis had high hopes that it would win a spot on the national network. Very soon afterwards a series with much the same format was made by a bigger company and shown throughout the country. There's a song in *Porgy and Bess* that has the line, 'No use complainin'.'

The Derby wasn't the only sporting event in 1966 which I associate with fanaticism on the part of a colleague. In late July I was appearing in a double bill at the Palace Theatre, Watford – a serious one act play by Friedrich Durrenmatt and an art nouveau musical by John Gould entitled *High Infidelity*. The Durrenmatt was called *Conversation at Night with a Despised Character* and has only two characters, a dissident professor in an unnamed East European country and the public execu-

189

tioner. The professor is alone in his flat when the man who has come to kill him enters rather clumsily through a window. Despite his errand he's a cheerful fellow prepared to indulge in a long philosophical discussion before dispatching his victim who has been expecting such a visit and is resigned to his fate.

The professor was played by André van Ghyseghem, a distinguished actor who, until we met, had no interest whatsoever in association football and at first found conversation about the World Cup which was being played in England something of a bore. There was a good deal of it between myself and others in the theatre who were keen fans. It was almost impossible to avoid the blanket coverage of the competition on TV with its late night recorded re-runs, and before long André became compulsively hooked.

By the time England reached the final with West Germany we had opened, and the evening after the semi-final he arrived at the theatre in despair.

'We're in the final and we'll miss it because of that bloody matinée!'

'No we won't, André,' I told him. 'I've got a portable TV – I'll bring it and we'll get here early, have a sandwich lunch, get dressed and made up, then we can watch the match and go straight on stage at five o'clock. The match will be over by a quarter to.'

The two teams were so evenly matched that it was almost more than we could bear to watch as Bobby Charlton, his brother Jackie, the magnificently toothless Nobby Stiles, the immaculate Bobby Moore, the speedy Geoff Hurst, the magical creator of space Martin Peters, and the rest of that gallant company did battle. At half time we could have torn the shrewd and perceptive Danny Blanchflower limb from limb for his pessimism about the outcome. Maybe as a great Northern Ireland player he felt detached, but as a Londoner who supports England – except when they're playing Scotland – I was incensed, feeling that any words which might carry to the England dressing room should sound a note of rallying encouragement.

Just as we were preparing to celebrate a famous one nil victory Weber equalised for West Germany in the last minute – putting the match into extra time.

'Cancel the matinée!' wailed André. But instead we had to

leave that epic half hour that brought Geoff Hurst immortality for the first hat trick in a World Cup Final and an England victory of 4–2. We faced a very sparse audience, mostly old age pensioners. At the end of the play the curtain came down as the professor stood ready for the downward thrust of my lethal looking dagger.

We had barely disappeared from the public view and the polite scatter of applause hardly begun before we abandoned all professionalism and any hope of convincing the audience that André was about to die by drowning the applause with a shout of 'What happened?' As that small audience thought about a cup of tea to while away the interval they must have clearly heard whoops of delight from the two actors who had tried to create suspense and a sombre atmosphere for the previous three quarters of an hour.

Perhaps that's why when the play was done later on BBC TV they passed over André and me in favour of a couple of struggling performers called Olivier and Gielgud.

*   *   *

The two other buffo roles I'd never had a chance to play were both in Donizetti operas, the title role in *Don Pasquale* and Dulcamara, the quack doctor in *L'elisir d'amore* – 'The Elixir of Love'.

They both turned up within year of each other. The Welsh National Opera had originally mounted a production of *Don Pasquale* for Geraint Evans and I had the tricky job of taking over the role for a revival. At the first rehearsal I met Bill Smith, the elderly Welsh business man whose love of opera and dogged determination had been the driving force behind giving Wales an opera company of which the nation in justifiably proud. He shook hands and said,

'My God, you're well preserved!' I was forty-eight at the time, so it was a somewhat startling remark. It must have been widely quoted in Cardiff because on the first night when Pasquale, preparing to meet the young girl he hopes to marry looks in the mirror and sings 'I am pretty well preserved', the laughter in the New Theatre was out of all proportion to the situation in the opera.

The first day that we rehearsed *Don Pasquale* in the theatre itself as opposed to a rehearsal room elsewhere in the city I had an eerie moment. The opera that evening was *La Bohème* and as soon as we'd finished our work on the stage in the late afternoon the crew had to set up the scenery for the first act of Puccini's famous opera. I left the theatre and went over to the nearby hotel where I was staying. When, an hour later, I looked for my vocal score to check one or two lines, I realised that I'd left it somewhere in the theatre. I went to look for it and my search took me across the stage which was almost dark. As my eyes became accustomed to the gloom it was as if I'd been disconcertingly transported back twenty years to my opera debut. I was at the Cambridge Theatre with everything exactly as it was on June 12th 1946 when I'd come through the attic door and thrown my hat in the air. I snapped on my cigarette lighter and the completely familiar surroundings seen again after so long had me near to tears.

I left the stage and examined the back of one of the canvas flats – sure enough it was still possible to see stencilled on the back the words New London Opera Company. How wise the Welsh were to have bought our old sets. They were the work of Alexandre Benois, Diaghilev's great designer.

Although I've had my fair share of coughs and colds which have meant occasionally having to miss a performance, I've been lucky many times that the worst day or two of these common maladies have struck when I didn't have to appear. I've been even luckier over first nights. I was chesty and croaky on the first night of *Don Giovanni* at my first Edinburgh Festival, but that was the only time I had a health problem on that all important opening performance until, a few days before the Pasquale in which I was strongly supported by Stuart Burrows, Michael Maurel and the Australian soprano Jenifer Eddy, I contracted a bad throat infection.

'I've just got to be able to sing on Thursday,' I told the doctor.

'OK,' he said, writing the prescription, 'you will.'

I did, but it was an evening when I felt curiously detached from what was going on round me. For such an important role first time through in public I had been strangely calm beforehand. Once or twice in the first act I was not quite in time with the music yet I was unworried by it – almost euphoric. There was nothing euphoric about the notices. One esteemed critic said that I seemed to be giving a private performance for my own benefit!

'What on earth did you give me?' I asked the doctor.

'An antibiotic, of course,' he replied.

'Well I gave a lousy performance.'

'You said you had to sing and you did, but I feared that you mightn't be too good – antibiotics are funny things and sometimes they can have a depressive effect.'

There was a second series of performances later in the year. I saw the critic who'd not only taken me to task, but expressed his disappointment that I'd not made more of a part that I might have been expected to attack with enthusiasm, sitting in the bar of my hotel. 'Have a drink,' I said.

'Thank you – I didn't think you'd want to speak to me, let alone offer hospitality.'

I explained that I agreed with his notice and told him what had happened. 'Promise me one thing – please come back and if possible persuade your colleague on the other paper to give me another chance.' He did so and was as good as his word. His name is Kenneth Loveland and fortunately he didn't have the embarrassment of having to pan me for a second time.

Pat brought the children down to see it and poor John, then seven, wept when Norina tore down the curtains and broke the ornaments in Pasquale's house. So far as he was concerned the old gentleman was a very thinly disguised Dad being badly treated.

Chapter 20

Murray Dickie, who despite being for many years a leading member of the Vienna State Opera is still an irrepressible, chirpy Scot rather below medium height with a personality that more than compensates for his lack of inches, came to London in 1967 with an interesting idea for a television series on operetta.

'You and I,' he said, 'could be seen in an open air restaurant in Vienna discussing the absurdity of the plot of, say, *The Gipsy Baron*, and then one of us would say, 'Yes, but it's worth wading through all that rubbish to hear'. . . and the camera cuts to a stage where the singers go into one of the celebrated excerpts. So the viewer gets an entertaining send-up of the plot from us and only the best bits of the music.'

It sounded excellent and we decided to try and sell it to Francis Essex at STV. He listened to us attentively. When we'd finished he smiled and said, 'What a lovely idea and how wonderful it would be if we only had the money to do it. Now, if you can think in terms of opera instead of operetta, a piano instead of an orchestra, our Glasgow studio in Hope Street instead of Vienna and an educational programme that's entertaining as well as instructive – well, we just might be in business.'

Murray turned to me and said, 'Ian, it's all yours,' and went back to Vienna.

It was a marvellous opportunity for me and I owe it entirely to Murray's original conception and his willingness to let me do it on this reduced scale without feeling that I was poaching in any way. I don't pretend to be an operatic expert but I know more about it than I do about operetta.

I was invited some weeks later to attend the press reception when STV's plans for the next year were announced by Lord Thomson. Towards the end of his statement which he delivered in his relaxed Canadian drawl came the sentence, 'On the cultural side we will mount a series called *Singing for Your Supper* – an introduction to opera introduced by Ian Wallace.'

I was standing next to Francis and asked him, 'Who's going to write the scripts for these programmes?'

'You are, of course.'

He made it sound like a silly question. I had a moment of panic. 'I've only written scripts for record programmes and odd bits and pieces for my one man show. A television series is something else. I wouldn't know where to begin.'

'Begin,' said Francis, 'by realising that you know more about opera than anyone else in our outfit.'

They were half hour programmes and there were thirty of them divided into three different stories. For the first I had the help of John Mulvaney, a Scots comedian who was my side-kick and asked the questions. There was a little about the history of opera, and the component parts – arias, recitatives, ensembles and so on. We had potted versions of the works being performed by Scottish Opera in that season and Peter Hemmings reported that we'd apparently helped the box office receipts to a significant extent. Sir David Webster, the Administrator of the Royal Opera House, made two journeys to Scotland to contribute, a number of famous singers including Charles Craig, Peter Glossop and David Ward came for very little money, and many young singers worked very hard and travelled long distances, to say nothing of the co-operation from Peter Ebert, Alexander Gibson and many others.

I had two producers. The first and third series were looked after by Brian Mahoney, thoughtful and reserved, the middle one by Brian Izzard, extravagantly extrovert. Both accepted my scripts and laboured mightily to make them work.

In one I was trying to make the point that since the invention of sound amplification, only two kinds of people were left whose voices had to carry over long distances without electronic help. I wanted then to cut to some film of the famous Sergeant Major Brittain drilling the Guards at Caterham. Unfortunately the piece of film that had been sent was quite hopeless. The commands were staccato and the soldiers were calling out 'One, two, three, one, two, three' as they did the drill movements. I wanted those sustained high pitched commands for which he was famous like 'Pre-e-e-e-e-e-e-esent heim!!!!' From that I wanted to cut to a tenor singing a similarly high note, showing that opera singers were the other kind of people who have to be able to make the voice carry unaided. Brian Izzard pointed out that we were to record the programme in a few hours, that it was Sunday and I was lucky to have that bit of film right or wrong.

I don't often blow my top, so when I do people are usually rather shocked. 'That bit of film will wreck the start of the show!' I was shouting, I'm afraid. 'We are in the city of Glasgow, which has a barracks at Maryhill. Ring them up and ask for a drill sergeant or sergeant major in uniform. If STV can't afford it I'll pay!' I had no idea what was the going price for warrant officers. Brian looked very unhappy and made a few remarks about spoilt prima donnas, which I knew better than to take too seriously, but I was very surprised when about forty-five minutes later a sergant major in full rig walked into the studio, came over to me, saluted and announced that he was reporting for duty. That was Brian's little revenge for my tantrum which I entirely appreciated. I can't remember that splendid man's name, but his word of command was exactly what I wanted and, if my memory is to be trusted, we cut to Di Stefano on disc singing the resounding *Vittoria! Vittoria!* from the second act of *Tosca* and it worked perfectly.

Perhaps the most memorable moment of the whole series (apart from one shot demonstrating my inability to cast a fly from a boat on Loch Leven to music from *HMS Pinafore* in a programme about opera in country arts centres) was recorded in our drawing room at home in London. It was a programme in which three generations of singers talked about their careers. The young singer just beginning was Josephine McQueen, the middle aged ones were Murray Dickie and myself and the singer looking back on a great career was Dame Eva Turner. It was impossible for her to get to Scotland, so it was agreed that I would interview her at my home and a film crew would be specially engaged for the job. In 1982 Eva celebrates her ninetieth birthday so she was then in her very late seventies.

She's an interviewer's dream. One question to set her going and you can sit back and listen to a conducted tour through a treasure house of golden reminiscence. With the energetic diction that she employs in speech as well as in singing she began by apologising for not being able to come to Scotland for the interview. 'You see tomorrow I have to fly to Tokyo to join the panel of judges who will adjudicate this year's *Madama Butterfly* competition.' I thought of my own apprehension about a flight to Glasgow and felt ashamed.

When I asked her about her career in Italy she responded with something quite unexpected. 'As you know,' she began, 'I sang with Arturo Toscanini at the Scala, Milano in 1924. Well, one day I went to his flat for an interview. We were talking when he said to me, "Come over to the window." When we looked out we saw the funeral cortège of Puccini passing by. When you think of the people Puccini knew, like Brahms, you realise that musicians are one big family.' It was exactly what I was trying to get across in this programme, and she managed it in a couple of sentences.

Pat had a delightful idea for when Eva's interview was over. She'd bought a bouquet so that we could present it and tell her that an interview should end with flowers, just like a performance of an opera. She seemed very touched and there was in her gracious acceptance of it something of the young soprano from Oldham receiving such tributes far from home at the height of her success.

Some of the programmes were networked – at a depressingly late hour. Culture seldom got a look in in those days before 11.30 p.m. at the soonest. But this produced letters from shift workers who were breakfasting at that hour – yes, breakfast TV for a minority of the population is nothing new. One letter from a miner was particularly rewarding. He began by saying that opera was something he'd never encountered before. 'Now,' he wrote, 'you have opened a window in my life.'

*　　*　　*

In July 1966 I was summoned, along with David Franklin, Steve Race, Frank Muir and Denis Norden, to the Paris Cinema, Lower Regent Street to record a pilot programme for the BBC – a quiz game called *My Music*. The producer was Tony Shryane and it had been devised by Edward J. Mason, the man responsible for *Dick Barton*, *The Archers* and *My Word* among many other radio programmes.

'The idea,' said Tony Shryane, 'is to bring together two professional humorists and two musical experts.'

I must have gone pale. 'I'm no musical expert,' I told him. 'I studied law and am a sort of self-made opera singer with very little other musical knowledge.'

I think he imagined I was joking or playing the false modesty card. 'I'm sure you'll find there's nothing to worry about,' he said in that reassuring manner doctors assume before the result of the X-ray has come through.

All too soon the plastic cups of coffee were drunk, the nervous conversational sallies were over and it was time to face the audience and the questions. I was aware that I was going to face them in the company of four taller men. At five feet ten and a half I could nearly look the six feet of Steve Race in the eye, but if Frank Muir and Denis Norden could be described as above average height David Franklin was an Everest of a man. Indeed after that first recording was over Pat said quietly on the way home, 'Tonight was the first time in nearly twenty years that I wondered if I'd married a midget.'

We knew that evening that we were playing for reasonably high stakes because the pilot was aimed at audiences both at home and abroad. In other words both Radio 4 and the BBC Transcription Service were interested in the success or otherwise of the evening's work. The Transcription Service sells radio programmes to broadcasting companies world wide, flying them out on tape or disc to their customers. This is quite different from the World Service which beams programmes in many languages including English to many countries from powerful transmitters in the UK.

My memories of that evening are naturally hazy nearly sixteen years later but I do remember confusing Beethoven's *Fifth Symphony* with Schubert's *Unfinished* and being relieved to identify a few bars craftily taken from a bridge passage of Mendelssohn's overture *Fingal's Cave*.

The moment when we realised that the programme had a fighting chance of success has already been recorded in Steve Race's excellent book *My Music* published in 1979. Steve, our ever present chairman, played a disc of a tenor singing *La Donna e Mobile* and sitting next to Denis Norden, whose question it was, I sensed his relief at recognising something familiar from a musical genre he would not claim as his own.

'Denis,' said Steve, 'translate into English "La Donna e Mobile".'

With no hesitation whatsoever the reply came, 'The bird's got a motorbike.'

Just as a sportswriter reporting a match involving my beloved Arsenal might record that a Pat Jennings save or a beautifully weighted cross from Kenny Sansom to Graham Rix turned the match, so that ad lib – received with rapture by a studio audience willing us to success – relaxed the tension and widened the scope of our answers with one inventive phrase. From then on if we didn't know the answer we could at least try to be amusingly ignorant and the public would enjoy both the frivolous answer and the sense of superiority when they knew the correct one.

When we heard that both Transcription and Radio 4 had accepted the programme we were elated. The similar *My Word* was already a firm favourite with listeners and maybe *My Music* could be the same. The financial side was (and is) unexciting, but a regular income, however modest, in this precarious profession is a pleasant phenomenon and recurring appearances on radio have other advantages.

How did I see my fellow protagonists in those early days? Ted Mason was a compelling figure. Bearded and possessed of a penetrating eye he was man of vitality and enthusiasm who had chosen to upturn his cornucopia of creative ideas in the vestibule of Broadcasting House instead of selling them to the highest bidder. As a consequence he was at this late stage in his life marginally bitter that so many good ideas had failed to make him a rich man. And yet . . . the wryness with which he spoke of it to me in a quiet corner of the pub in Northumberland Avenue where we used to repair before early recordings of the programme in the old Playhouse Studio near the Embankment made me think that he had a great affection for the BBC and might well have been unhappy in a more commercially rewarding environment where he'd have been less of his own boss.

Tony Shryane, his collaborator in so many successful enterprises, is a quiet, shrewd observer of his fellow man and I'm sure he'll forgive me if I liken him to the landlord of a perfectly run pub who creates an atmosphere where his customers feel able to talk freely. Like such landlords, he's got us discreetly summed up, though I'm sure his conclusions will never reach the public domain!

David Franklin was a broadcaster of exceptional gifts which might never have been revealed if his career as an operatic bass singer had not been abruptly ended by a large but benign growth in his throat. Its removal left his splendidly sepulchral speaking voice unimpaired but his days of sustaining such roles as Baron Ochs in *Der Rosenkavalier* or even the much shorter Commendatore in *Don Giovanni*, which he'd sung with such distinction at Glyndebourne, were irrevocably over.

With courage and resilience he set about making a second career as a writer, lecturer and broadcaster. During the seven years he sat on Frank Muir's left for *My Music* recordings, contributing fruity, articulate answers, especially when he had no idea of the right one, he was doing all sorts of other broadcasts on both radio and television. He introduced opera programmes from Sadlers Wells or the Coliseum off the cuff with incisive prose and deadpan wit; he lectured on a singer's life carrying on a bantering dialogue with his recorded voice on a tape machine, he won awards for autobiographical programmes on both media and he also chaired a famous radio show called *Twenty Questions* with a schoolmasterish urbanity that came naturally to a man who had been a schoolmaster before anything else. For some listeners and viewers he was pomposity personified, but the majority recognised the warmth and common sense behind his Pooh Bah facade and their instinct was correct.

One evening Steve asked me to identify an opera from one note and one word. The word was 'Si'. As I'd sung in the opera many times I knew it was the moment in *Don Giovanni* when in a cemetery the statue of the Commendatore accepts the Don's invitation to supper. (This, incidentally, is a good example of Steve's constant effort to try and ask questions within the area of our knowledge.) Giving my answer I added that I was pretty sure that the recording was the pre-war Glyndebourne production with David Franklin in the role. I went on to say that there might be people listening who didn't know what a fine operatic career David had had before he was forced to retire nearly twenty years earlier.

The next morning the phone rang about ten o'clock. 'Bill here.' (He had been christened William and was Bill to his friends.) 'Just wanted to thank you for what you said about me last night. Couldn't trust myself to speak about it then. I might have made a fool of myself and shed a tear. See you next week.' The dialling tone resumed before I could reply.

Unfortunately the pressures of increasing success were making demands on his reserves at a time when his health was already giving rise to some anxiety. One evening in 1973 I gave him a lift from the Commonwealth Institute, where we'd recorded two programmes, to the Great Western Royal Hotel at Paddington where he was spending the night before going by train to Torquay for a lecture the following day. On the way he said, 'Tell me something. Does your chap get more tense as we get near the end of the programme?'

'I've not really thought much about it,' I replied, 'but now you mention it I think perhaps he does.' My chap, of course, being Denis – and I had noticed that in those early days he added a good deal more to the doodle on the scribbling paper provided by the Corporation and smoked with a little more intensity in the last ten minutes.

'So does mine. Yet I feel more relaxed. Why is it do you think?' I ventured to suggest that we were not expected to make the audience laugh and if and when we did so it was a lucky bonus. Frank and Denis, on the other hand, as professional humorists, would always be trying to work towards some sort of high note on which to go out. Achieving that depended entirely on the fall of the cards and their inspired response to it.

'Yes, of course that must be it. We've got to sing at the end, but we don't have to write the song on the spur of the moment.' When we arrived at the hotel Bill was in sparkling form. I'd managed to shoehorn him into Pat's mini and he now found getting his six feet and at least five inches out of it something of a gymnastic feat.

'This is quite a tricky delivery,' he declared. 'It may have to be a caesarian through the roof!' He bade me a cheerful goodnight.

Next morning he woke to find himself paralysed down one side and when I saw him in hospital he looked like a tree that had been struck by lightning. It was a severe stroke and though he made some progress and entertained hopes of being able to return to work – even if it meant a wheelchair – he never did and died about a year later still only in his middle sixties.

Bill and I had sung with Glyndebourne at Edinburgh as long ago as 1948 and it had been a comfort to me in my first panel programme to be confronted with an old friend. As well I had worked on one or two television shows where the music had been provided by Steve Race and his Orchestra. Chairing a panel game is a hazardous occupation requiring special skills. To do it for sixteen years, and set the questions for the majority of that time must surely qualify for an entry in the more respectable parts of the *Guinness Book of Records*.

Steve is a proud son of Lincoln and his musical pedigree is

impeccable – a Fellow of the Royal Academy of Music who decided to tilt his shining freelance in the field of jazz without ever losing his interest in the whole spectrum of music. His instrument, of course, is the piano, yet in the first few series he only had a celeste with which to supply musical illustrations. Now he manages to turn ninety degrees from question sheet to keyboard either to tax our ear and memories with his ingenious piano medleys of tantalisingly tip-of-the-tongue, nearly remembered tunes or to accompany our end-of-programme vocal efforts. That turn to the piano is harder than it looks or sounds, being mental as well as physical, for Steve no longer plays the piano regularly in public. Even so he reveals his technical mastery by affecting instant transpositions from the planned key should any of us suddenly feel the need for a change. This has been known to happen in mid song! There are many household names in the world of outstanding accompanists who would blench at what Steve does with ease in this respect without tremor or protest.

It's been well publicised that we have prior knowledge of our final songs, though for the first few years this was not the case – which gave rise to some embarrassing moments. I recall Ted Mason approaching me in that pub near the Embankment and saying in a stage whisper, 'Your first song tonight is *Cushy Butterfield* so that won't give you any trouble.'

'Ted, I don't even know the tune let alone the words!'

'But you must; it's a Geordie song.'

'I know it is but my name's Ian Wallace not Owen Brannigan.'

Ted clutched his brow. 'Oh, God! well do the best you can.'

It was a case of saying to Steve when the moment came that I'd have to sing something else.

Now we each have a day's conference with Steve once a year when we choose twenty-six songs for the next series, but we never rehearse them on the day, leaving plenty of room for spontaneity such as the evening when Steve in a rare moment of aberration started the introduction to *The Fishermen of England* in a key at least a third too high for me. I gamely embarked on a solo that was bound to end in strangulated disaster. The audience loved it and we didn't re-record it in the correct key – after all our job is to entertain the public and one way of doing it is to have the occasional musical equivalent of a slip on a banana skin.

For the first few years I felt slightly in awe of Denis and Frank though they were always extremely friendly and generously appreciative of any comic sallies – most of them accidental – which I perpetrated. By the time we assembled for that famous pilot they had ended the partnership that had brightened our lives with *Take It From Here*, *Whacko!* and other comedy series, and when they arrived for the pre-recording refreshment thoughtfully provided by the BBC that first evening – and indeed every recording since – they were soon locked in conversation as if they were catching up in fifteen minutes on all that had happened during their voluntary separation. They still give me that impression today. I sense that they are complementary even after going their separate creative ways for so long.

Their seemingly inexhaustible ability to use the English language as an instrument of ad lib humour must make them consistently two of the funniest men in England during a sustained period of about thirty years. I freely confess to feeling elated on the rare occasions I've made them laugh out loud. Humorous writers tip their hat to a good joke but don't laugh quite so easily as other folk.

I managed it once during our first 'away match', that is, a recording done somewhere out of London or un-BBC like the Royal Academy of Music or Sadlers Wells.

We found ourselves in Birmingham Town Hall with an audience of two thousand and having to project more like stand-up comics than the quiet, laid-back chaps we really are.

There was a round of nursery rhymes on record to identify. I felt very confident having just accomplished the first ten years of parenthood. When I heard mine I knew at once what it was – or thought I did.

'Oh yes,' I cried, 'that's "The wife wants a child, the wife wants a child, my husband's lost his fiddling stick . . ."' the gale of laughter engulfed us and I saw that Frank and Denis were shaking with mirth, '" . . . and doesn't know what to do."' More frenetic laughter from the assembled multitude.

Afterwards Frank observed as we came face to face, 'Very

funny and dirty with it.' I still don't know what the correct answer should have been – I thought I'd got it right.

John Amis joined us in 1973. He was another old friend and of a size suitable to have weighed in for a contest with Bill Franklin on equal terms. Not only physically – both have found little to inspire them in Gilbert and Sullivan and both have shown a tendency to challenge the chairman on points of detail.

John is a kindly man of considerable erudition and his store of anecdotes is coupled with an outstanding talent for mimicry that goes largely unnoticed because his subjects are only known to a fraction of the listeners. It's the classic case of, 'If you knew my uncle Fred you'd realise how like him that is.' John 'does' famous foreign conductors and certain English composers to the life; indeed if he ever decided to try his hand at politicians Mike Yarwood might well pay him a large sum to leave the country.

Before deciding to devote his life to being a broadcaster, lecturer and writer about music he thought seriously about a singing career, studied and made a start. He could certainly have pursued it further had he felt inclined, as he reminds us at the end of each programme, and there must be few people around who could match his skill as a siffleur.

As TV viewers know John is a flamboyant dresser and only the other day in the warm-up before the show (when the ad libs are sometimes topical and occasionally rabelaisian) he complimented Denis on a new suit. Denis looked across at John's sartorial flight of fancy, a jacket apparently made of the sort of ticking that is associated with a pillow's underwear and said, 'Yes, it is a new suit, and as you can see I donated the lining to John.'

We have an unwritten rule that when one of us is telling a story the others don't interrupt. Denis once broke this rule to brilliant effect when I was talking. It was in one of the first of our televised programmes. I was telling a story about a performance of *La Bohème* near the start of my career in which the Polish bass Marian Nowakowski was taking part.

'We were in the last act,' I said, 'and Mimi was dying. Nowakowski and I as Colline and Schaunard were striking attitudes of grief, leaning against a chest of drawers when he turned to me and said, "Pssssst".'

204

'And were you?' asked Denis.

I and the audience were convulsed – in fact I giggled for the rest of the show including my song at the end. Denis was abjectly apologetic afterwards and pleaded tiredness after a difficult day. Far from being upset I was delighted at his intervention, which made marvellous television and gave me a story I've dined out on ever since.

Listeners to the radio version of the programme didn't hear Denis's interjection. Tony Shryane edited it out while Douglas Hespe, our television producer, left it in for the viewers. Why the difference? The viewers could see I was amused by it and took no offence whatsoever. Radio listeners unable to see my face might not have been so sure.

How did we feel about the transfer to television? Most of us were unsanguine to say the least, feeling that five middle aged men scratching their noses were unlikely to inspire a wholesale switch on. We were all TV animals in one way or another and my impression was that if we started playing to camera we'd lose our touch for the radio listener.

It is perhaps even now not too widely known that the cameras come and eavesdrop our radio recordings, so that the two are substantially the same – except for visual rounds including photographs, pictures and weird musical instruments that would be meaningless on radio. Our reservations and apprehensions were both stilled by Douglas Hespe, who at the outset was sensitive to the programme's radio tradition and sited his cameras so unobtrusively that we do not and cannot play to them.

When I saw the first telerecording, however, I was uncomfortable and wanted to hide under the sofa. Next day Frank rang me about something else and at the end of the conversation asked, 'Did you catch us on TV?'

'Yes.'

'What did you think?'

'It was a bit like watching a football match where no one wanted to win and didn't give a damn about the spectators.'

'That's what I thought,' he said, 'but maybe that's what the public likes.'

As we're still at it (at the time of writing) I suppose he must be right, but there's no doubt that the TV audience is not for the most part the radio one and many of them are unaware of our radio history. Many of our listeners prefer to stay that way and who would blame them, except that they deprive themselves of occasional glimpses of our delicious scorer and programme secretary, Leonie Lawson, who is as good for our morale as the solid core of supporters who find their way to our recordings even when London is blanketed in snow or shrouded in mist. Under those conditions we are sometimes down to the number associated with the survivors of the Charge of the Light Brigade and they are as much a part of the show as the recording vans outside.

I am often asked by members of the public with a mischievous turn of mind to comment on the singing of Frank and Denis. Frank has an extrovert style that can take a song by the scruff of the neck and give it a new and effective impact, but he's equally at home in a quiet sympathetic number. Perhaps his vocal reputation can best be illustrated by the fact that in the very week that this is written he was offered the part of the Major General in an American production of *The Pirates of Penzance* to be staged at Drury Lane five days before they offered it to me. We both turned it down for one reason or another. To put this in perspective I ought to add that before they got around to Frank and me they had had refusals from singers like Spike Milligan and Frankie Howerd.

As for Denis, he is undoubtedly the most improved singer in the country. I am quite serious about this. When people make jocular remarks about his singing to me I suspect they've not heard the programme recently. The days when he would sing a few lines in a bunch of keys and sign off with a crisp ad lib are in the past. My son John after watching one of Denis's songs on the last TV series commented, 'Put him in a white tie and tails, Dad, and you've got a song and dance man.' I should add that I can take no credit. I don't teach singing, not even to my old friend.

* * *

Though I'd sung my last performance at Glyndebourne in 1961, the old warrior was recalled in 1968 for a special assignment. The management had decided to form a touring company to give young singers who had graduated from the chorus or had impressed at audition a chance to sing principal roles under the Glyndebourne banner in selected towns and cities in Britain. The sets and productions would be the same as those used in the main season – adapted where necessary for the touring theatres.

I was to sing Dulcamara in *L'elisir d'amore*, the idea being that such a buffo role might best be done by someone with experience who could give the young singers backing and support. This admirable idea had only one snag. I had never sung Dulcamara in my life and to make matters worse Signor Badioli who'd sung the part in the main season had brought a wealth of comic business to the part – none of which had found its way into the stage director's book and all of which he'd taken with him back to Italy.

My powers of invention were hardly equal to the demands of this flamboyant role, but on the first night at the Theatre Royal, Newcastle-upon-Tyne I faced a further hazard which almost ended in disaster.

Dulcamara, a quack doctor, entered in a caravan drawn by a donkey – a real one. In each city we had a donkey audition. It was too complicated and costly to tour our own. The Geordie animal did a competent dress rehearsal, but on the opening night it pulled the caravan a few feet on to the stage and stopped dead. No amount of pulling or shoving from the chorus, who were taking most of the weight of moving the vehicle anyway, could shift it. The caravan was supposed to come right downstage and turn round, so that I could fling open the door and start selling my bottles of medicine to the gullible townsfolk. But we were stuck right upstage with the door of the caravan facing the back cloth.

The only way to save the situation was to unhitch the donkey and drag the caravan down to its right position carrying out an elaborate U-turn. Before all this could be achieved, the music had reached my aria, which I had to begin through a side window far from the orchestra and the audience, lit by a lamp an enterprising electrician had re-angled with his bare hands. No wonder one critic wrote that I settled down after a shaky start. The donkey, of course, stole the scene. It's good to recall that two of the young singers in that cast were Jill Gomez and Ryland Davies whose careers have since taken them to the top of the profession – and even better to be able to record that Glyndebourne Touring Opera, which started with that recalcitrant donkey, is flourishing fourteen years later.

At one rehearsal some members of the chorus asked me when I'd first sung for Glyndebourne. When I told them it was at the 1948 Edinburgh Festival there was a gasp. 'That was before we were born,' they told me.

*   *   *

Soon after I got back from the tour which, as well as Newcastle included Manchester, Sheffield and Oxford, I had a phone call from Peter Plouviez, General Secretary of British Actors' Equity of which I'd been a member for over twenty years.

'Are you free tomorrow at 9.30 in the morning to go and see Vic Feather at TUC Headquarters in Great Russell Street?'

'What on earth for?'

'This is the year of the TUC Centenary and there's to be a big celebration in Manchester on 1st June – they want you to be the link man for all the speeches and music.'

Incredible! I had faced some outlandish challenges since my first play in Glasgow wearing a spinal support, but this really took the biscuit. Only four years had passed since I'd been recruited to help the Tory Party, now I had an early morning appointment in one of the enclaves of their principal opponents.

Vic's office was large. The walls were covered with paintings while more canvasses were propped at the wainscoting. As I sat down on the opposite side of the desk where he was crouched deep in paper work, one of the phones on his desk rang.

'Hallo, Fred,' he said, taking a cigar at least six inches long from his mouth. Whoever was at the other end sounded excited and angry. A resigned expression clouded the rugged, good natured face of the Assistant General Secretary of the TUC, and he had time to pull at least twice on his cigar before Fred subsided. His black hair and the aroma of smoke reminded me of my occasional visits to my father's office in the City as a boy. At length he spoke.

'No, Fred, don't do it. Go back and have another meeting. Take my word for it . . . what? No, no, no. There'll coom a time, Fred, boot not now, there's a good lad – call me later.' He put down the phone with a shake of his head. 'What the pooblic

208

don't realise is that we spend more time stopping strikes than starting 'em!'

'Now, Ian, you know why you're here?' I indicated that I had no more than the bare bones of it. 'Well, I'll be quite frank. You're not the first choice. We had recommended to oos a yoong lad with brilliant ideas who was going to do a pageant of all the hoondred years history of the Movement in the arena of King's Hall at Bellevue, Manchester. I thought it sounded great oontil I found that he was going to have a scene showing why the TUC supported Collective Security in the thirties. He was proposing to stage woon of Hitler's Nuremberg Rallies with an actor dressed as the Fuehrer shouting at the top of his voice and all our trade unionists, who'd coom in booses from all over Britain for this loovely happy day, were to shout out "Sieg Heil! Sieg Heil!" You might as well ask 'em to roosh into Westminster Cathedral and shout "To hell with the Pope!"'

Even at this early stage I found myself liking this warm forthright, north country man, but I had to get one little matter out of the way. 'Mr Feather, I'm a loyal member of my union and have been for twenty years, but I have to tell you that I'm not a Labour man.'

'I don't care if you're a white Baptist, you're the chap we want for this job. You see the TUC represents trade unionists of all political persuasions. At this do Harold'll be Prime Minister and make the big speech. To be perfectly frank it'd be all the same to me if it was Ted.'

I was to write a linking script outlining the history of the TUC since its founding in Manchester in 1868 (the year my father was born) and I was to choose suitable music to intersperse it for brass band (in close collaboration with Mr Brass Band himself, Harry Mortimer) and the Rossendale and Felling Male Voice Choirs. I was also to introduce the main speakers and maybe sing a song or two myself. The whole thing was to be televised.

'We'll stoof the idea of a pageant,' declared Vic, 'boot near the end of your words and the music I'm arranging for hoondreds of kids to coom into the arena dressed as miners, nurses, mechanics, postmen, engine drivers, condooctresses of booses – to represent every kind of worker you can think of – the new generation going into our second century.'

'What a super idea!' I exclaimed. Vic would have been a brilliant impresario. I told him so and he reddened with pleasure.

'Boot that's not all. You remember Low the cartoonist and how he always portrayed the TUC as a great big loombering cart horse? Well I want the children to be led by a loovely white horse, slim and elegant – the TUC with a fresh, new image – and you can paint the picture in your script.'

'Where will you get it?' I asked him.

'By a piece of loock Bertram Mills will be in Blackpool that week. Woon of those Liberty Horses will do. I'll fix it.' As I left him I commented on the pictures. 'Yes, I'm a great art loover and all this stoof in here is entries for an exhibition of workers' paintings I'm organising. Not bad are they?'

I wrote the script, conferred with Harry Mortimer, whom I knew well from singing and compering at Brass Band Festivals in the very hall where on June 1st we'd be staging this historic event, and returned to Great Russell Street a few weeks later to read it to Vic. He was to all intents and purposes the General Secretary, as George Woodcock was about to retire and Vic succeeded him soon after the Centenary was over.

He only made two script changes. As I read out my introduction to one of the early speakers I used some form of words like – highly respected and much beloved.

'Read that again.' I did. 'Coot out mooch belooved – he's a pain in the neck.'

Later in one of the historical passages I used the word protection.

'Find anoother word for protection. You may not know it boot there's a family called Kray who are about to stand trial for a protection racket and I think soom of them'll be going down. We don't want any clever dick making comparisons.' Then he looked sad. 'We'll have to forget that idea of the horse. The circus won't play. They say that with all the kids rooning about it might panic and soomebody might get hurt. We can't risk that, so there we are.'

I felt so sorry for him. It was such a good idea – both funny and moving, the best of all combinations to make a public impact.

A night or two before the great day Pat and I were at home

watching the television news. One item was the triumphant return to the city of Manchester United proudly bearing the European Cup. The crowd, it was said, was well in excess of 100,000 and their bus was only able to move at all because ahead of it, surrounded by cheering jostling supporters, were half a dozen mounted police – at least one riding a quite unruffled white horse! I gripped Pat's arm. 'Of course!' I shouted and leaped for the phone. She thought, not for the first time, that I'd gone off my head. Before I could lift it off the hook it rang.

'Ian, are you watching the telly?'

'Yes, Vic.'

'What do you do to get a bloody police horse? Dial 999?'

It made all the difference.

The start of the ceremony was slightly marred by a clash that had taken place a day or two earlier in the House of Commons between Harold Wilson and Jim Callaghan over the vexed question of an incomes policy. As a result some of the delegates were not exactly in holiday mood when they arrived at the hall. I could see Vic dashing from one group to another breathing words of reason and successfully defusing any unfortunate tendency towards a slanging match. Somehow when Harry Mortimer and the Men o' Brass struck up with *Congratulations* everyone suddenly realised what the day was all about and settled down to enjoy both the speeches and the music. But the dramatic entrance of the white horse and the children was the high point, as we all knew it would be – and that was a hundred per cent Vic's idea. It succeeded in making everyone in that hall feel a pride in belonging to a movement that had played such an important part in the social history of the previous hundred years.

There was one disappointment. We had all understood that the BBC would be televising the entire ceremony. I had given a copy of the script to Ray Colley, the TV producer, and spent time describing to him the way it would all work. Perhaps he couldn't bring himself to tell us bluntly that the BBC weren't interested in anything except one or two of the speeches, which was all they transmitted. Nor did the press give coverage to anything other than the Prime Minister's speech. Maybe what we were doing was no more interesting to the general public than any other centenary celebration – except that about 12,000,000 of them might have liked to share the afternoon with the couple of thousand of their brother and sister trade unionists in the Kings Hall.

There was a celebration dinner in the evening at which I was asked to tell a few stories, and then I drove through the night south east right across England to the north Norfolk coast where the previous year I'd bought a little house in a small village between Cromer and Sheringham. We've holidayed there ever since. It's so hard to plan in advance in my disordered existence and for some time Pat and I had been hoping to discover a place not too far from London where we could go at literally a moment's notice when a day or two – or a longer time off – was possible.

For the first few years Rosie and John had to be ferried each day to the Cromer Junior Tennis Tournament for a week near the beginning of August, we explored the Broads in a small motor launch I bought, and only sold because we couldn't bear the thought of it sitting waiting for us so often in vain. But we still go to Catfield Staithe and Hickling Broad – or I do – and putter away up the dyke in my nine foot fibre glass dinghy with the outboard. The rest of the family are not quite so keen on it.

Pat and I love to birdwatch at Salthouse or Cley or just to walk along the beach from West Runton in either direction; we hit a golf ball at Sheringham or sit in our minute garden and do nothing whatsoever. When we're not there dear friends keep an eye on it for us – and a close eye at that, which is a great comfort.

Rosie and John don't seem to have outgrown it and these days sometimes go up there on their own – and we seem to be gradually acquiring a circle of friends and acquaintances who would take the loneliness from retirement if an old strolling player like me ever got around to it. I doubt it, though each time I leave the village to return to London, I do so with increasing reluctance.

Chapter 21

There's not much more to tell that wouldn't be a repetition of the sort of things I've already described. Scottish Opera fulfilled an ambition of mine to play a Gilbert and Sullivan Opera on the stage – as opposed to concerts and records when, later in 1968, they presented *The Gondoliers* in a Victorian setting. I don't know whether the Duke of Plaza Toro is really my part, but that's the one I played. Peter Hemmings suggested that I should write an encore verse for the duet *Small Titles and Orders*, which began,

> 'I'm perfectly willing
> To earn the odd shilling
> As guide to the ducal apartments.
> There are guard dogs to baffle
> All those who would snaffle
> Â cannon ball from the escarpments.'

Then on the night when the Queen and Prince Philip paid us a visit there was a special one,

> 'We're all of a flutter
> Our knees turn to butter
> When we're entertaining the Monarch.
> We organise banquets,
> Air monogrammed blankets
> And polish the spare room with Ronuk.'

Appropriately my opera career ended so far as Scotland was concerned with my two old friends *La Cenerentola* and *Il Barbiere*. We toured the latter as far afield as Oban, Kelso and over the border to Barrow in Furness. But I wasn't quite through with Dr Bartolo.

Il Barbiere was presented at Brighton Festival in 1971, produced by Sir Tyrone Guthrie – far from well and barely able to speak because of a heavy chest cold and tracheitis. At lunch-

213

time each rehearsal day he was too tired to talk to the cast and he and I went to a pub away from the rest for a pie and a half of bitter while he quietly reminisced or sat silent.

Like so many artists he could rally for the time he was working and, though it wasn't his most inspired production, it was lively and he obviously enjoyed working with a largely young cast and conductor John Eliot Gardiner. On the last day of rehearsals in London before we went down to Sussex he said to me, 'I've been so unsociable to those dear people, let's all have lunch in a pub together today.'

It was a happy relaxed hour of cheese sandwiches, pints and a miraculously quiet corner where no one had to shout to be heard. All singers are fascinated by actors and I believe the converse is true. They plied him with questions about Guinness, Gielgud, Richardson and Olivier. Someone said, 'What's the most important quality an actor needs?'

'That's an easy one. Survival.'

He deliberately prescribed for me a dressing gown so long that it trailed on the ground always threatening to trip me up on the many steps and stairs of the set. It was a typical Tony Guthrie ruse to extract a little extra from the performer. I was so happy to be working with him again that my protests were barely audible – though I did persuade Tanya Moiseiwitsch, his devoted designer, to snip off about three inches.

I invited him and his wife Judith who was almost as tall as Tony to come and have dinner with Pat and me at home, never thinking he'd feel up to it. To our delight he said he'd like it very much. Judith arrived at the rehearsal room carrying a shirt in a plastic bag. Tony was always a casual dresser at rehearsals.

As I drove up Haverstock Hill Judith remarked that as a young girl she used to swim in the ladies' pond in Kenwood. We had finished work early and I knew that Pat would not be expecting us for a while. I drove to Kenwood and reversed the car along a path bearing a notice 'No Cars' as far as the gate to the pool. Until we arrived there Judith hadn't realised what I was doing and probably thought this odd backward journey was a sign of Scots eccentricity. Suddenly she recognised where she was.

'Oh if only I had a costume I'd go in now!' she cried.

'Thank God you haven't,' said Tony. 'She'd do it, you know, if she had.'

I started back for the road, hoping not to encounter a keeper or other arm of the law.

'Don't worry if we do. You can pretend you're Italian and Judith and I will refuse to utter a word. That'll get us through.' The plan didn't have to be put into effect.

When we got home Pat said, 'Tea or Scotch?'

'Scotch, please,' replied Tony, 'but first I must change my shirt and have a wash; Judith, where's the plastic bag?'

'I have it,' she responded rather tartly, 'but the hypocrisy of it – trying to convince the Wallaces that you dress for dinner. Why, you've even had me put in a tie, and when did you last wear one of those I'd like to know?' It was a delicious scene between two articulate and devoted people.

In the end Pat said, 'Why not take up a Scotch for while you're changing?'

'There's a kind, sensible girl. That's what we call at home – one for the soap dish.'

After *Il Barbiere* was over Tony and Judith went back home to Ireland. Two weeks later after breakfast he went into his study to read his letters. When Judith came into the room shortly afterwards it was to find that he had died sitting in his chair. Not many months later she joined him.

At Tony's memorial service in St Paul's Church, Covent Garden, the Actors' Church, Sir Alec Guinness began the address, 'As I came into the churchyard I saw that a great tree had fallen.'

* * *

The last ten years or so have been, in musical terms, an endless series of variations on familiar themes. I must confess I'm happy on an opera stage, even more so on one where I can speak and sing and – because it's how I began I'm always interested in doing a play with no singing at all; but by 1970 I had manoeuvred myself into a position where I was known for versatility, so that most of the work I was offered was for one night stands. I wasn't happy about it, but it was a situation of my own making and reluctantly I gave up trying to keep a foot in other camps and accepted dates as much as a year ahead without attempting to have release clauses in the contract in case a play or a film should come up in the mean time. Most concert-givers would not accept that sort of condition anyway.

I also changed my agent. Richard Stone had looked after me for more than twenty-five years and in that time had become one of the most successful and respected members of his profession. His clients include Benny Hill, Dave Allen, Terry Scott, Hugh Lloyd, Lance Percival and Jon Pertwee – a formidable list. We became close friends. I am Timothy Stone's godfather, Richard is John's, but as time went on the bewildering variety of my work – much of it in the musical field – made it difficult for a theatrical agent to represent me beyond keeping my diary and handling enquiries. The agency was not geared to develop the musical side, yet unless I took the unwise step of giving up concerts there was little they could do to help me in the theatre and elsewhere – a sort of Catch 22 situation. For all parties there had been nothing quite like it before.

When an enthusiastic young concert promoter called Raymond Gubbay pointed out that in the course of a year roughly half my work had been either in his promotions or had arisen through his contacts the moment to make a move, painful though it was, had arrived. Raymond concentrated me firmly in the concert field for much of the time and the results were excellent. Not only did he find me a great deal of work from other sources but he devised and promoted concerts for me all over the country. G and S, opera, operetta, musicals and a Scottish evening were all grist to both our mills. Though I was no stranger to London's Royal Albert, Festival and Queen Elizabeth Halls, I now became something of a regular, particularly in Raymond's Gilbert and Sullivan promotions.

I speak of all this in the past because a couple of years ago he decided to give up the agency side of his activities to concentrate on concert promotion – much of it bringing large scale attractions from abroad – so once again I was in search of a manager. The association with Raymond was of the happiest and I still appear in his promotions from time to time, recently producing and singing in *Trial by Jury* at the Queen Elizabeth Hall, but I've fallen on my feet now. I've gone back to a theatrical agency presided over by the prestigious and elegant Terence Plunket Greene (no relation to the singer). He took one look at me and consigned me to the girl who has been his first lieutenant since she joined him at the age of nineteen – Ginette Chalmers, who has flair for finding and opening new doors, looks after my complicated diary and charms all my customers whether they like the sound of the fee or not!

Simultaneously with all this concert activity I'd become a radio script writer in the field of record programmes, mostly light classical, both for the BBC and the British Forces Broadcasting Service. The latter required long links between each disc in hour long programmes, but I always enjoyed working under the benevolent and merry eye of Roy ffoulkes – one of the most knowledgeable and enterprising of music producers. Why the BBC doesn't snap him up I'll never know. At one time I was writing an average of one and a half presentation scripts a week (all involving research) as well as chasing round the country singing.

Though many of these programmes were for Radio 2 and the World Service of the BBC, there was the intermittent pleasure of writing a dramatised narration for a sequence of operettas and reading or rather performing it on Radio 3. Monica Cockburn and later Robert Bowman, both BBC light music producers, recorded the music of the operettas in English, often casting me for one of the singing roles. It was then my job to write the story from the point of view of the character I had sung – or from whatever other standpoint made dramatic sense. I could speak over bridge passage music (though never when anyone was singing) and if some dialogue was necessary I played the parts myself stepping forward, as it were, from being the narrator. Each of them was many days' work, listening to the tapes of the music, poring over ancient librettos and plot summaries, trudging across Hampstead Heath cudgelling out a way to start, writing timed speeches to fit the music and when it was finished rehearsing the different speaking voices for the characters who would speak through me. We did *A Night in Venice, The Arcadians, Wiener Blut, Frederika, Zigeunerliebe, Lilac Time, Boccaccio, The Drum-Major's Daughter* and others. I love this sort of work and both Monica and Robert gave me my head. The only mild disappointment was that Radio 3 nearly always put them out in the afternoon – several on a summer bank holiday afternoon!

Anyone who has done a great deal of sound broadcasting has respect and affection for the many BBC producers whose friendliness and capacity for making artists feel relaxed is one of the secrets of radio's success and survival. More than that they are sometimes instrumental, as in the case of those operettas, of encouraging you to do something you'd never even considered. Barry Knight and David Rayvern Allen are two more who've introduced me to new radio ideas while Tony Shryane, as well as being the *My Music* producer, has for a long time been quietly giving me more faith in myself as a performer. Like Rodolfo Mele he's been one of my great encouragers and I'm deeply grateful. I suspect quite a few of the Archer family could tell the same story.

Throughout the 1970s I was my own boss and, though away from home a good deal, mostly for short periods, I had as much time as many fathers with Pat and the children. Yet even with all this activity there were times when I was slightly depressed, feeling that I ought perhaps to be bold and turn down the substance of endless scripts (not the operettas) and concerts for the shadow of that elusive theatrical career.

There were and are two great compensations. Travelling to my engagements all over the country is exhausting but it reveals what a beautiful country we live in. So often eccentric scheduling involves cross-country journeys far from motorways and trunk roads. It becomes especially noticeable when the route takes you from east to west, rather than north to south. Almost every region has pleasant surprises and the variety of scenery is infinite. I adore Scotland – all of it – Spey Bay, St Andrews, Sauchiehall Street, but it's through work not holidays that I discovered the Yorkshire Dales, the Peak District, North Wales, Shropshire, Northern Ireland, Exmoor and west Cumbria. I long to return to them and many other places without the preoccupation of the evening task ahead.

The second? To be walking along a street in a strange town and feel a detaining hand on my arm. 'I'd just like to thank you for all the pleasure you've brought me over the years,' says a total stranger with a nervous smile. It's warming to feel among friends wherever you go – nothing quite like it.

.

Chapter 22

When you're as far into a book about your life as this, apart from feeling exhausted, you remember the critiques you've read of other people's referring to unconsciously self-revealing passages. No doubt the reader will have spotted those in this book. As they're unconscious I won't, but if I've given a conscious impression that I've not enjoyed the last dozen years, that would be misleading. Concert audiences all over the country ·have given me generous receptions and the other singers I've worked with, mostly much younger than myself, have been excellent company, making very light of the considerable age gap; but for a great many of these concerts, and always with the one man show, the loneliness of the solo performer is a contrast with the years when I was always working in a company with many other people.

The same thing applies to presenting record programmes. Research and script writing is a solitary business, especially for someone who feels that it might be more fun, however modestly, to be making history in the musical field instead of listening to others doing so.

Ironically, the exciting days for me in the seventies were very exciting indeed. I felt sometimes like an old warhorse, kept in the stable and paraded on special occasions like the BBC TV production of *The Mikado* when I played Pooh Bah and enjoyed the whole thing from the first rehearsal to the post recording party just as if I had been back at Glyndebourne. Even playing the small part of Antonio, the gardener, in a TV production of *The Marriage of Figaro* gave me pleasure out of all proportion to my share in a production that was conducted by Sir Charles Mackerras, produced by Basil Coleman and included such excellent singers as Elizabeth Harwood, Norma Burrowes, Thomas Allen and John Shirley Quirk. A Gilbert and Sullivan Prom, before the BBC planners lost their nerve and killed them off, was as exhilarating for the singers as a sauna, and though Sir Malcolm had passed from the scene Marcus Dods has a similar capacity for bringing out the lyrical beauty and comicality of Sullivan's scores.

There was one very sad day in 1972 when I came to Glasgow to record a radio programme for Eddie Fraser. He'd succeeded Howard M. Lockhart (the man who gave me my first break doing the play in the spinal support) as chief variety producer for BBC Scotland, and he was prepared to bring me – a London Scot – up to Glasgow and other Scots locations times without number to sing with the BBC Variety Orchestra – either in my own right or as a guest in the many singing series he presented on both radio and television featuring Kenneth McKellar, Moira Anderson, Helen McCarthur and Bill McCue. During the run of *Fanny* he came to London and made a series, recorded in my dressing room, in which I talked to London Scots and sang the songs they requested. A simple idea, but excellent publicity for me. He called it *A Scot in Drury Lane.* Though he was a producer there was something of the impresario about him and he saw the potential of the artists I've mentioned very early in their careers. Without the enormous boost they received from the chance to sing a wide variety of songs for half an hour once a week on the air for three months at a time, they might have taken a little longer to reach the top.

He'd asked me to do a special programme of my favourite music and suggested that I might like Ken McKellar and Helen McCarthur to be my guests. I took this as a compliment. I'd so often been theirs.

When I arrived at my hotel the night before the recording there was a message from the BBC that Eddie had been taken ill and was in hospital but that the programme would go ahead as planned.

Next morning we were rehearsing with another producer when he came into the studio and told us that the hospital had telephoned with the news that Eddie had died within the last hour. We were stunned. All work on the programme stopped and we decided to meet half an hour later to decide what to do. We all adored Eddie, a perky Glaswegian, rather short, with a comedian's face and the sort of straight unruly brown hair that however it was combed always had a wee bit sticking out at the back. He loved all of us and had the invaluable gift of candour which artists need and so rarely get.

My reaction was to go ahead and record the programme as a tribute to a man whose epitaph could have been 'The show must go on', but Ken was adamant that we should do no more that day as a mark of respect. He knew Eddie far better than I did and felt that if we'd attempted it our emotions might well have got the better of us. The show was recorded a few weeks later.

Perhaps in later years Eddie became a little possessive towards some of the artists he'd helped on their way and would have liked to play some sort of managerial role in their careers. This may have been an embarrassment, but the BBC's policy of retiring all producers at sixty often strands first class people still fitted to do great things in a limbo where their only chance of work is on a freelance basis for the employer they've served so long. It's not easy for them to find other work and he was undoubtedly trying to create fresh outlets for his fertile store of show business ideas.

Eddie was special and I hope that one day someone will do a programme about him and what he did, not only for Scots singers but the whole spectrum of Scottish light entertainment.

*　　*　　*

In the autumn of 1975 John Calder published volume one of these outpourings under the title *Promise Me You'll Sing Mud*. I'd appeared a number of times at his arts centre Ledlanet, a Victorian baronial mansion near Milnathort in Kinross-shire – and the stories in my one man show gave him the idea that I ought to write a book. It took me several years – I often had to lay it aside for months at a time because of other work. This one has taken less than a year despite other work, but much of it was written in the solitude of Norfolk or, taking a leaf out of Robert Morley's book, in an end of the garden summer house with heat and light but no phone.

I'd never penetrated Capital Radio's studios in the Euston Road before, though I'd been next door several times to Thames Television. It was late afternoon on a day in February 1978 and before going there to be interviewed by Michael Aspel for a programme called *Help Line* on coping with a long illness such as I'd had during the war, I'd been asked to call in and talk to Raymond Gubbay at his office a little way up Tottenham Court Road. After we'd discussed one or two business matters he said, 'I'm off to the Albert Hall. I've a concert there tonight, so I'll walk you as far as Warren Street tube station.'

We parted outside.

'Well,' said Raymond, 'what dull lives you and I lead at present – I'm off to make sure my orchestra has enough stands and the right music, and you're going to do a radio chore for nothing.'

'Never mind, Ray,' I replied, taking up his tone of mock depression, 'we never know what's round the corner.'

To my surprise he roared with laughter – put his arm round my shoulder and said, 'Good luck to whatever it is,' and left me. Raymond is a warm, friendly man but doesn't usually embrace artists in the street.

The girl in reception at Capital told me to go up the stairs and along the corridor. 'Someone'll show you where to go.' Raymond had laughed out loud; she seemed to be trying to control a fit of the giggles.

The door of the studio was only partly shut because heavy cables lying along the corridor disappeared into it and through the crack I could see that Michael's sanctum was brilliantly illuminated. I pushed open the door and was mildly surprised to see a man with the sort of hand-held TV camera that provides those graphic touchline shots in *Match of the Day*.

'Well,' I thought to myself, 'Michael must have been talking to Abba or the Rolling Stones and they haven't had time to clear away all the media gear.' Even when that tall Irish fellow with a red book stepped out from behind the door I didn't get it. I'd played minor roles in *that* programme for Michael Flanders, Albert Semprini and Jimmy Shand and I really believed for a moment that Eamonn Andrews had popped over to say hallo before dealing with his victim for the evening. It was only when he uttered the words, 'Ian Wallace, international bass baritone, this is your life!' that I took it in.

My first reaction – apart from a certain weakness at the knees, was that I must ring Pat and tell her I'd be late home. Within seconds I realised that she must have known, as did

Raymond, which was why he'd shown affection and amusement at my remark about the unpredictability of life.

Pat had known for nearly three weeks and keeping it from me meant that she lost half a stone in weight. The task wasn't made any easier by my going down with flu and lying in bed beside the phone! Unlike some victims I found the experience happy and moving.

The *My Music* team and Tony Shryane were all there, so were Donald Swann and the faithful David Money, playing me in with a duet version of 'Mud' to meet Madeleine Christie, my first leading lady in the play I'd done for Howard Lockhart, who appeared on film; Jimmy Edwards, whom I'd known at Cambridge; the historian John Ehrman, a close friend at school and university; Hubert Wood, the surgeon who'd looked after me when I was on my back; John Partridge, whom you've met already; Robert Morley, wearing his beret from *Fanny*; my dear friend Sesto Bruscantini who'd flown in from Rome; Sister Turner who'd been the ward sister for those twenty months I'd lain on my back; and of course Pat, Rosie, John and my mother, eighty-seven in a gold dress bidding fair to steal the show.

They'd tried to persuade Carl Ebert to fly from his home in California, but his doctor decided that it was a bit too much for a man of ninety. Sir Robert Birley, my old headmaster at Charterhouse, was snowbound in Somerset. Bless him, despite severe arthritis he'd volunteered to be airlifted in a helicopter, but they were too busy rescuing stranded motorists and dropping fodder to sheep and cattle.

Pat and Rosie made a bid to get the Arsenal first team squad along, which I'd have loved, but hardly surprisingly, they had more important things to do that day. Had I known, I'd have settled for just one of them, any one, but at that time preferably Liam Brady.

I was so thrilled that what had seemed to me a very fragmentary sort of career had been rated in someone's mind sufficiently noteworthy to be acknowledged in this way. The party afterwards was an unforgettable reunion and the night the programme was shown produced phone reunions with friends, some of whom had been out of touch for years.

Incidentally everyone at Thames looked after my family and friends with a delicacy and tact on which they all commented later. But it was all down to Pat to decide whether I'd like it or not. As usual she made the right decision – even if it cost her a great effort to keep it from me. Afterwards she told me, 'I had to tell so many lies, I felt sure you'd see through them.'

'Darling,' I replied, 'since I've believed everything you've told me for thirty years, why would I suddenly start questionning you now? I'd be more likely to think to myself, poor old thing, she's getting a bit eccentric in her middle age.'

Tailpiece

I was tempted to call this an epilogue, but at a mere sixty-two it could be that the best is yet to come.

The day Eamonn handed me the red book I'd been lunching with representatives of the National Westminster Bank (yes, they were in the secret too, apparently) because they'd agreed to sponsor various recitals organised by the Incorporated Society of Musicians – a professional society with about six thousand members made up soloists and music teachers. I'd been an inactive member for many years and to my amazement in 1977 they'd asked me to chair their solo performers section. I'd decided to devote my year of office to seeking sponsorship to help our activities on behalf of young artists, and Natwest proved a generous and discerning patron.

In 1979 the ISM took the unprecedented step of electing as President a man who'd never seen the inside of a drama school or a music college until well into middle age, and then only as a visitor. It was the greatest compliment that I could be paid by a profession that had already given me so much.

The job involved travelling all over the country to visit as many of our fifty centres as possible as well as chairing innumerable meetings and committees. Perhaps at last the part of me that was from my tone deaf, businessman-turned-politician father came into its own, and if I never do anything else of significance I can take some satisfaction from helping to bring about a closer understanding between our professional society and the Musicians' Union. Their General Secretary John Morton has the aspect of an Old Testament prophet and elder statesman rolled into one and on our first meeting uttered the splendid sentence, 'Forgive me if I'm rude but it does save time.'

Before my year as past President was up a similar agreement with Equity was on the way and I'd like to think that our small Society helped the two performers' unions to collaborate more closely with one another and to view us with tolerance and understanding. If that result does eventually emerge it will have had much more to do with the fact that our General Secretary, Susan Alcock, beguiled the MU and Equity deputations – all male – with her mixture of femininity and total grasp of her subject. I merely softened them up with one of the most pleasant experiences in London – lunch at the Garrick Club – where it is forbidden to discuss business!

So, within a year or two at this late stage I had professional respectability thrust upon me. And, though never a student in either establishment, found myself invited to the Royal College and the Royal Academy of Music to adjudicate and lecture, receiving with gratitude an honorary membership from each. After working for thirty-five years as an unqualified quack, it was a heart warming recognition, even if I do fear that at one of these adjudications I'll make some awful mistake and give the prize to the wrong person.

*   *   *

The vision in the shaving mirror looked pale and drawn.
    'Surely you'll pack it in now and start teaching?'
    'Never.'
    'Why not?'
    'I'm not qualified.'
    'You've not been qualified for anything else you've done, so what's the problem?'
    'I'm the only one who's been at risk. I'd never dream of trying to develop young voices with my lack of expertise.'
    'Pompous, but probably wise. What then?'
    'I can still sing a bit and in 1980 I did a funny play at Guildford called *Consider My Position* by John Graham.'

'Oh yes?'

'I played an irascible Scots doctor and I grew a moustache which came in white – it made David Lumsden laugh!'

'Who's David Lumsden?'

'A great friend, but that's not the point. I started out to be an actor, maybe I'll end up one.'

'Are you saying this may not be the end of your story?'

'Well, with Rosie starting a career in social work, and the Stargazers getting into the charts first go off. . . .'

'Who are the Stargazers?'

'The group for which John plays the saxophone. All sorts of exciting things seem to be happening to them and funnily enough all this family success has rubbed off a bit on the old man.'

'What are you talking about?'

'For the first time in my life I've got a recording contract too. Always been freelance before.'

'What sort of records?'

'Ballads to start with on those budget albums you can buy in all sorts of shops and later on hymns – so I'll be able to sing at my own funeral.'

'What does Pat think of it all?'

'Poor soul, she says that three careers in one household still means an awful lot of cooking and ironing.'

At that moment I heard our cocker spaniel Patch barking furiously – a gentle animal, she only does that when the letters come through the slit in the front door. I hurried downstairs – there's always the chance that lying on the mat is another fascinating offer.

226

INDEX